Enigma Books

Hitler's Contract

Also published by Enigma Books

Giorgio Fabre

Hitler's Contract

How Mussolini Became Hitler's Publisher

The Secret History of the Italian Edition of *Mein Kampf*

Introduction by Susan Zuccotti

Enigma Books

Enigma Books
580 Eighth Avenue, New York, NY 10018
www.enigmabooks.com

Original Italian title:
Il Contratto. Mussolini editore di Hitler
Published by Edizioni Dedalo srl, Bari © 2004

Translated by Robert L. Miller

ISBN 1-929631-37-5

Printed in the United States of America

Library of Congress Cataloging-in-Publication Data

Fabre, Giorgio.
  [Contratto.]
  Hitler's contract : how Mussolini became Hitler's publisher : the Italian edition of Mein Kampf / Giorgio Fabre ; translated by Robert L. Miller.

    p. : ill. ; cm.
  Translation of: Il contratto : Mussolini editore di Hitler. Bari: Dedalo, c2004.
  Includes bibliographical references and index.
  ISBN: 1-929631-37-5

1. Hitler, Adolf, 1889-1945. Mein Kampf--Translations into Italian--History and Criticism.   2. Publishers and publishing--Italy--History--20th century. 3. Government and the press--Italy--History--20th century. I. Title. II. Miller, Robert L. (Robert Lawrence), 1945-

DD247.H5 F337 2005
943.085

Table of Contents

Abbreviations

ACS .... Archivio Centrale dello Stato, Rome
A.S. Ba .... Archivio di Stato, Bari
A.S. Ge .... Archivio di Stato, Genoa
A.S. Mi .... Archivio di Stato, Milan
A.S. Ts .... Archivio di Stato, Trieste
ASDMAE   Archivio Storico Diplomatico del Ministero degli Affari
                         Esteri, Rome
ACDEC .... Archivio della Fondazione Centro di documentazione
                         ebraica contemporanea, Milan
AUCEI .... Archivio dell'Unione delle Comunità ebraiche italiane,
                         Rome
BAK .... Bundesarchiv, Koblenz
SPD .... Segreteria particolare del Duce
CO .... Carteggio Ordinario
CR .... Carteggio Riservato
PCM .... Presidenza del Consiglio dei Ministri
MCP .... Ministero della Cultura Popolare
MAE .... Ministero degli Affari Esteri
MAI .... Ministero dell'Africa Italiana
MI .... Ministero dell'Interno
MPI .... Ministero della Pubblica Istruzione
DGSE .... Direzione Generale della Stampa Estera
DGAP .... Direzione Generale Affari Politici
DGPS .... Direzione Generale di Pubblica Sicurezza
DGAC .... Direzione Generale dell'Amministrazione Civile
DGDR .... Direzione Generale della Demografia e Razza
DGSI .... Direzione Generale dell'Istruzione Superiore
DAGR .... Divisione Affari Generali e Riservati
DPP .... Divisione Polizia Politica
Gab .... Gabinetto
UCI .... Ufficio Centrale Investigativo
UC .... Ufficio Cifra
UCII .... Unione delle Comunità israelitiche italiane

DDI..................I documenti diplomatici italiani (Rome, Libreria dello Stato, Istituto Poligrafico e Zecca dello Stato, 1952 and ff.)

O.O. ....B. Mussolini, *Opera Omnia,* edited by Edoardo and Duilio Susmel, 35 vols. (Florence: La Fenice: and Rome: Volpe, 1951–1980)

PDI...................*Il Popolo d'Italia*

Introduction

by Susan Zuccotti

For at least forty years after the Second World War, many Holocaust historians accepted a mistaken set of assumptions about Italian Fascist racism and anti-Semitism. The Italian anti-Jewish laws imposed in 1938 and 1939, it was believed, were only a bland version of anti-Semitic measures in effect elsewhere in Europe by the late 1930s or early 1940s. Mussolini himself never truly believed the racist and anti-Semitic rhetoric he began to sputter only in 1938. He issued his anti-Jewish laws unexpectedly that year under German pressure or, at the very least, in an attempt to ingratiate Hitler and solidify the Axis alliance. Italian Jews and non-Jews alike were astonished and disoriented by the laws, which they never expected. But Mussolini remained indifferent about his new program. The laws were never seriously enforced in Italy, and exemptions were liberally granted.

To some extent, these assumptions were based on some of Mussolini's most public postures. After all, the Duce had long had a Jewish mistress, Margherita Sarfatti, editor of the art and literature page of his *Popolo d'Italia* and a coeditor of *Gerarchia*, the Fascist party's monthly ideological review. Also, in the spring of 1932, before Hitler came to power in Germany, Mussolini informed the German journalist Emil Ludwig, "Anti-Semitism does not exist in Italy.... Italian Jews have always behaved like good citizens, and as soldiers they have fought courageously. They hold important positions in the universities, the army, banks." Then in July 1934, in a moment of anger after Austrian Nazis had assassinated Chancellor Engelbert Dollfuss and Austria seemed about to be overrun by the Germans, Mussolini made his colorful comment, "Thirty centuries of history permit us to regard with supreme pity certain doctrines supported beyond the Alps by the descendants of people who did not know how to write, and could not hand down documents recording their own lives, at a time when Rome had Caesar, Virgil, and Augustus." A few months later, in December 1934, Mussolini even permitted young Jews from Vladimir Jabotinsky's revisionist Zionist organization to enroll at the Italian Maritime School in Civitavecchia, where they formed a special section and ultimately became the nucleus of the Israeli navy.

Also influential in the formation of these assumptions were some of the post-war memoirs of Italian Jewish survivors, who wrote about their experiences just before and during the conflict. Many of the

Italian Jews who survived the German occupation that began in September 1943 did so because they received remarkable help from sympathetic Italian non-Jews. Understandably grateful, they tended to focus on the positive rather than the negative, remembering more about Italian citizens who had helped them during the war than about Mussolini's persecutory program before it.

Assumptions of a benign official anti-Semitism in Italy began to crumble in the mid-1980s. First to fall was the idea that Mussolini's anti-Jewish laws had been bland. Information about the content of the laws had been available from their onset, of course, but for years after the war, scholars had not emphasized their harsh reality. When I, along with a new generation of Italian scholars like Michele Sarfatti, began to reevaluate the laws in the 1980s, it became apparent that they were as onerous as any in Europe. To the dismay of the Vatican, for example, inter-marriage between Jews and non-Jews was made illegal in Italy in 1938—a prohibition never decreed in France when Pétain's Vichy regime issued its own racial laws in October 1940 and June 1941. All Jewish children in Italy had to withdraw from public elementary and secondary schools; at the university level, Jewish students already enrolled could continue, but no new students could be admitted. Again, such a decree was never issued in Vichy France. A strict *numerus clausus* was imposed on students in French universities, but Jewish elementary and secondary school children attended classes regularly, even wearing the Star of David in the northern zone, until they either went into hiding or were arrested after the summer of 1942.

Foreign Jews in Italy in 1938 had an especially hard time. All of them were required to leave the country within six months of Mussolini's September 1938 decree. Worse, Jews who had been naturalized after January 1, 1919, lost their citizenship and were regarded as foreigners. In France, recently naturalized Jews were never denied their citizenship *en masse*, but passed before a review board, which sometimes preserved their status. Nor were all foreign Jews ever required by a single decree to leave France, although when deportations began in mid-1942, the fate of many of them was far worse than that of Jews who left Italy in 1938 and 1939.

Mussolini's anti-Jewish laws imposed other restrictions on Italian Jews in 1938 that were similar to those in the Third Reich at the time and in German-occupied countries and Vichy France during the war. Jews were prevented from owning businesses and properties over a certain value, and banned from the armed forces, banks, insurance companies, and public administration. They could not teach in public schools or work as notaries. Only those with special exemptions could work as journalists, doctors, pharmacists, veterinarians, lawyers, accountants, engineers, architects, chemists, agronomists, and mathematicians. Italian Jews could not employ non-Jews as domestic servants, own radios, place advertisements or death notices in the newspapers, publish books, hold public conferences, list their names and numbers in telephone directories, or frequent popular vacation spots. Local ordinances were often even more severe, or just plain petty. In Rome, poor Jews could not even continue their traditional activities as ragpickers. Clearly, the laws were as cruel as those anywhere else in Nazi or Fascist Europe.

Equally brutal was the Italian definition of Jews—a distinction determining those to whom the laws would apply and, in the long run, life and death. In Italy, as in other countries with anti-Semitic laws, all individuals with two Jewish parents were considered Jewish, even if they had converted. Individuals with one Jewish and one half-Jewish parent—that is, with three Jewish grandparents—were considered Jews, while those with three "Aryan" grandparents were also "Aryan." Those with one Jewish and one non-Jewish parent—that is, with two Jewish grandparents—were not considered Jewish only if they had been baptized before October 1, 1938, or at birth. These definitions did not differ greatly from those in effect in the Third Reich at the time. The chief difference was that while in Italy a baptized half-Jew was declared a full "Aryan," in Germany he or she was a *Mischling* of the first degree. An individual with only one Jewish grandparent in Germany was a *Mischling* of the second degree, restricted, like all *Mischling*, but usually not deported. In Italy, that same individual was "Aryan."

While clarifying the harsh content of the Italian racial laws, historians in the late 1980s also began to look beyond assumptions of non-enforcement. As they did so, a far more complex reality emerged.

Survivor memoirs had already indicated that individual Jews had lost jobs, property, and the right to attend public schools. But in 1994, Adriana Muncinelli published a study making it clear that educational administrators in the Province of Cuneo in 1938 and 1939 had zealously enforced proscriptions on Jews in the public schools, removing even those with Jewish-sounding names. Many of their victims may not have been Jewish for generations, if ever. Evoking the possibility of similar harshness elsewhere, Muncinelli's work reminded scholars of the value of local studies. In 1998, Giorgio Fabre's examination of Fascist censorship, *L'Elenco*, revealed the extensive cooperation of Italian publishers with Mussolini's proscriptions on books by Jewish authors. The pervasive publication in Italian newspapers and journals in the late 1930s and early 1940s of vicious anti-Semitic propaganda also became increasingly evident.

Nor were Italian policies exempting "worthy" Jews from the racial laws more generous or more liberally granted than similar programs in other countries. The Italian laws defined as eligible for exemption the immediate families of Jews killed, wounded, or decorated while fighting in Libya, World War I, Ethiopia, and Spain, along with the families of men who volunteered for service in those wars. Individuals and their families who had participated in Gabriele D'Annunzio's occupation of Fiume in 1919, joined the Fascist party between 1919 and 1922 or during the second half of 1924 (after the murder of Socialist deputy Giacomo Matteotti by Fascist thugs), or been wounded in the Fascist cause, were also eligible. So too were individuals with exceptional merit of a "civic nature," a quality left undefined in the original statutes. But the word "eligible" was key. Exemptions were not granted automatically. Those who considered themselves "worthy" had to apply and submit to a demeaning evaluation, which often ended in rejection. Furthermore, exemptions did not apply to all the racial proscriptions. Exemptees could retain their property, businesses, and certain professions, but even they could not teach, send their children to public schools, or work in banks or public administration. By January 15, 1943, the Office of Demography and Race at the Ministry of the Interior had examined 5,870 applications for exemption. Of these, they had granted 2,486 and refused 3,384. They can hardly be accused of excessive generosity.

Compliance with the anti-Jewish laws seems to have been almost complete in the public arena. All Jews, with the exception of a handful of pre-enrolled university students, were ejected from the public schools. All Jews, with the exception of a couple of thousand *discriminati*, as exemptees were called, lost jobs in the prohibited professions and their property and businesses over a certain value. All Jews naturalized after 1919 lost their citizenship. Books by Jews were not published. In only two areas was a degree of non-enforcement observable. The majority of Italy's roughly 10,000 foreign Jews left the country, as required, but those who could find no place to go were not dumped over the frontier, as happened with Polish Jews in Germany in

October 1938. Furthermore, in an effort to placate Italian shipping and tourist industries, foreign Jews from elsewhere in Europe, especially the Third Reich, were granted temporary transit visas, considerably confusing the situation. Second, the Fascist program of forced labor for Jews, inaugurated in May 1942, was enforced only half-heartedly, because Italian non-Jews disliked the sight of clearly middle-class Jewish city dwellers digging ditches and picking fruit, and because the government was preoccupied with other matters.

If enforcement of the anti-Jewish laws in the public sphere was virtually complete, however, it is more difficult to determine what was happening behind the scenes. Many Jewish memorists record that Italian non-Jews quietly disapproved of the racial laws and helped their Jewish neighbors in a myriad of small ways. Lawyers and journalists sometimes allowed their Jewish colleagues to work without attribution, for payment off the books. Non-Jewish domestic servants sometimes remained with their Jewish employers. But at the same time, we read of innkeepers in vacation resorts who refused to receive Jewish families who had been their guests for years. Enforcement in this gray zone remains elusive.

If historical appraisals of the content and enforcement of the Italian anti-Jewish laws have changed through the years, so too have descriptions of the evolution of Mussolini's ideas and policies on racism and anti-Semitism. It is in this area that Giorgio Fabre makes his valuable contribution here. Between 1997 and 2002, historians like

Gianluca Gabrielli, Barbara Sorgoni, Giorgio Fabre, Michele Sarfatti, and Giulia Barrera wrote of the Duce's racist rhetoric just before and during the Italian invasion of Ethiopia in 1935, and of barriers to blacks entering Italy in the 1930s. Co-habitation of whites with blacks was prohibited during this period, and a novel about a torrid love affair between a white Italian woman and a black man was the first to be censored on racial grounds in April 1934. But following these studies of Mussolini's anti-black attitudes, Giorgio Fabre introduces in this book much startling new material on Mussolini's racism and anti-Semitism. Fabre argues convincingly that the anti-Jewish laws of 1938 were neither sudden, unplanned, nor unexpected.

Consider first Mussolini and racism in general. Fabre shows that the Duce agreed to publish Hitler's *Mein Kampf* within weeks of the Fuhrer's rise to power in January 1933, and paid an exorbitant fee for the privilege. More significant, he reveals that Mussolini was contemplating the introduction of racist ideas in his own country at that time, fully five years before he is usually considered to have done so. The author traces the phrases in the Duce's personal summary of *Mein Kampf* that he underlined, portraying him as far more interested in Hitler's racism than in his aggressive posturing. He also studies Mussolini's speeches and writings for *Il Popolo d'Italia* as early as March 1934, detecting numerous references to a "pure Italian race" and frequent disparagement of racial mixing in the United States and France.

Regarding Mussolini and an anti-Semitic program, Fabre traces the origin back to at least 1933. He unearths instructions from the Duce to journalists, advising them not to cover specific Jewish subjects. More serious are the purges of Mussolini's Jewish staff members and others, including Margherita Sarfatti, as early as 1933; the beginning of restrictions on foreign Jewish university students; and the Duce's demands in 1934 for religious censuses to determine the number of Jewish stockbrokers, journalists, and public officials in Italy. A discreet, erratic, but surprisingly comprehensive elimination of Jews from the public sector followed, at least four years before it was previously believed to have occurred.

Content, enforcement, and emergence of Fascist anti-Semitism—all have been subject to recent scrutiny and reevaluation. But Fabre's work raises one other question for future consideration. If Mussolini's "softening up" of public opinion regarding the Jews went on for so long—and indeed, Fabre argues elsewhere that it began even earlier than 1933—what was the effect on the Italian people? Recent scholarship has unearthed copious evidence of anti-Semitic rhetoric in the nineteenth and early twentieth centuries emanating from the Roman Catholic church in Italy, which blamed Jews, Liberals, and Freemasons for the unification of the country and the loss of the Papal States in 1870. Most Italians seem to have been unwilling to abandon their patriotic fervor and adopt the political stance of their priests, but anti-Semitism was nevertheless not unknown to them. When Mussolini began his campaign to prepare his countrymen for the anti-Jewish laws, as Fabre shows, he was not introducing alien concepts. Yet the significant help given to Jews during the German occupation by Italian men and women at all levels of the society, including the army, diplomatic corps, and even occasionally the Fascist party, suggests that he failed to convince them.

Perhaps Giorgio Fabre and other talented scholars will address themselves to this issue as well, and surprise us yet again. In the meantime, we are grateful for this new work, and read it with pleasure.

Susan Zuccotti
New York City
January 2006

Chapter I

Contacts

By the time Major Giuseppe Renzetti wrote to Mussolini on February 3, 1933, the Germans had already come to a decision regarding *Mein Kampf*. However, Renzetti was given the news to be transmitted to Rome only on the 3rd.

What the Germans wanted, and Renzetti was reporting in writing, was that the book written by the new Reich Chancellor, Adolf Hitler, be translated into Italian for them to make some money from the sale of the copyright. A Nazi representative was about to travel to Italy for that purpose. Renzetti therefore wrote to Mussolini.[1] The news came from Hitler's secretary, Rudolf Hess, who told Renzetti that the Nazis needed money to finance the tough electoral battle the Party was up

1. Doc. A1 and photo.

against and this was simply one more opportunity to raise the badly needed funds.

Renzetti was a major in the Italian army's Alpine corps and had been president of the Italian Chamber of Commerce in Germany since October 1930, when Mussolini had received him in Rome and named him as his point man with Hitler and the Nazis.[2] Any information given to Renzetti would certainly reach the Duce's desk almost instantly and receive the attention it deserved.

On February 3, 1933, Hitler had been in power for just four days. As soon as he became Chancellor he decided to hold general elections on March 5. Even Renzetti, who had the Nazis' full attention at the time, had suggested something of the sort. Those elections were key to paving the way, as they ultimately did, for the Nazi party's rise to total and unassailable power.

The Nazis feared the elections and were gearing up, seemingly without knowing how to go about it—or so it appeared. At a Cabinet meeting on February 2, the day before Renzetti sent his message, Interior Minister Wilhelm Frick recommended that the government allocate as much as one million marks for its own propaganda, but the idea had been rejected by Finance Minister Schwerin von Krosigk.[3] The Nazis at the time had no assurances that they could count on the

---

2. The best biography of Renzetti is part of the book by Federico Scarano, *Mussolini e la Repubblica di Weimar. Le relazioni diplomatiche tra Italia e Germania dal 1927 al 1933* (Napoli: Giannini, 1996). But see also Federico Niglia, *Il maggiore Roma-Berlino. L'attività di collegamento di Giuseppe Renzetti fra Mussolini e Hitler,* "Nuova storia contemporanea," July–August 2002, pp. 69–81.

backing of large industry. Better still, according to information coming from Berlin, it appeared that Hitler didn't want private contributions, which was why Renzetti was writing to the Italian dictator, asking the Duce to favorably consider the request to either purchase the rights to the book on his own or to persuade a trustworthy Italian publisher to finance it. Basically, Mussolini was being asked to make a substantial contribution to the upcoming Nazi election campaign.

Renzetti wrote that Max Amann, Hitler's personal representative, was already on his way to Italy to discuss the matter. Upon reading the message Mussolini ordered that Amann be immediately received. Gaetano Polverelli, who was in charge of the Press Office since Mussolini at that time was also Minister of Foreign Affairs, saw to it without delay.[4]

At that time Max Amann[5] was not just another Nazi functionary. He had been Hitler's commanding officer and comrade-in-arms during the First World War and was an extremely loyal—and it seems rather brutal—follower since the political beginnings, as well as the managing director of the Party's publishing company, Franz Eher Verlag, of which Hitler was the main owner. Eher Verlag also owned the Party's newspapers and magazines including the official Nazi mouthpiece, the daily *Völkischer Beobachter.*

---

3. Ian Kershaw, *Hitler 1889–1936: Hubris* (London: Allen Lane, The Penguin Press, 1998), p. 730
4. Doc. A2.
5. See photo.

Max Amann had also been the publisher of *Mein Kampf* since inception while Rudolf Hess had acted as one of the editors of the text. Amann was also the administrator with power of attorney overseeing the Führer's personal property.[6] Politics at that time was already a rather expensive activity and major politicians all had personal administrators to handle their affairs. Mussolini also had a counterpart of sorts to Max Amann in Giulio Barella, administrator of the newspaper owned by the Duce, *Il Popolo d'Italia,* and the man in charge of the dictator's personal finances. The fascist leader was therefore well aware of the "high cost" of politics, which essentially meant the financial requirements of propaganda. He had said as much just a few months before to Prince Starhemberg of Austria, who was requesting funding for his political party.[7]

Later, in December 1933, Amann would become the most important man in the German press as president of the Reichspressekammer, the regulating office of Germany's newspapers, something akin to being the "czar" of Nazi and non-Nazi publishing. He took advantage of his powerful position to acquire great personal wealth, and after the war the Americans discovered that his bank account had increased from 108,000 marks in 1934 to 3,800,000 marks in 1943.

---

6. On Amann see also Oron J. Hale *The Captive Press in the Third Reich* (Princeton: Princeton U.P., 1964), pp. 21–29 (figures on income are on p. 25). See also the entry by Hermann Weiss in *Bibliographisches Lexicon zum Dritten Reich* (Frankfurt am Mein: Fischer Tachenbuch Verlag, 1999), pp. 21–22 and I. Kershaw *op. cit.* p. 300.
7. See Ernst Rüdiger Starhemberg, *Between Hitler and Mussolini. Memoirs* (London-New York: Hodder and Stoughton, The Cooperation Publishing Company, 1942), p. 92.

The man who was traveling to Rome was therefore one of Hitler's best qualified representatives. The book he was representing was a memoir that he had worked on and that featured him in some ways. In *Mein Kampf* Hitler praised Amann's "extraordinary ability, his industry and scrupulous conscientiousness" and spoke highly of his success in bringing "order and neatness" to the Nazi party's administration.[8]

As part of his credentials for the trip to Rome, Amann brought with him the power of attorney bearing Hitler's signature, a document he was to leave with the Italians.[9] As his report to Mussolini documents, Polverelli closely repeated Renzetti's message, namely, that "a lot of money was required" to fund the election campaign and that the sale of the rights to *Mein Kampf* could make a difference in solving that pressing problem. This was the reason for Amann's trip to Italy.

On that occasion, however, Amann also imparted insights into German politics. For example, he described the Nazi leadership's state of mind and how they were ready to do anything to hang on to their newly acquired power. Could it be that in repeating such anecdotes he was seeking to ingratiate himself? Or was it a gesture of extreme deference, even genuine admiration and trust, towards the Duce as the great precursor of the Nazi era? Those feelings were broadly shared at the time within the Führer's entourage. This was clearly and rather openly a very self-conscious kind of confidential talk, intended to create an atmosphere of trust and convince the Italians to provide the

---

8. Adolf Hitler, *Mein Kampf* (Boston-New York: Houghton Mifflin, 1999), pp. 592–593.

funding, since the Germans were clearly extremely anxious to receive that money.

---

9. See photos and Doc. A3.

Chapter II

A Book No One Had Read

The saga of the Italian translation of *Mein Kampf* began immediately upon Hitler's rise to power. From the start it was clearly more a political than a purely publishing venture.

We know very little about the transmission of the text of *Mein Kampf* itself. Nazism's seminal document, which was also Hitler's autobiography, was originally published in two volumes, the first in 1925 and the second in 1927. It would be a mistake to believe that it immediately became the famous "black book" of humanity. In its first years the book had a limited readership in Germany, Italy, and elsewhere. Although Adolf Hitler had been politically active and was known internationally after the First World War, especially following the stunning results of the 1930 elections, the book's fortunes were, to say the least, rather mixed.

A few examples will easily show that the book generated limited interest in Italy.[10]

During the early months of 1931 Giuseppe Renzetti began negotiating for a translation of the book by the official fascist publishing company, *La Libreria del Littorio*,[11] but without much success. This came at the major's own initiative, with the assistance of a civil servant at the Ministry of Foreign Affairs, but with neither the backing of the Duce's private staff or of the dictator himself. Other writings by Hitler had reached the Duce's private secretariat at the time but these were routinely ignored, even if they dealt with Italian Fascism.[12] There

---

10. See the attacks such as the one by Ivo Pannaggi, "In Germania," in *L'Ambrosiano*, January 8, 1931. In an article from Düsseldorf, Pannaggi claimed that the Nazis were simply a new version of "the prewar nationalists" and ridiculed their racial theories.

11. The mention of *Mein Kampf* is part of a report by Renzetti to the head of Mussolini's Press Office, Lando Ferretti, dated February 12, 1931 (quoted in F. Scarano, *Mussolini e la Repubblica di Weimar, cit.* p. 190): "The publisher of Hittler's [*sic*, as Renzetti this time used to spell his name] book (*Mein Kampf*) Eher Verlag, Münich, Tiergatenstr. 15—, is expecting the request from the Italian publisher (Libreria del Littorio) regarding the already discussed translation. Please remember that Comm. Parini asked me to have 5 or 6,000 lire available following your request." BAK, collection N.1235 (Nachlass Renzetti), f. 3/ Korrespondenz 1931. It appears that "the already discussed translation" was in fact the translation of the complete version of *Mein Kampf*. Piero Parini was the general manager of Italians overseas (*L'amministrazione centrale dall'Unità alla Repubblica, le strutture e I dirigenti. I. Il ministero degli Affari Esteri*, edited by Vincenzo Pellegrini [Bologna: il Mulino, 1992], p. 148). The Libreria del Littorio went into bankruptcy at that time. See the report drafted later on by the owner Giorgio Berlutti for Mussolini in ACS, SPD, Co, b. 1406, f. 513.494. Rome. Libreria del Littorio ora Unione Editoriale Internazionale.

12. We refer specifically to Hitler's preface to *Die Revolution des Faschismus* by elementary school teacher Vincenzo Meletti, the translation of the book *Civiltà Fascista* (Nuova Italia) and published in German by Eher Verlag. Two copies of the book

was virtually no interest in any of Hitler's writings in Italy in the early 1930s.

An article published by Gino Cucchetti, the Bolzano correspondent of *Il Popolo d'Italia*, on July 22, 1931, may be considered particularly significant at the time, since the author had established good personal relations with Hitler himself.[13] Writing in the Duce's newspaper, Cucchetti described how the Nazi leader had just "sent a brand new complimentary copy of his new book, *Mein Kampf: My Struggle.*" Cucchetti wrote that *Mein Kampf* was a newly published work, while the definitive version had already been in print for four years—something he was simply unaware of. He described the content of the book rather succinctly as being written "in a flat but consistently lively and polemical style" and "dealing with issues of political parties, racial, and class struggle and the importance of minorities."

Italian interest in Hitler himself was to grow in the course of 1932, especially at the time of the March elections, which was a turning point

---

were sent to Mussolini's secretariat in May 1931 but the Duce did not see the book and it was probably not brought to his attention. For its arrival at Mussolini's private secretariat (May 8, 1931) see ACS, SPD, Co, b. 1900, f. 529.856 Meletti, Vincenzo, Insegnante, Perugia. The book was also sent to the Ministry of Foreign Affairs, but it was also not seen officially by the Duce at that location. The thank-you letter written by the Italian Consul in Münich to Eher Verlag (May 27, 1931) is in the file and only mentions the thanks from the head of the minister's cabinet. The letter is in ASDMAE, MCP, DGSE, b. 368, f. Mein Kampf (Max Amann).

13. G.c., *Adolfo Hitler ed il "Sud Tirolo." "La Direzione del Partito Hitleriano condanna le recenti manifestazioni di Innsbruck,"* PDI, July 22, 1931. Gino Cucchetti had already interviewed Hitler for *Il Popolo d'Italia* on May 12, 1931 (*Con Adolfo Hitler alla "casa Bruna"*), but made no mention of *Mein Kampf*, which he was not aware of. The July 22 article was reprinted without changes in Gino Cucchetti *L'Alto Adige nostro (Scritti*

in the success of the Nazi party. Suddenly many articles were being published about Nazism and a few books about the Party's leader also appeared in Italy.[14] The most noteworthy translation from the German was of the book *Hitler* by Theodor Heuss, published in April 1932 by Bompiani, a few months after the German edition. The author, a moderately anti-Nazi liberal, would later become president of the German Federal Republic. The Italian edition translated by a newsman at the *Corriere della Sera* was so riddled with mistakes that it amounted to an abridged approximation bordering on fraud. For example, any mention of the relationship between Nazism and Fascism had been omitted.[15] Even the innumerable quotations from *Mein Kampf*, which

---

politici e letterari, 1922–I-1932-X). "Brennero," Bolzano s.d. [but 1932], pp. 264–268, but without the adjective "new" (p. 264).

14. For books see *Inchiesta su Hitler* "Nuova Europa," Rome, n.d. [1932], already published in the magazine edited by Asvero Gravelli, "Antieuropa"; Pietro Solari *Hitler e il Terzo Reich* (Agnelli: Milan 1932). See also the short announcement of the PDI on February 16, 1932, regarding the translation of Meletti's book that mentioned "Adolf Hitler's magnificient introduction." See also the interview by Carlo Scorza on April 29, 1932, and published in Carlo Scorza, *Fascismo idea imperiale,* tip. (E. De Gasperis: Rome, 1933), pp. 80–87.

15. The preface by the translator Renzo Segàla was added on April 20, 1932. For the German edition see Theodor Heuss, *Hitlers Weg. Ein Historisch-politische Studie über den Nationalsozialismus* (Union Deutsche Verlagsgesellschaft: Stuttgart, 1932). The original edition of the book was seen by the Head of the Government's Press Office and the parts that may have been of interest to the Duce were underlined. The list of the points that had been underscored was passed along to Mussolini with the book and is in ASDMAE, MCP, DGSE, b. 428, f. Hitler ed avvenimenti dei nazional-socialisti in Germania. 1932 [Hitler and National Socialist events in Germany. 1932]. The list bears the annotation: "viewed by S.E.C.G." (Sua Eccellenza il Capo del Governo.) [His Excellency the Head of the Government.] That copy with the same underlinings made by the Press Office (and a note of possession dated January 16, 1932) is part of the Mussolini Collection (ACS, Biblioteca, Coll. Mussolini, n. 129). The only underlining that may actually be by Mussolini (p. 54) is under the name of Sonnino,

were part of the original German edition, had almost all been cut. Mussolini too had superficially perused that biography at some point.

By 1932 Hitler was on his way to becoming a well-known figure in Italy for his ideas and his anti-Semitism. His book, however, was much less known. Even among Italian political functionaries knowledge of the text of *Mein Kampf* was limited and largely secondhand. One or possibly even two copies in German reached the Ministry of Foreign Affairs in 1932, but without generating any notice; not a single copy was to reach the Duce's desk.[16] There is also the biographical file created by the diplomatic history section of the Ministry of Foreign Affairs at the beginning of February 1933 a few days after Hitler became chancellor. The Nazi leader is described as being an untalented man and *Mein Kampf* is not even mentioned.[17]

At the beginning of 1933 in Italy *Mein Kampf* was just a thick book by an emerging politician very few people knew anything about. If Mussolini did pay attention to the text it was because of his awareness of Hitler,[18] not because of *Mein Kampf*, which remained virtually

---

identified by Heuss as one of the Jewish political leaders in the history of Europe (together with Disraeli and Gambetta).

16. The first copy was mailed to the ministry on March 14, 1932, by Carlo Barduzzi, consul in Cologne. There is no confirmation that it in fact did reach Rome, in any case it was not received at the ministry. The second copy was mailed on May 19 by Pittalis, the consul in Münich and placed in the archives without being shown to Mussolini. ASDMAE, MCP, DGSE, b. 428, f. Hitler ed avvenimenti dei nazional-socialisti in Germania. 1932. [Hitler and National Socialist events in Germany. 1932].

17. ASDMAE, MAE, DGAP 1931-1943, Germany, b. 12.

18. Regarding the many indications of Mussolini's at least cursory knowledge of Hitler before 1932 we note a little known fact in this book involving a detailed journalistic biography of Hitler published by a Berlin daily, the *Deutsche Allgemeine Zeitung* on

unknown and was thought to be of little or no interest. This was the context in which the negotiations began.

October 10, 1930. The article was seen by Mussolini who read German and who carefully underlined it especially the various elements of personal information: that Hitler was Austrian, was a bachelor, had been destitute and had very little education, had been wounded during the war and had a passion for history. Mussolini vigorously underlined a sentence that summed up Hitler's thinking about social democracy in that it used terror but could be broken by "an even greater form of terror." The article was a contribution from Münich by Alfred Detig, *Wer ist Hitler?* The article with the pencil marks is in ASDMAE, MCP, DGSE, b. 107, f. 1930. Hitler, Adolf.

Chapter III

Financing

The entire story may appear rather simple to us today. Yet at the time it was kept secret and has remained totally unknown until now. It was, however, far from being a clear-cut matter. One detail will suffice to show why: based on the documents we have found the Germans had not been completely truthful with the Italians when they began the negotiations. They had actually lied quite a bit. The Nazis, who were a rather young group of men both politically and in terms of their actual age, were feeling their way around on the threshold of power. However, just like any new group of upstarts thirsting for their spoils, they were already extremely aggressive and rather cynical.

During his meeting with the Italians on February 9, Max Amann failed to mention another key issue: a few days before, Hitler had decided to forego his salary as Reich Chancellor. According to official statements issued on that occasion, Hitler's compensation was to be distributed among the families of the "Nazi fighters" of the SS and SA who had been killed during the street battles of the preceding years. Hitler was to retain only his income as a writer, generated for the most part from sales of *Mein Kampf.*

The news was formally released by the Nazi party Press Office on February 6 but had been leaked[19] the day before and it is very possible that Rudolf Hess already knew by the 3rd. The matter, however, was never brought up with the Italians nor did they mention it.

Yet this was a piece of news of some importance. Prior to coming to power Hitler's personal expenses—including apartments, automobiles, employees (secretaries, aides, bodyguards, hairdressers)— were extremely high.[20] It was also very clear that he had no intention of reducing those costs nor did he do so once he became chancellor, despite the statements that were made in February 1933. Perhaps he harbored a "royal" vision of power or, in simpler terms, like many twentieth century leaders, he had a petty bourgeois craving for "aristocratic" privilege and creature comforts.

---

19. The announcement was published on the front page of the *Völkischer Beobachter* of February 7, 1933 (*Adolf Hitler verzichtet auf sein Reichkanzler-Gehalt*, see Oron James Hale, *Adolf Hitler: Taxpayer,* in "The American Historical Review," 60, July 4, 1955, p. 838). For the informal announcement see the Berlin correspondent in the London Times of the 5th published on the 6th (Election moves in Germany, p. 120).
20. Henry Ashby Turner Jr., *German Big Business and the Rise of Hitler* (New York-Oxford: Oxford University Press, 1985), p. 153.

Public statements to the contrary, it is very likely that Hitler quite simply could not or would not do without his salary as Reich Chancellor. During the months and years that followed he continued to collect his salary, as recorded in his income tax filings.[21] This will explain why some time later, when the issue of how the Nazi leader's income should be assessed for tax purposes, his entourage concluded that shielding the royalties from *Mein Kampf* was a top priority. A bitter struggle began with the German tax office on the assessment of the royalties as completely tax free. In the end Hitler managed to prevail.

The second point the Germans failed to mention to the Italians— closely related to the first—was the ambitious promotional effort for *Mein Kampf*, connected to the Nazis and Hitler's need for money at that time. The plan existed for some time, at least since January 27, 1933, when Hitler and his advisers discussed the marketing the book in various countries. It was on that same day in Berlin that Hitler reviewed the power of attorney document made out to the managing director of the Nazi party's publishing company, Franz Eher, which had first published *Mein Kampf.* This was the same document that Amann had left behind in Rome. The original power of attorney that was being renewed was actually dated two years earlier—we shall see later the kind of problems this was to create—and had no relationship to the sale of the rights to the "book," but referred only to the "newspaper" exploitation of the book overseas.

---

21. On the issue of his salary and tax exemption, see O. J. Hale, *Adolf Hitler: Taxpayer*, cit., pp. 838–841.

Amann, however, had not traveled to Italy simply to offer to publish extracts of the book in newspapers, as stated in the power of attorney. He came, as Renzetti had announced, to negotiate the publication of the book itself. Why did he then decide to leave this oddly inappropriate power of attorney with the Italians? Why hadn't a new power of attorney been signed by Hitler rather than renewing an old one? A mistake is always possible, naturally. Nazi bureaucracy was certainly not, contrary to popular belief, a paragon of efficiency and precision, especially within the group immediately surrounding Hitler. Furthermore the period immediately following the rise to power was a time of confusion. A different explanation, however, may also be possible.

What remains unstated, but was clearly implied in documents published later on, was the fact that Amann's undertaking was of an extremely serious nature for a number of reasons the Italians were well aware of. The first was that the Germans—whether they were in a tight spot or not—were attempting to raise money not by soliciting donations from a private person but rather from what was for all intents and purposes a foreign government and a regime, however friendly it may have been. The funding, barely veiled by the proposed publishing contract, was in fact the real motivation behind the deal. The Germans were ready for anything, which was all the more serious because—and this is the second point—precedents for such a scheme actually did exist.

Since the late 1920s Hitler and the Nazis had been accused by two German newspapers, one socialist and the other Catholic, as well as by Albrecht von Gräfe, a former member of parliament who had been linked to the Nazis, of being subsidized by fascist Italy. These accusations were so persistent in 1929 that Hitler brought a legal action for slander and in May of that year, after a trial in Munich, he was declared "free from any suspicion," while his accusers were found guilty. The case went to appeal in 1930 and Hitler was cleared of any wrongdoing and acquitted for the second time even though many rumors persisted. The Italian dictator was well aware of these proceedings since he had personally followed those events through the reports filed by the consulate in Munich.[22] On that occasion Max Amann was one of the witnesses testifying on Hitler's behalf.

Now, a few years after those events and using his own men, one of them having testified as a character witness at his trial, Hitler was *truly* requesting financing from Mussolini, perhaps to secure a personal "stake" but also clearly with campaign expenses in mind. The fact that he was proceeding in such a roundabout manner—using extremely trustworthy Party men like Hess and Amann, and avoiding traditional diplomatic channels, which he clearly didn't trust—was nothing

---

22. As a source it is preferable to quote the reports of the Italian consulate regarding this trial (that took place in the Münich court between May 6 and 14, 1929), ASDMAE, MAE, DGAP 1919–1930, Germany, b. 1181, f. Processo Hitler [Hitler Trial.] The reports include the "visto" [seen] markings by Mussolini. On both trials see F. Scarano, cit., pp. 114–115, 188–189. But see also Meir Michaelis, *Mussolini and the Jews. German-Italian Relations and the Jewish Question in Italy. 1922–1945* (London-

unusual. There are no known German documents (at least as of this writing) about this event. On the other hand, two Italian witnesses, Renzetti and Polverelli, corroborate one another as trustworthy minor officials who could not be expected to lie to the Duce. It seems likely then that a request for funding, and a scandalous one at that, was clearly taking place.

The Führer's men therefore conducted the negotiations with extreme caution: they had traveled directly to Rome to discuss the matter with the Italians, thus avoiding any written communication. There had been no correspondence nor had any third party served as intermediary. Furthermore, as we shall see later on, apart from the contract and the receipt, which Hitler did not sign and that was a document simply recording an ordinary publishing transaction, the Italians had nothing more tangible than their own notes to go by. The only document signed by the Reich Chancellor was that strange, incorrectly worded power of attorney, which may have been an intentional mistake.

It is hard to believe that a man of Amann's experience would travel from Munich to Rome to secure such an extraordinary commitment as the Duce's personal financial backing while forgetting to bring along the proper power of attorney. On top of that, the power of attorney stated that Hitler was selling rights that were far less important than those of the book, namely, the reprint rights "for foreign newspapers."

Oxford: The Institute of Jewish Affairs, The Calerendon Press), 1978, p. 46. Michaelis reproduces some of the comments by Italian dailies.

If the document were to surface suddenly in the future it would be considered of minimal importance. Dated 1931 and renewed only in 1933, the power of attorney predated Hitler's rise to power and therefore had or appeared to have little real value.

Chapter IV

Money and the Nazis

The Nazis had not limited their search for the sale of translation rights to *Mein Kampf* to the Italians. Between February and April 1933 the Nazis had also signed a contract with Hurst & Blackett publishing for the British edition.[23]

The differences between the latter negotiation and the one conducted in Rome are particularly revealing. Hurst & Blackett purchased the first option from the British literary agent Curtis Brown, who controlled the rights that had remained unsold for several years. The sale, however, was not made very quickly but only after long

23. James J. Barnes and Patience Barnes, *Hitler's Mein Kampf in Britain and America. A Publishing History 1930–1939* (Cambridge et al.: Cambridge U.P. 1980), pp. 5 ff. I thank

negotiations and the involvement of Hans Wilhelm Thost, the London correspondent of the *Völkischer Beobachter.* The German publisher, meaning Amann, finally gave his approval for a sale that did not include the full text but only an abridged version. Berlin also decided which parts of the text were to be abridged.

It was Berlin—and therefore Amann and Hitler himself—that decided the British edition should not be complete. On the other hand, the negotiations with Italy proceeded quickly, directly, in a friendly atmosphere and an abridged edition was never even mentioned. The Germans never clearly explained why Great Britain was to get a watered-down version of the text and Italy was not. It is very likely they feared that the many pages of warmongering would best be cut to avoid getting a bad reception in London.

Amann was therefore offering the complete edition to the Italians. Mussolini's reaction to the offer came instantly: he gave Polverelli written instructions to transfer 250,000 lire to Munich[24] because Franz Eher Verlag was located there. The amount in lire was transferred by the Ministry of Foreign Affairs through Under Secretary Fulvio Suvich in the form of a check drawn on the Banco di Napoli.[25] On the 13th— perhaps a few hours after Mussolini had spoken with Major Renzetti,

---

Professor Barnes of Wabash College (Indiana) for graciously allowing me to include information contained in his book (e-mail of May 1, 2001).
24. See photo.
25. Suvich's authorization to pay exists. It is in ASDMAE, MAE, Gab. 1919–43, b. Gab. 125, f. Documenti sottratti dai fascicoli originali dal prof. Enrico Serra [Documents taken from the original files by Prof. Enrico Serra.]

who had traveled to Rome to receive his orders[26]—the check was delivered to the Italian Consul General in Munich, Francesco Pittalis.[27] The Duce acted expeditiously once he had decided to allocate the funds.

The operation was to remain completely confidential and extreme care was taken to ensure that as the buyer the Fascist government would never be connected to the recipient, Adolf Hitler, at any point in the future. The "pay off" was to be remitted anonymously and in cash. Even the receipt Amann was to sign[28] did not specify the amount paid or the identity of the purchaser, an exceptional measure of caution being at work in this case.

The amount was in itself significantly larger than the customary advances paid at that time in the publishing industry, not just in Italy but also abroad. A few simple comparisons will confirm this.

In 1933 two hundred and fifty thousand lire[29] equaled 53,625 marks.[30] Hurst & Blackett paid an advance of 2,611 marks, after expenses, to Franz Eher Verlag for the English rights to *Mein Kampf* for the edition published in London in October 1933.[31] The amounts

---

26. Mussolini received Renzetti at 4:30 p.m. on the 13th. See ACS, SPD, CO, b. 1310, f. Udienze Febbraio 1933 [Audiences February 1933].

27. See Doc. A4.

28. See Doc. A5.

29. See Doc. A11.

30. In 1933 the exchange rate was a minimum of 4,44 lire to the mark and a maximum of 4,69 lire. In this case it was set at 4,60 lire. For exchange rates see Ufficio Italiano dei Cambi, *I cambi delle principali valute in Italia 1918–1993* (Bari: Laterza, 1994), p. 198.

31. The numbers are provided (out of context) in J. J. Barnes and P. Barnes, *op. cit.* For the British publisher, pp. 16–17, and the American, pp. 78, 82.

received by the German publisher for the English rights up to December 1938 came to a total of 12,193 marks. Given the meager British sales of the book by Hurst & Blackett in later years and the problematic transfer of royalties to Germany during the war the total amount paid may not have been that much higher.

The same abridged edition was sold to the Houghton Mifflin Company in the United States with a royalty contract based on a percentage of sales and an advance of $500. The American publisher paid Eher Verlag another 5,668 marks at the end of 1936 once the first printing of just over 7,000 copies had sold out. Another 2,318 marks were paid after expenses in March 1938 and 6,858 marks in March 1939. A total of approximately 15,000 marks in all. In each case the payments represented about one-fourth of the amount Mussolini paid up front. The contract was, however, very unusual by Italian publishing standards as well. Drawing comparisons with other "rich" contracts of the time, we find that the popular novelist Guido Da Verona received an advance of 42,500 lire[32] in 1930 from Unitas Publishing. In 1934 Mondadori paid an advance of 1,000 pounds sterling (equal to 12,000 marks) to Stefan Zweig for his biography *Erasmus of Rotterdam*, plus a yearly ten percent royalty.[33] In both cases the amounts are about one-

---

32. A.S. Mi, Pretettura, Gab., 1st payment, b. 423, f. Casa Editrice Unitas pubblicazione libro intitolato "Promessi Sposi" di Guido da Verona [publication of the book entitled *Promessi Sposi* by Guido Da Verona.]
33. As written in the contracts records of Zweig, reproduced in *Stefan Zweig. Instants d'une vie. Images, texts, documents*, rassemblés par Klemens Renolder, Hildemar Holl, Peter Karlhuber (Paris: Stock, 1994), p. 112.

fourth of the total advance allocated for the Italian rights to *Mein Kampf.*

If on the other hand we consider the actual subsidies paid for books published in Italy, the unusually large amount of 100,000 lire that Mussolini paid a few years later in 1939 for a book by Giovanni Papini immediately stands out. It should be said however that this amounted to a subsidy intended to support a "historical" and ultra-fascist publisher such as Vallecchi, that was in deep financial trouble.[34]

Another one-time financing overseas appears two years later, specifically in November 1935—to the pro-fascist French daily *L'Ami du Peuple* in the amount of 500,000 French francs (407,000 lire).[35] Another key comparison must also be made: in October 1936, when the Nazi regime was in full swing, Amann offered to an ecstatic Joseph Goebbels a 250,000 marks advance plus a yearly stipend of 100,000 marks for the rights to his existing and future diaries.[36] It was by any terms of comparison a truly gigantic amount of money. Compared to the Goebbels advance Mussolini's 53,000 marks was not an indifferent amount. It corresponded after all to the purchase of translation and publication rights in a single country for a single book, *Mein Kampf,* which had already been published several years before. The 250,000 marks paid to Goebbels plus his "stipend," besides being clearly both

34. Giorgio Fabre, *L'elenco. Censura fascista, editoria e autori ebrei* (Turin: Zamorani, 1998), p. 13.
35. ASDMAE, MCP, DGSE, b. 509, f. *L'ami du peuple*, Taittinger, Henry (telegr. of 4 and 8 November).

income and a gift from the state for one of the new regime's highest ranking political figures, was also an investment in a totally exclusive new book inclusive of all future rights.

The Duce's payment of 53,625 marks was not simply very substantial; it was also unrelated to the customary market cost of the rights to the book and could only be justified—and for the Italians this would be the true motive behind Hitler's request—as an attempt to help the Nazi leader win the German elections. The proof that this was a likely scenario can be found in the funds set aside at that time to help Chancellor Englebert Dollfuss of Austria, who had asked for financing through Prince Starhemberg. Only ten days after the meeting with Amann, on February 17, 1933, Mussolini decided to pay up to 5,000,000 lire to help the Austrians.[37] The money had been requested and was being provided to stem the dangerous rise of the Nazis in Vienna. The Duce, faced with a long line of people demanding financial help at that time, secretly approved the different amounts in each case.

In other words—and this not intended as irony—the Duce gave the Führer money once he came to power; it was a personal form of funding that had very strong political underpinnings and enormous consequences. The actual amount in and of itself was very high if as

36. Elke Frölich (ed.), *Die Tagebücher von Joseph Goebbels. Sämtliche Fragmente,* vol. 2, 1.1.1931–31.12.1936 (Münich: Saur, 1987), p. 704.
37. DDI, VII s., Vol. XIII, pp. 109–10 (regarding the conversation between Suvich and Starhemberg with the amount), p. 203 (for the delivery of the funds, March 9, 1933).

payment of a copyright advance, but at the same time it was tiny as a contribution to political propaganda, and a mere pittance compared to what the Austrians were getting to prevent the Nazi tide from reaching the Italian border.

If news of the financial help given to the Nazis by the Fascists was making the rounds at the time, no hard evidence to the rumor can be traced.[38] After the war a few Italian diplomats hinted at such funding, but apart from the lack of credibility of some of these "eyewitnesses," the money they were referring to was given during the period of the rise to power of the "Hitler movement" long before 1933.[39] The financing discussed was never revealed by anyone nor did anyone ever find out about it. Even Fulvio Suvich, who was more than a witness and who actually played the role of intermediary in the transaction, was careful never to mention the episode, even indirectly. It was carefully kept secret during the entire post-war period.

According to Renzetti's memoirs, which are now available in the German archives in Koblenz, this was not the only funding the Nazis

---

38. These documents include those quoted by Leopold Steurer in his interview: Fabio Gobbato, "Mussolini finanziò Hitler," *L'Adige*, August 15, 2003. These are in ACS, MI, DGPS, DPP, f. materie, b. 43, f. C 11/30. Germania. Movimento Hitleriano [Germany. Hitler Movement] sf. 1. These are, however, simply reports of rumors from the Italian police.

39. See Raffaele Guariglia, *Ricordi 1922–1946* (Naples: ESI, 1950), p. 75, discusses the "considerable help" provided to the Nazis competing with those given to the Heimweheren. Giuliano Cora, "Un diplomatico durante l'era fascista," in *Storia e politica*, a. V, f. I, January–March 1966, p. 90 (Cora refers to a moment immediately following Hitler's failed Munich putsch of 1923 and says that he learned about the Italian funding from Bavarian government sources); Pietro Quaroni, "L'Italia dal 1914

had requested of the Italians.[40] A previous request never came to fruition, while the second actually did succeed. An account of the operation was to remain confidential and hidden in the Italian archives. Giuseppe Sapuppo, a government official who handled the file, did leave a paper trail of the matter in the archives and later wrote that "the decision to buy the translation rights to *Mein Kampf* [...] was a matter of political expediency."[41] It was intended as a show of Fascist support for the new power the Nazis represented. It was not an inordinately large amount, but what could one expect from a book deal? Hitler had made a bold request, had he not?

Furthermore, and formally with this secret money, Mussolini was acquiring the rights to the masterwork of Nazism; it was further proof of his keen interest in Hitler's ideology. After all, such exchanges and courtesies were rather common. Later on, in July, through Renzetti's efforts, a book by Italo Balbo was published and serialized in the Nazi paper, *Völkischer Beobachter*, the contract had probably been signed prior

---

al 1945," in *Nuove questioni di storia contemporanea*, Vol. II (Marzorati: Milan 1968), p. 1225 (the Hitler movement had received assistance "at various times").
40. Renzetti in his memoirs mentions a request for a second funding. Renzetti writes: "It has been said that Mussolini financed the Hitler movement. This is not true, he never gave anything. And I must say in all truthfulness that the Nazis never asked for anything. I will discuss two exceptions later on, one for the translation rights to Mein Kamps [*sic*], which was fulfilled; and another one, barely attempted, which I didn't even transmit." (BAK, collection. 1235 (Nachlass Renzetti), f. 16/ Memorien.) F. Scarano, *op. cit.*, p. 190, refers to this passage without quoting it. There is nothing further in Renzetti's memoirs regarding both funding attempts.
41. Doc. A34.

to the negotiations for *Mein Kampf*.[42] Balbo's advance—the amount is significant when compared to that paid in Italy for *Mein Kampf*—was 6,770 lire. At that time Balbo's career was at its zenith and his fame spanned the world immediately following his second celebrated transatlantic flight.

---

42. Renzetti passed on news of the publication to Mussolini's secretariat in a communication of July 15, 1933 (the book was published the following day). ACS, MCP, Gab., 1° versamento, Reports (1922–45), b. 3, f. Report. n. 20. "Giuseppe Renzetti maggiore: relazioni sulla situazione politica in Germania e sul contenuto dei suoi abboccamenti con Hitler, Göring ed altri ufficiali nazisti." The book was *Der Marsch auf Rome*, published by Kittler with a preface by Göring. On July 24, Renzetti informed Martelli, head of Balbo's cabinet, that he had sent (as an advance) a check for lire 6,770 (1,500 marks). BAK, collection N. 1235 (Nachlass Renzetti), f. 5/ Korrispondenz [1933].

Chapter V

The Protector

The check was finally sent to Munich on February 13, 1933; on the same day Mussolini received Major Renzetti and gave him instructions on what to tell Hitler. This conversation, along with the one held on the following day, was recorded in a note taken probably by Under Secretary Suvich, who was also present.[43] The Duce spoke freely: he "ordered" that Hitler give von Papen, whom the Führer did not trust, some responsibility; he approved the idea, already discussed with Amann, that the Nazis should win the elections by "any means

---

43. Regarding Renzetti's meetings with Mussolini and the Hitler-Mussolini relations during this period relating to the issue of the "Jews," see Giorgio Fabre, "Mussolini e gli ebrei alla salita al potere di Hitler," in *Saggi sull'ebraismo italiano del Novecento in onore di Luisella Mortara Ottolenghi*, ed. by Liliana Picciotto, *La rassegna mensile di Israel*, January–April 2003 (Vol. LXIX, n. 1), pp. 187–236. We quote pages 224–225 here.

possible"; he suggested firmly putting an end to the political murders that were bloodying the entire country; finally, he voiced his opinion that since the Germans wanted an anti-Semitic policy they should "gradually and without any kind of violence eliminate the Jews from all positions of importance." Less than one year before Mussolini had reassured journalist Emil Ludwig about his own attitude toward the Jews in an interview that was given worldwide distribution.[44] Now the Duce was making very different and secret suggestions that would be repeated several times later on. Mussolini wasn't simply issuing orders to his diplomats and representatives, he was also imparting copious "advice" to Hitler himself. Renzetti, as a faithful underling, was sure to pass along the advice as he received it.[45]

After some ten years of authoritarian government the Duce must have thought this was the way things should be done. He had already behaved that way in the past—at least since August 1931 when through Renzetti he had offered Hitler detailed advice on political action.[46] But

44. For the statements made to the German journalist, see Emil Ludwig, *Colloqui con Mussolini. Riproduzione delle bozze della prima edizione con le correzioni autografe del Duce* (Milan: Mondadori, 1950), pp. 72–73 (first edition, 1932, pp. 75–76). Regarding the fact that at that time (March–April 1932) Mussolini was certainly saying some untruths on the issue of the "Jews," see Annalisa Capristo, "L'esclusione degli Ebrei dall'Accademia d'Italia," *La rassegna mensile di Israel*, September–October 2001, pp. 1–27, in particular pp. 1–6.

45. In a report dated May 14, 1933, Renzetti criticized the measures enacted by the Nazis against the Jews and wrote: "And so we agree with the Duce whose thoughts I transmitted clearly to Hitler in the past and more recently." DDI, VII s., vol. XIII, p. 655 (report from Renzetti to Mussolini's secretariat drafted that same day). But on the subject see G. Fabre, *Mussolini e gli ebrei, cit.*, pp. 190–194.

46. For 1931 see the June 20, 1931, letter from Giovanni Capasso Torre (who was also the former head of the Duce's Press Office), the consul at Munich, where he says

that was prior to Hitler's rise to power and now that he was the Reich Chancellor his Italian protector simply continued to act as though nothing had changed. To top things off Mussolini felt even more justified in his display of superiority since he had just received a call for help. Italian historian Renzo De Felice[47] has written that Mussolini wished to "remain free of any specific commitment" during the early stages of the Nazi party's growth and Hitler's ascent. But this doesn't appear to be the case. True, Mussolini was cautious, but he didn't proceed with the "extreme caution" De Felice wrote about elsewhere. He conducted secret diplomacy enabling him to take bolder positions and was ready to provide the cash to help his German friends even though it had strings attached and was competing with the funding he sent to the Austrians.

This signaled the start of an intense "patronizing" effort by the Duce through his institutions over a period of several months, aimed at the new German regime and even more at Hitler himself. Italy was the only world power that not only showed no hostility towards Nazi Germany but actually took a favorable view of the new regime through

---

he transmitted to Hitler the "advice" personally given to him by Mussolini (to move the Party's headquarters from Munich to Berlin). ACS, SPD, CR, b. 71, f. 442/R Hitler, Adolf. Führer. sf. 1. But see also Renzetti's letter to the Press Office dated August 19, 1931, where on Mussolini's orders he sent a newspaper article from *La Libertà* for Hitler to read (but the letter was not sent). ASDMAE, MCP, DGSE, b. 110, f. 1931. Very confidential and classified envelope for His Excellency Orsini Baroni (mail drop for Renzetti). See also Renzetti's reports to Mussolini on June 21 and October 25, 1932, regarding passing on other "advice." DDI, VII s., Vol. XII, pp. 144–145, 462–464.

47. Renzo De Felice, *Mussolini, il Duce. I. Gli anni del consenso. 1929–1936* (Turin: Einaudi, 1974), p. 441.

a number of specific actions.[48] Mussolini made sure the help he was giving did not go unnoticed and took the liberty of imparting advice on every issue from foreign policy—he even suggested with whom the Germans should seek alliances and whom they should avoid[49]—to internal security and economic policy.

The Italian dictator then attempted to weigh in even on Nazi anti-Jewish policies. Mussolini at that time was committed to defending the political Four Power Pact against Nazi violence and excesses. However, he discouraged the Nazi anti-Jewish position only in part by concentrating on calming down its most openly virulent manifestations. Once public acts of violence by the Nazis against the Jews did in fact begin to recede, Mussolini asked the German ambassador to avoid going too far in the opposite direction, thereby avoiding the image of backing down in the face of a "power" such as that represented by the Jews.[50]

We now have additional evidence hidden within these files relating to the funding. The Germans came to see the Duce, asking for money, and furthermore, no one could predict they wouldn't do so again in the future. Mussolini agreed to pay an amount far exceeding what the Germans imagined they could raise through the straightforward sale of

48. For the events recounted here see G. Fabre, *Mussolini e gli ebrei, cit.*, pp. 194–198.
49. See the "very confidential" telegram from Mussolini to Ambassador Cerruti of February 21, 1933, where the Duce gave a whole list of hints to be given to Hitler regarding the attitude he should adopt toward France, England, and the USSR. The text is in ASDMAE, MAE, DGAP, 1931–1943, Germany, b. 12. Reproduced in DDI, VII s., Vol. XIII, pp. 123–124.
50. G. Fabre, *Mussolini e gli ebrei, cit.*, pp. 203–204 and 235.

book rights. But one may logically assume that in turn they would expect to obtain even more to cover their election costs. The Germans had asked first and this encouraged Mussolini to think that he could broaden his influence as the "chaperone" or, better, as the "godfather" of a movement that was considered genuinely "Fascist" and in fact viewed as the heir to Fascism itself. Mussolini in effect had risen to the challenge with great and perhaps excessive cunning.

Chapter VI

Trust Among "Wiseguys"

Strangely enough in the weeks that followed the Germans took a seemingly incomprehensible attitude towards the entire matter of the *Mein Kampf* translation by completely ignoring it and remaining aloof.

For starters, the Germans allowed the set date of March 5 to slip by because it was election day and culminated in a triumphant Nazi victory while still failing to achieve an absolute parliamentary majority. Before that date no one came forward to collect the funds the Italians had provided, which in theory were meant to finance the elections. The Italians went to great pains to make sure that the money would arrive before the 5th, uselessly as it turned out, and Polverelli, head of the

Press Office, even called Munich to follow up.[51] One of the key players in the whole affair was beginning to become increasingly elusive. Max Amann, to whom Consul General Pittalis was to hand over the money coming from Rome, systematically skipped all his appointments with the Italians.[52] As Pittalis reported: "He is hesitant and is making excuses." Less than one month after visiting with Mussolini, hat in hand, the Nazis seemed to have forgotten the entire agreement.

What had changed in the meantime? Quite simply this: a far less dangerous form of financing than that offered by Mussolini was now available to the Nazis in Germany itself. Even before the elections the pressing need for money had been considerably reduced: Hitler had managed to secure funds from contributors he probably didn't even want in the first place. The captains of German industry, under the guidance and influence of Hjalmar Schacht, had met at Hermann Göring's residence on February 20 and agreed to cover any financial shortfall the Nazis were to incur by pledging a contribution of 3,000,000 marks.[53] As if this were not enough, on the following day the German cabinet reversed itself regarding its previous decisions and agreed to back Hitler's Nazi party propaganda effort using state funds.[54]

Mussolini's money was therefore no longer required. The Nazis had come with a pressing request and the Duce had responded with a half measure. At that point they found a solution to their problem through

---

51. See Doc. A6
52. Docs. A7 and A9.
53. H. A. Turner, *op. cit.*, pp. 329–332.

different sources. Finally, it was only on March 19 that Amann paid a visit to Consul General Pittalis, displaying a very different attitude. According to Amann the entire matter was now "taking on the appearance of a political affair," rather than a simple publishing or financial agreement.[55] What he really meant was that he was no longer pleased with the way things were going.

It is impossible to know what Pittalis meant exactly when he wrote "the appearance of a political affair," which could have referred to many different things. There is no way of knowing whether in the meantime the Nazis had found out about the huge Italian funding provided to the Austrians and whether Amann was venting his displeasure about it. It is also possible that he could have been referring to the potential acute embarrassment of his boss, who was involved in heavy political financing—but wasn't this what he had actually lobbied for in the first place? He could also have been hinting that the amount of money offered was too low—following his conversation with Amann, Polverelli had noted[56] that the Nazis "needed a lot of money." It could have meant the opposite since so much money provided for only one book could become embarrassing: but this last assumption appears to be highly unlikely.

It must be said that during the next phase of the negotiations no one ever commented that the amount in question was excessive for a

---

54. I. Kershaw, *op. cit.*, pp. 447–448.
55. Doc. A7.
56. Doc. A2.

book deal—and the Nazis were hardly the kind of people to feel disconcerted about being given too much money. Once they unsuccessfully attempted to set up a kind of little financial lifeboat in Italy events quickly made the exercise moot and even embarrassing so they were understandably distancing themselves from it as much as they could. Whatever the case may be, the Germans let the date of the general elections slip by without making contact. Only later by mid-March, after insistent reminders from the Italians—once they were fully cognizant of the amount agreed upon that was placed at their disposal—did the Germans prepare a draft contract both in German and Italian which they sent to Rome.[57]

The draft reached the Italian Ministry of Foreign Affairs where it was immediately examined by the legal section that came up with many objections and restated many clauses in the contract.[58] The intent of the exercise was to clearly indicate that the transaction was to appear as a *sale* made by Franz Eher Verlag, rather than a *purchase* by an unidentified and as yet nonexistent Italian publisher. The Germans' strategy was to offer a standard publishing contract intended for another publisher in order to prevent it from becoming a "political matter." The Italians then rewrote the contract, making the Fascist government rather than another publisher the purchaser of the book rights.

---

57. Docs. A10–12.
58. Doc. A13.

The comments provided by the Italians can essentially be reduced to two. The first dealt with the issue of the power of attorney that, as the legal section duly noted, was meant to cover only non-German newspaper extracts of passages from *Mein Kampf.* The legal section observed that a different power of attorney was required, using tighter language, regularly stamped by a notary public, and not just a blank piece of paper such as the one provided; furthermore, the document should specifically mention book rights and not newspapers.

The second comment was more political than legal. Based on existing Italian law, Italy enjoyed freedom of religion with equal rights among individuals belonging to "the religions authorized within the Kingdom." Law number 1159 of June 24, 1929, stated in article 4 that "religious diversity shall not impede the exercise of political and civil rights." While the legal section at the ministry agreed to the German request that the translator of the book be an Italian citizen—obviously to avoid using an anti-Nazi German—it was unacceptable that the person should be of the Jewish faith or "race" as it was specified in the document. There was, however, a way around this, as the legal section suggested, that was both honorable and sufficiently anti-Semitic: the publisher acquiring the rights would sign a separate undertaking agreeing to not have "an Israelite" as the book's translator.

The Germans—perhaps for purely diplomatic reasons—had been very accommodating regarding any control over the translation. The German draft of the contract mentioned that it would be "possible" to have a German translator recommended the publisher to check the translation. Franz Eher Verlag had simply stated that it would be "willing" to provide such a person. The legal section at the ministry took a very clear position on this clause, offering language that gave total freedom of choice for potential German assistance to the future Italian publisher, who could "as it finds it necessary and convenient, decide to use the services of a person enjoying the trust of Fr. Eher publishing company" and "shall be free to accept or reject the corrections or changes proposed by that person." The Italians were therefore already defending their future and the as yet unidentified publisher.

Did Mussolini personally examine the text of the German contract and the Italian proposal? It is difficult to be absolutely certain, but in all probability he did, because some of the legal section's pages of comments are underlined. Those pencil marks could very possibly be his own since he was following the matter closely as it reached an extremely critical stage. On the other hand, it is very clear that the suggestions made by the legal section were accepted "in toto" in the revised Italian version of the contract that was quickly sent to Munich on April 10, 1933.[59] The only detail omitted at this point was the possibility of a separate agreement regarding the exclusion of any Jewish translator; the new text of the contract made no mention of the translator, nor, from what we can tell, did the Germans insist on that clause. But the Germans were once again dragging their feet despite

---

59. Doc. A14.

solicitations from Rome about putting the last touches on the contract;[60] the final text would require more time. They procrastinated by delaying making any decision and began discussing a few minor points, such as their insistence on keeping the faulty power of attorney. The Italians immediately conceded that issue, stating they were ready to move ahead.[61]

The contract was finalized only on June 6[62] even though it was dated May 30, and only then were the papers signed by Max Amann,[63] both in German and Italian. It was forwarded to Rome, along with a receipt,[64] probably signed by an Eher Verlag administrator, with the notation: "translation and publishing rights for Italy for the book *Mein Kampf* by Hitler."[65] It was the same contract the Italians had offered, which had been drafted in Rome and that the Germans had agreed to with some difficulty but in the end accepted in its entirety. One detail reveals that the bilingual text was actually the one drafted by the Italians: the date in the German column bears mention of the year of the Fascist Era. On the other hand, on the Italian side no publisher's name was entered. The Germans were therefore signing off in the dark, so to speak and even though they had been overpaid they were agreeing to hand over their precious text to the Italian authorities. The story had now truly become a "political matter."

---

60. Doc. A17.
61. Docs. A 20 and A21.
62. Doc. A 23.
63. See photo.
64. Doc. A25 and photo.

The Italians were also "boxed in" in a way, since they were committed to publishing the most important text the Nazis had produced. That obligation was now in the hands of the Germans in the form of a contract, which they were to use, as will become clear later.[66] If faced with potential complaints the Italians would have their hands tied and they would not have been able to avoid publication; they would have been compelled to publish or risk creating an international incident. At the end of September, the Germans announced with some fanfare the coming publication of the Italian translation.[67] This was perhaps a way to avoid stirring up the "political matter" that Amann feared so much. Whether secret or not, the contract remained an agreement reached with another government, whereas the other "foreign" contracts for *Mein Kampf* had been signed with private companies; the one with Houghton Mifflin was signed on July 29, 1933. With Italy it was to be a very different story indeed.

The whole episode plays out like a silent and robust enough war among "wise guys" intent on making the most of the situation: Mussolini seeking to affirm his right to influence a restless new foreign political movement that he felt he somehow patronized, while Hitler and his men were attempting both to fill the coffers for what promised to be a difficult election and broaden their political and ideological influence abroad while making money as well. As things turned out

---

65. I owe the interpretation of this sentence to Dr. Valentina Cuomo.
66. Doc. A63.

Mussolini missed an opportunity. Either because his offer was too small or because his attitude had been too "overbearing," whatever the reason his attempt to manipulate Hitler had failed. The golden opportunity that fell into the Duce's lap to influence Hitler did not materialize. The Germans turned out to be smarter by avoiding an outright political contribution but still managed to get some money for the book and apparently a personal "stipend" for Adolf Hitler himself.

The Italian dictator on the other hand wound up only holding a secret receipt from a publisher, the Italian rights to *Mein Kampf* and the obligation to publish the book. Mussolini was also fully aware that he had provided only a portion of funding after the election, which didn't allow him to fully take advantage of his involvement from a political and diplomatic point of view. Mussolini therefore only managed to provide some help for the efforts and the wallet of his "pupil" and new rival. Even though no specific numbers are available, the information provided by the newspapers at the time clearly illustrates the unusual success of the sales of *Mein Kampf.* In Germany during the nine months from the beginning of the year sales had climbed from 287,000 copies, sold during the entire period before that, to 850,000 copies and possibly even 1,000,000 copies by the end of 1933.[68] According to

---

67. This news (along with that of the imminent publication of the Dutch edition) was reported in the *Times* of September 27, 1933 (p. 9, col. g).
68. The number quoted in Hitler's "Honorar Buch" at Eher Verlag is 854,000 copies sold as of November 17, 1933 (O. J. Hale, *Adolf Hitler: Taxpayer, cit.*, p. 837). For the totals, see "The Story of Mein Kampf," in *The Wiener Library Bulletin*, VI, 5–6, September–December 1952, pp. 31–32. Instead the *Times* on October 23, 1933 ("Herr Hitler's Foreign Policy," p. 10, col. d), spoke of sales going from the spring to

other estimates by the end of 1945 in Germany alone some 10,000,000 copies had been distributed and sold, to which foreign sales must be added.[69] The book had been translated into sixteen languages, including Chinese by 1936.[70] Distribution of the book was a matter of prestige for the Nazi regime.

In 1941, citing the "British press," some writers stated that between 1936 and 1938 Hitler had made 72,000,000 French francs in royalties, plus 12,000,000 marks that were used to pay for the lavish refurbishment of his estate at the Berghof.[71] By the end of the war there were some five million marks in Hitler's account with Eher Verlag, a huge balance from which he had drawn regularly and rather copiously.[72] Other Nazi leaders also incurred steep expenses—and posted equally steep earnings; money seems to have been a very high

---

October 1933 from 380,000 to 1,500,000 copies. Again on September 27, 1933, the *Times* announced that by October 2 one million copies would have been sold (p. 9, col. g).

69. For a summary evaluation see I. Kershaw, *op. cit.*, pp. 242–243.

70. The news of the publication of a Chinese-language edition in Nanking is in the *Times* of February 28, 1936 (p. 15, col. g). The publication was requested by John Otway Percy Bland, friend of the famous forger Edmund Backhouse (Hugh R. Trevor-Roper, *Hermit of Peking: The Hidden Life of Sir Edmund Backhouse* (New York: Alfred A. Knopf, 1977), p. 32

71. M. J. Benoist-Méchin, *Chiarimenti sul Mein Kampf di Adolfo Hitler* (Milan: Garzanti, 1941), pp. 6–7. Benoist-Méchin claimed that Hitler made 18 million French francs in 1936, 24 million in 1937 and 30 million in 1938.

72. O. J. Hale, *The Captive Press, cit.* pp. 315–316. Hale was the American officer who interrogated Amann at length after the war on the German press and reported the following information: Hitler had 5,525,811 marks in his account, Göring 67,861, Goebbels 135,164, Rosenberg 85,673. It was known that Hitler withdrew 569,212 marks in 1943, Göring 210,600, Goebbels 244,212 and Rosenberg 254,908.

priority among the National Socialist elite.[73] Relatively generous and among the first to tumble in from abroad, the Italian payment was funneled into Hitler's private account.

---

73. In general, for the issue of "Hitler's money" and the money of other Nazi leaders, see with some reservations, Wulf C. Schwarzwäller, *Hitlers Geld. Von Armen Kunstmaler zum Millionenschweren Führer* (Weisbaden: Vma-Verlag, 2001).

Chapter VII

Availability

The progress of the Italian translation of *Mein Kampf* is a fascinating tale—and not just from the point of view of publishing history. Since the book was undoubtedly a political document anything associated with it would be political as well. The Italian Ministry of Foreign Affairs, true to the letter of the contract, immediately began a search for an Italian publisher. This negotiation, aside from being favorable, had the backing of the top echelons in Rome, ensuring that the book would actually be translated and published.

The Duce was determined that the book should benefit from solid professional oversight and a broad readership, so Mondadori naturally became the first choice—at that time it was already Italy's largest and most successful publisher. Owner and founder Arnoldo Mondadori was contacted through his brother Bruno, head of the company's Rome office.[74] Only a short time before, in June–July 1932, Mondadori had published a book of interviews with Mussolini by Emil Ludwig, and the Duce held the company in high esteem and thought the publisher to be personally loyal, as well as being very savvy. Mussolini was therefore determined to use "his" publisher, rightly believing that he would provide the book with the best distribution. After a rather long wait, Arnoldo came back with an answer[75]: it was a flat no, offered politely, but a refusal nonetheless. His excuse was that his company was heavily committed to too many projects at the moment, such as, for example, printing books for the Fascist party and the various government ministries, it would therefore be unable to fulfill all the pending requests.

Mondadori also mentioned that he had been aware of the book for some time. Had he wanted to translate and publish it he could have done so on his own but that did not happen. One reason for his refusal was the book's size and the fact that at least part of the text was "of local German interest." Finally, he mentioned studies written about Hitler that were "less extensive," that had "even been published by other Italian publishers." No doubt he was referring to the anti-Nazi book *Hitler* by Theodor Heuss, published by Bompiani. This last remark strengthens the thought—which was almost certainly the

---

74. Docs. A24 and A26.
75. Doc. A26.

case—that Arnoldo was using it as an excuse to avoid a book that could become the source of innumerable problems.

Mondadori at that time was already deeply committed to publishing titles opposing the Nazis through a feisty editor in the German section of the "Medusa" book series, Lavinia Mazzucchetti. Mondadori was also publishing, or about to publish, books by several anti-Nazi German writers, some of whom were Jewish. One of these was clearly Emil Ludwig and Mondadori had already published several biographies he had written, as well as his *Talks with Mussolini* (English title) in 1932. Arnold Zweig was also a Mondadori author since 1930 (*La questione del tenente Grisha—The Case of Sergeant Grisha*); Vicki Baum (*Elena Willfüer, Stud, chem.—Chemistry Student Helen Willfüer*) in 1932; Lion Feuchtwänger—the first volume of his "Trilogy of Joseph" *La Fine di Gerusalemme—The End of Jerusalem*, was published by the "Medusa" book series on April 1, 1933.[76] Finally, Nobel Prize winner Thomas Mann had been lured to Mondadori[77] from another publisher, Corbaccio, just

---

76. The book also announces the imminent publication of a book by Arnold Zweig, *Giovane donna del 1914* [Young Woman of 1914].

77. The information comes from Lavinia Mazzucchetti. See Thomas Mann, *Lettere a italiani*, introduction and notes by Lavinia Mazzucchetti (Milan: Il Saggiatore, 1962), p. 29. See also the letter from Mazzucchetti to Mann dated March 14, 1933, mentioning Mondadori's intention to take on the German author and steal him from Corbaccio, *cit.*, in Lucia Giusti, "Aspetti della ricezione della letteratura tedesca moderna in Italia negli anni Venti-Trenta," in *Editori e lettori. La produzione libraria in Italia nella prima metà del Novecento,* edited by Luisa Finocchi and Ada Gigli Marchetti (Milan: Angeli, 2000), p. 257. Regarding relations with Ullstein there is information in a letter from Enrico Bemporad to Mondadori himself dated March 7, 1933, regarding the exclusive to a book by Vicki Baum. See *Non c'è tutto nei romanzi. Leggere romanzi stranieri in una casa editrice negli anni '30,* edited by Pietro Albonetti (Milan: Fondazione Arnoldo e Alberto Mondadori, 1994), p. 74.

a few months before in the spring of 1933. Mondadori was about to finish the translation and to publish his *Le Storie di Giacobbe—The Tales of Jacob*; the book was eventually published on November 30, 1933. There was also the rather friendly business relationship between Mondadori and anti-Nazi Berlin publisher Ullstein. Under these circumstances, it was likely that the publication of *Mein Kampf* could be perceived as potentially creating too many problems and enemies for Mondadori. All these reasons could well have motivated Mondadori to take a position that was completely out of character and reject a request that had been made by the Duce's office.

The Press Office, acting through the prefect of Milan—once again very confidentially[78]—then turned to the next candidate as publisher, also considered very trustworthy, Valentino Bompiani. The offer was very clear: Bompiani would handle all translation and printing expenses and in exchange keep all revenues. The publisher's response on July 27 was very positive.[79] Once a copy of the German edition reached the publisher's office at the beginning of August,[80] the work of assessing and preparing the translation got under way.

Bompiani didn't ask any contract related questions about *Mein Kampf* and the ministry did not volunteer information regarding the negotiations that had already taken place.[81] Bompiani remained, it appears voluntarily, in the dark concerning any prior history, even

---

78. Doc. A27.
79. Doc. A28.
80. Doc. A30.

confirm his agreement, possibly given on the same day, to publish the "national edition" of Mussolini's complete works. In his telegram Hoepli also noted that "other European countries and Colombian continents [i.e., the Americas] are surrendering to the new ideologies that you have proclaimed and enacted under the name of Fascism." The entire world, Hoepli wrote emphatically, was becoming Fascist, and with that he was clearly referring to Nazism and Nazi Germany. No information is available regarding those negotiations but they obviously couldn't have been an accident. Together with the translation of *Mein Kampf,* the summa of Hitler's thought, Mussolini was launching the official "edition" of his own works, which would obviously require several large volumes, many more in fact than the two of *Mein Kampf,* bringing together texts that preceded those written by Hitler by several years. Mussolini, in other words, was about to embark on publishing his own "opus maximum."

By August Bompiani had started working on the translation. In early September the publisher wrote another letter to the Duce's Press Office.[83] Following a careful evaluation of the work he was now convinced that it was necessary to modify the project somewhat, meaning that he recommended translating only part of the book rather than the entire text. He would concentrate on the theoretical and ideological sections of the second volume of the German edition. The idea was to write only a summary of the more autobiographical first

---

83. Doc. A33.

volume, while keeping the most racist chapter, entitled "Nation and Race," in its entirety. With those changes *Mein Kampf* could then be published in a single-volume edition rather than in two volumes, which according to Bompiani, could not be marketed to a "broad readership." In the same letter the publisher was requesting assistance in securing a special introduction to be written by Hitler himself.

Bompiani and Mondadori had therefore reached the same conclusion. Bompiani was being handed the book without having to pay any royalties but he still had to shoulder all other expenses and could presumably see his way to a guaranteed profit; however, such a dense and turgid book, as evidenced by the German edition, would be unlikely to make that possible. This was his personal conclusion. At the end of July the London *Times* published a number of extracts of *Mein Kampf* from the "authorized English edition," thereby announcing the book's publication that took place at the beginning of October. There was no mention of an *abridged* edition, nor had anyone brought up the issue; Bompiani's idea of "reducing" the book's size had not been suggested by another example but was generated internally within his company.

Bompiani's letter reached the desk of Galeazzo Ciano, who had just replaced Gaetano Polverelli as head of Mussolini's Press Office on August 2.[84] Polverelli's deputy Giuseppe Sapuppo, who was specifically in charge of handling the foreign press, brought the letter in question to

___

84. Mussolini's handwritten communiqué for that same day in ACS, SPD, CO, Zinc box, sc. 9, f. 11.4.3.

Ciano. Unlike Polverelli, Sapuppo had retained his position.[85] He filled Ciano in since the new man had no knowledge of the matter. Ciano then went to the Duce—who was also his father-in-law—to get his opinion. Mussolini immediately agreed to have the book condensed but he still required that the proposal be sent to the German publisher; he also agreed to ask Hitler to write a special preface.[86] A few days before[87] Mussolini had also approved an edition for the blind following a German request but perhaps this was just one more trick: to approve something while not actually carrying it out.[88]

This issue deserves careful attention: Mussolini agreed to make the Italian edition of *Mein Kampf* more manageable. This could have meant that he had reached the conclusion that the book was too "heavy," something that may not have displeased him that much. The proposal had come from the publisher, however, without any pressure from Italian officials, or from the Germans.

A few months later, in June 1934, when the Bompiani edition had been in print for a month and a half, a French court issued a ruling on a pirated translation of *Mein Kampf* in the law suit brought by Franz Eher Verlag against les Nouvelles éditions latines. The French publisher—it was pro-fascist and not at all hostile to the book—had published a

---

85. Doc. A34.
86. Doc. A35.
87. Docs. A31, 32, 36.
88. It seems that this Italian edition never came to pass. There is no evidence that Bompiani ever received the actual permission.

complete and unabridged translation without the author's permission.[89] The lawyers for les Nouvelles éditions latines put up a spirited defense, which they lost and that ultimately the Nazis won, using the argument that *Mein Kampf* was a political manifesto rather than a simple work of literature. It should therefore be known and distributed in its complete and unabridged version even more so because the author was the head of a state that only a few years before had been at war with France.

This could all appear to be yet another chapter in *Mein Kampf*'s publishing history that didn't concern Italy or its translation, when a direct relationship in fact did exist. During court proceedings the French attorneys insisted on the difference between the French translation and the abridgements—those were the words they used— "as they were offered officially to the French and the Italians" was nothing but a device to hide the text itself. In France, therefore, the Italian and British versions were singled out as a text that the Germans had deliberately truncated. There is no record of any Italian reaction to those totally unjustified statements at that time. While the French attorneys were correct regarding the English translation, they were certainly mistaken about the Bompiani edition, which the Germans had

---

89. For the account of the trial and the judgment, "Au tribunal de Commerce. La traduction de Mein Kampf," *Le Temps,* June 20, 1934, p. 8. Regarding the pro-fascist stance of the publisher, who attempted to obtain Mussolini's authorization—it was not extended—to translate one of his books, see ASDMAE, MCP, DGSE, b. 171, f. *Vita di Arnaldo* di Benito Mussolini.

though he had to believe that some kind of transaction had taken place. Such details, however, probably didn't warrant much investigation at that point and the contract with Franz Eher Verlag continued to remain completely secret.

It should be pointed out that the query sent by the Press Office—the government and Mussolini himself were actually peddling and pushing for a translation of *Mein Kampf*—was extremely clear and that besides a prefect, it had been sent to two major publishers, one of them Mondadori, which happened to be Italy's largest and most important company. The discretion surrounding the operation was indeed impressive but the publishers and their staff were at least kept informed—this staff was not just another group of employees: they represented an intellectual elite removed from political power, that was finding out long before anyone else that the Fascist regime was warmly sponsoring the publication of Hitler's book. It is legitimate to wonder whether some individuals may have ventured beyond the bare facts sensing that all this could possibly have some kind of political and ideological significance and imagine what the consequences could possibly be.

Finally, something happened that was probably more than just a mere coincidence. The day after Bompiani's letter of acceptance arrived, Mussolini received a telegram from another prestigious publisher.[82] It was the old publisher Ulrico Hoepli, who was writing to

---

81. Doc. A62.
82. ACS, SPD, CO, b. 1042, f. 509.164. Hoepli, Ulrico. Casa editrice.

originally offered to the Italians in its entirety. The Italian publisher had actually offered to make cuts to the text and had done so innocently.

Giuseppe Renzetti with his wife Susanna *(at his right)*
meeting with Hitler in 1933.

Il Segretario particolare di Hitler mi ha oggi comunicato che il Direttore della Casa editrice nazionalsocialista di Monaco, il Signor Hamann si reca in Italia allo scopo di venedere ad una Casa editrice italiana i diritti di traduzione e poi di vendita del libro di Hitler "Main Kampf". Lo scopo della vendita sarebbe quello di ottenere dei fondi da impiegare nella lotta elettorale che come è noto, verrà iniziata fra qualche giorno.

Nel dirmi questo, il Dott Hess mi ha pregato di interessare le Superiori Gerarchie per far facilitare il compito dell'Hamann. Si sarebbe vivamente grati al Capo del Governo italiano qualora Egli potesse accordare alla Casa editrice italiana da scegliere o all'Haman stesso, una certa somma.

Hitler non vuole ricorrere a bancheri o a industriali per racimolare i fondi necessari per la lotta. Gli è pertanto che mobilita tutto quanto è possibile per averne attraverso vendite di librie ecc.

Poichè io ritengo che l'esito delle elezioni dovrebbe essere favorevole ai nazi e date le simpatie che questi hanno per l'Italia, subordinatamente passo la richiesta fattami con la preghiera di volerla accogliere benevolmente.

L'Hamann parte oggi stesso per l'Italia e scenderà a Roma all'Albergo Flora ove resterà in attesa delle persone con le quali egli dovrà trattare, Persone che dovrebbero venire fissate dalle Superiori Gerarchie.

Egli non vorrebbe restare a Roma più di due o tre giorni dato che qui lo attendono i lavori per la lotta elettorale che si inizierà in questi giorni.

(G. Renzetti)

Renzetti's memo of February 3, 1933, with Mussolini's notations.

Max Amann, c. 1935.

ADOLF HITLER

KANZLEI:
MÜNCHEN 2, BRIENNERSTR. 45
FERNSPRECHER 56065-67

MÜNCHEN, DEN ....

V o l l m a c h t

Der Direktor des Verlages Franz E h e r Nachf.
G.m.b.H. M ü n c h e n , Thierschstrasse 11
Herr Max A m a n n
ist berechtigt, von meinem Werke "Mein Kampf" das Verlags-
recht für ausländische Zeitungen, das ich mir in dem Verlags-
vertrag mit der Firma Franz Eher Nachf. G.m.b.H. ausdrücklich
vorbehalten habe, als mein Bevollmächtigter zu veräussern.
München, den 1. Oktober 1931.

Diese Vollmacht hat heute noch volle Gültigkeit.
Berlin, den 27. Januar 1933.

Hitler's power of attorney dated October 1, 1931, and renewed on January 27, 1933.

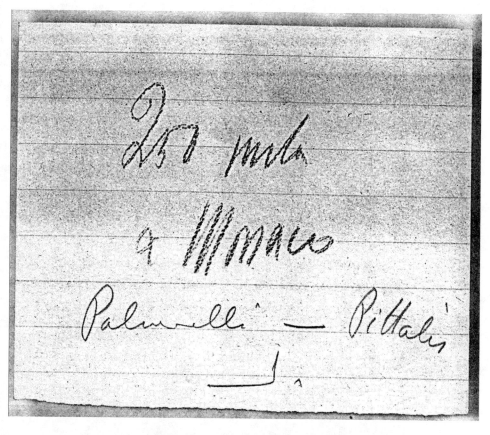

above
Mussolini's handwritten note to Polverelli and Pittalis with the amount to be sent to Franz Eher Verlag and with the added initials of Fulvio Suvich.

below
Hitler's signature.

Amann's signature on the contract for the translation into Italian of *Mein Kampf*.

QUITTUNG.

Nº _____   Für RM 5 3 6 2 5.—

Von Kgl. Italienischen Generalkonsulat München

für Übersetzungs- u. Veröffentlichungsrechte für Italien an dem Buche Hitler „Mein Kampf".

Reichsmark Fünfzigdreitausendsechshundert

Zwanzigfünf

erhalten zu haben, wird hierdurch bescheinigt.

München den 6. Juni 19 33

Frz. Eher Nachf., G. m. b. H.

Receipt issued by German publisher Franz Eher Verlag, Munich,
to the Italian Consulate General in Munich.

Völker, die für erhabene nationale Ideen kämpfen, sind lebensstark und zukunftsreich. Sie halten ihr Schicksal selbst in Händen. Jhre gemeinschaftsbildenden Kräfte sind dann nicht selten Werte von internationaler Geltung, die für das Zusammenleben der Völker untereinander segensreicher wirken, als die "unsterblichen Ideen" des Liberalismus, die die Beziehungen der Nationen verwirren und vergiften. Faschismus und Nationalismus, in ihrer weltanschaulichen Grundhaltung innerlich verwandt, sind berufen, einer fruchtbaren internationalen Zusammenarbeit neue Wege zu weisen. Sie in ihrem tiefsten Sinn und Wesen begreifen, heißt dem Frieden der Welt und damit der Wohlfahrt der Völker dienen.

Berlin, den 2. März 1934.

above
Hitler's original signed preface to *La mia battaglia,* published by Bompiani in 1934.

opposite
The original 1934 cover of *La mia battaglia.*

HITLER
LA MIA BATTAGLIA

BOMPIANI

Italo Balbo in 1933 with Mussolini *(center)* and Fascist party secretary Achille Starace *(left).*

The original cover of the 1941 complete edition of the translation of *Mein Kampf* as
La mia vita, La mia battaglia published by Bompiani.

The 1938 advertisement for *La mia battaglia.*

Traduzione dal tedesco
DEL PROF. BRUNO REVEL
dell'Università Bocconi di Milano

Enigma Books

The copyright page of the 1941 edition of the complete Italian translation of *Mein Kampf* with the translation credit given to Bruno Revel.

Fulvio Suvich *(left)* at a meeting in Germany with Rudolf Hess in 1933.

Alfred Rosenberg in 1941.

Under Secretary of the Ministry of the Interior Guido Buffarini Guidi *(center)* with Himmler in 1938.

Chapter VIII

Cutting the Text

By mid-1933 political relations between Italy and Germany had gone through some sharp changes, mostly because of frenzied German moves on the international scene. The Italians were the object of a few egregious insults: Germany, for example, was putting intense pressure on Austria with its talk of an *Anschluss* between the two countries. This was obviously an unacceptable outcome for Italy. Another source of irritation came at the League of Nations in Geneva where, after opposing the signing of the Four Power Pact on European disarmament for the longest time, an initiative that Mussolini had warmly endorsed, Berlin simply omitted giving Rome any advance warning of its intention to walk out of the League.

Even more disturbing was the fact that the Duce was finding out month after month that Fascism was losing its influence in Germany. Nazism was beginning to find its own way and Goebbels was busy creating institutions similar to those existing in Italy—for example, worker's recreational associations modeled on the Fascist "Dopolavoro"—claiming that these were purely German creations. Then the "Society for the Study of Fascism," which was extremely friendly towards Italy, was simply shut down without a word of warning to its Italian counterpart.[90] There was also a marked increase in the number of statements coming out of Germany regarding the superiority of the Germanic race that greatly irritated the Italians. Mussolini penned several unsigned editorials in his newspaper, *Il Popolo d'Italia*, from August to December 1933 where he openly ridiculed this trumpeted "racial superiority."[91]

In spite of all these signs Mussolini's staff continued to actively monitor the progress of the translation of Hitler's book. No unfavorable political clouds were allowed to darken the preparation of the Italian edition, not even during the most awkward moments.

As for Bompiani's two requests—to cut the text and obtain a new preface by Hitler—these would be given different answers in the

---

90. The initial information was sent by Renzetti to Rome on November 29, 1933; as for the news that the Society had been disbanded he included it in the report of December 6, 1933. Both reports are in ASDMAE, MAE, Gab. 1919–43, b. Gab. 359.
91. See: "Berlino che decade" (August 18) and "Culle e bare in Francia e in Germania" (August 20). See in Benito Mussolini, *O.O.*, Vol. XXVI, pp. 41–22 and 42–43. As well as "Razza" (September 14), "Non una, ma cinque" (November 3),

coming months. The Germans for their part took a long time to provide an answer and Amann was once again making himself scarce and unreachable,[92] until finally on October 27 he signed a generic authorization to abridge the work "of those sections of lesser interest to Italian readers" as he wrote to Italian authorities,[93] leaving the matter exclusively for the translators to decide. But as previously noted the Germans by then were accustomed to the notion of an abridged edition.

The real problem turned out to be Hitler's preface. At first, on October 17, the Chancellor told Ambassador Cerruti that he would "gladly accept" the offer.[94] But when he actually had to deliver the preface Hitler also used a whole series of excuses and procrastinations. His indecision was the main reason for the unusual delay in publication of the Italian edition. *Mein Kampf* had become in the meantime a worldwide "issue": once translated it created violent political and popular reactions in many countries. The Czechoslovakian Ministry of the Interior had banned the book in September because of its aggressive remarks about German minorities living in that country; a Polish judge in Katowice had ordered the book seized because it

---

"Ambrogio romano non teutone" (December 6). See *O.O.*, Vol. XXXVII, *Appendice I. Scritti (1907–1945)*, pp. 406, 407–408, 411–412.
92. Doc. A43.
93. Doc. A44.
94. Doc. A39.

contained statements offensive to the Polish nation.[95] And in England all hell broke loose.

The *Times* began a strong campaign attacking the book and followed its various fortunes internationally. It was at this time, and because of the London newspaper, that *Mein Kampf* came to be known as the "black book" of humanity. Starting in early July the *Times* published a series of long extracts that had aroused British public opinion.[96] For months thereafter the *Times* used the book in various articles as proof that Hitler had nothing but malevolent intentions. To top this off the actual "abridged" translation was published at the beginning of October, becoming the target of innumerable attacks because the cuts were viewed as proof of bad faith—that is, they were meant to hide the book's true nature.[97]

The bad reputation *Mein Kampf* had earned was only due in small part to the anti-Semitism and racism it so copiously served up. The aggressive and warmongering intentions it expressed and the passages calling for Germany to rearm were received with much more alarm. A British anti-German conditioned reflex was mostly at work, for this was a book calling for war written by the head of a government of a country that only a few years before had started a world war it had then lost. The book was deemed to be less a racist and anti-Semitic

---

95. Two articles ("Newspapers Suspended in Czechoslovakia" and "Herr Hitler's Book Banned in Poland") in the London *Times* on September 27, 1933, p. 11, col. b.
96. It was published on the 24th (with an editorial as the introduction), 25, 27, and 28 of July.
97. For a list see J. J. Barnes and P. Barnes, *op. cit.*, pp.18–19.

statement and more a revenge-seeking manifesto; it had the same dangerous effect, as the *Times* wrote in one of its editorials, of the old "furor teutonicus" of the pan-Germanists that permeated the nationalist sentiments of the First World War.[98]

In other words the articles published in the *Times* and other dailies expressed traditional anti-German sentiment, rather than anti-racist outrage, and a defense of the Jews. This took place both when the initial extracts of the book were published and later when the volume itself reached the bookstores. The same scenario played out in France as well. Months after the book had been illegally translated and ordered seized, a booklet was published in Paris defending the right of any Frenchman to have access to and to read *Mein Kampf*. By reading the book—it explained—Frenchmen would be forewarned because they would understand that Hitler viewed France as a "mortal enemy"; but they would have also been able to admire the "correctness" of his point of view, and this was not at all meant in irony, when it referred to the Jews, Freemasons, Bolshevism, and pacifism.[99]

But perhaps the most violent protests against the book took place in October 1933 when the plan for general disarmament was being discussed at the League of Nations in Geneva. On October 14 Germany, as previously mentioned, decided to leave that international

---

98. "Herr Hitler's Responsibility," *Times*, July 28, 1933, p. 15, col. c.
99. Ch. Kula and E. Bocquillon, *Mein Kampf (Mon Combat) par Adolf Hitler ou Le livre interdit aux français. Analyse du livre interdit*, Confédération de Groupements de Contribuables, Paris, May 1934. I thank Stefania Montecalvo, who was key to locating this text.

organization. The move provided one more occasion to attack *Mein Kampf*: it was immediately pointed out—and Hitler had to defend himself publicly on this—that the portions of the text dealing with German rearmament had been cut in the English translation, which had been authorized by Berlin as an abridged edition.[100] It was easy for the Germans to denounce this translation of *Mein Kampf* as nothing more than a warmongering forgery, but its true international notoriety was completely political and originated in the nationalist-inspired clashes leading up to the First World War.

Did these reactions come to the attention of the Italian government? It doesn't appear to be the case, for Rome was not yet fully aware of the book's existence. As we mentioned before not much was known about *Mein Kampf* and this situation would continue for a long time. Even as late as May 1933, Gaetano Polverelli, then head of the Press Office, who had spoken with Amann and was himself a veteran newsman, was still referring to the book as a "biography."[101] Basically, he hadn't read it and knew very little about it.

The reports provided by Italian diplomats were sparse, to say the least, and had a tendency at that time to play down negative reactions to Nazism abroad. Dino Grandi, for example, the Italian ambassador reporting from the London embassy, failed to inform Rome of the violent reactions to the book during the publication of extracts by the

---

100. See the two articles in the *Times* dated October 21 ("Germany and Peace," p. 10, col. d, with Hitler's answers at a press conference) and of October 23 by P. J. Hartog ("Herr Hitler's Foreign Policy. An Omission from English Version," p. 10, col. d).

Times in July, and after distribution in the bookshops in October. The same happened with Ambassador Bonifacio Pignatti in Paris. This neglect would continue until the Italians both in Paris and London finally understood that the publishing event had become political. The realization of that fact had to wait until Pignatti found out about the existence of a French translation that the German embassy in Paris knew nothing about and that, as we know, turned out to be unauthorized,[102] and when by pure coincidence Grandi found out from a conversation with a book dealer in Piccadilly that the English edition was selling very well.[103]

British diplomats by comparison were discussing the book much more intensely: in April 1933 the British ambassador to Berlin had given the Foreign Office a detailed description of the its content.[104] But no comparable dispatch can be found in the Italian diplomatic reports coming from Berlin. This is quite understandable. The British viewed any document, and that book in particular, as particularly useful to illustrate the thinking of a man such as Hitler, who was still a complete mystery. The Duce, the Italian ambassador to Berlin, and the Ministry of Foreign Affairs didn't need an old source like *Mein Kampf* to be enlightened as to Hitler's *current* thinking. Thanks mostly to Renzetti, Italy had direct, broad, and up-to-date information unavailable to the British.

---

101. Doc. A17.
102. Doc. A48.
103. Doc. A50.

Foreign reactions in any event had absolutely no impact on Italy. The translation of this problematic book went ahead unimpeded. The political gesture of facilitating the translation was more important than any detailed knowledge of the text, to which the Italian government had acquired the rights. The actual publication of the book was awarded to a private publisher, who was also spending his own money, thus allowing everyone to retain more or less complete freedom of action.

---

104. J. J. Barnes and P. Barnes, *op. cit.*, pp. 21–23.

Chapter IX

Race

Mussolini and the Italian leadership were to take a closer look at those pages only several more months later. In any case Bompiani informed Rome that he was very close to publishing the book[105] between December 16, 1933 and the beginning of 1934. It was during this time that experts at the Ministry of Foreign Affairs had prepared and sent to their superiors a series of excerpts representing the first translation of *Mein Kampf*.[106] The ministry prepared a terse translation of the selected passages with a few additional comments. The topics selected were those likely to be of interest to the Italian ministry, with particular emphasis on contemporary politics: Hitler's

---

105. Doc. A49.
106. See assembled documents in Appendix B.

ideas on Austria, Italy, France, and England, and a particularly long and detailed excerpt on racism and the Jews.

This "translation" was delivered to the ministry's top personnel following the trip to Germany that Under Secretary of Foreign Affairs Fulvio Suvich took at the end of 1933. During his visit he also met with Hitler on December 13 and heard the Chancellor repeat some of the points stated in his book.[107] Was it because of what he heard during that conversation, or due to the international issues raised by the book that prompted Suvich to seek more information? It would only be at the end of 1933 that the Italian dictator's entourage would be able to take a closer look and actually find out at first hand that the book was not simply one more odd text but a relevant political document having worldwide ramifications.

There was, however, another reason for curiosity about *Mein Kampf* relating to the Duce's personal interest. At that time Mussolini was reading up on issues of race, in particular the theme of the Jews and the clash and crossbreeding among races. The diplomatic service was helping him by assembling information on the subject and in acquiring or refining new ideas.[108] *Mein Kampf* would therefore be highly useful to complete his research, along with other books.

---

107. Fulvio Suvich, *Memorie 1932–1936*, ed. by Gianfranco Bianchi (Milan: Rizzoli, 1984), pp. 246–258.

108. Armando Odenigo, consul at Bratislava, spoke to Suvich about "the various publications on the issue of race as it is now being understood and discussed in Germany." Suvich was eager to find out for himself—perhaps following a request by Mussolini—and gathered more information from the consul and Odenigo on November 22, 1933, suggesting how important were Gobineau's writings. The entire

There are two other encounters with books that can be accurately dated and show once again Mussolini's sharp interest in sweeping political-theoretical definitions. The first notation is his reading between November 14 and December 14, 1933, of Oswald Spengler's latest book, the first volume of *Jahre der Enscheidung* (*The Hour of Decision*).[109] On December 15 (the dates are of interest as they are all extremely close to one another) Mussolini's review of this book in *Il Popolo d'Italia* was published anonymously, but was rather easy to identify.[110] Following his suggestion the book was then translated by Beonio Brocchieri and published in 1934 by Bompiani.

As the "anonymous" reviewer of *Il Popolo d'Italia* was to point out, Spengler's book praised the Duce very highly. The also formulated important worldwide "strategic" points that must have left their imprint in Mussolini's mind, such as "Germany is once again taking up

---

correspondence in ASDMAE, MAE, Gab. 1919–43, b. Gab. 125, f. [Pubblicazioni sul problema della Razza] [Publications on the issue of Race].

109. A copy of the book reached Mussolini on November 14 after having been confiscated by the Italian police from a package shipped to a German man residing at Verona. Mussolini kept the book, showing his interest. ACS, MI, DGPS, DAGR, F4, b. 39, f. *Jahre der Enscheidung. Erster Teil.* Libro di Spengler Oswald edito a Monaco [Book by Oswald Spengler, published in Munich]. It is known that another copy of the book was sent by Spengler himself directly to the Duce in August 1933, but obviously it had not been read. ASDMAE, MAE, Gabinetto 1919–43, b. 2462, f. Spengler Oswald.

110. "Spengler" in *O.O.*, Vol. XXVI, pp. 122–123. In the course of the book review and therefore quite openly, Mussolini suggested that Beonio Brocchieri should translate the book. Beonio Brocchieri was received by Mussolini on November 16. For the documents on the translation: ACS, SPD, CO, b. 2477, f. 554. 885. Beonio Brocchieri prof. Vittorio. Mussolini, in the *Taccuini* by Yvon De Begnac (*Taccuini mussoliniani,* edited by Francesco Perfetti [il Mulino: Bologna, 1990], p. 594); claimed that J. Evola had helped Beonio Brocchieri.

its historical position as a border nation against Asia."[111] However, the Duce essentially focused on two main ideas. The first was Spengler's critique of the idea of "racial unity," "a grotesque phrase considering that races have been mixed for thousands of years." It was, or appeared to be, critical of German racism and was heartily underlined.

Mussolini then turned to the second issue, a theme he had already dwelt upon five years before in a famous article he had written on an essay by Richard Korherr,[112] the future Nazi statistician of the "final solution": "What is Spengler's thesis? It goes like this. The world is threatened by two revolutions, one white and one colored. The white one is 'social,' resulting from the catastrophic collapse of the eighteenth century and the new dominance of the masses, especially the faceless and soulless ones piled into the big cities, something that took place during the period of liberalism, democracy, and universal suffrage, what may be referred to as nineteenth century demagogy. The other revolution is that of the colored peoples, who are infinitely more prolific than the white race—enough as to eventually drown it. The question for us twentieth century Europeans is: what should we do? Spengler fails to provide an answer to this painful question." The

---

111. Six years later Mussolini quoted Spengler on this specific point ("Germany's mission is simply to defend Europe against Asia. This is not just Spengler's thesis.") in his letter to Hitler dated January 3, 1940. See DDI, IX sg., Vol. III, p. 22.

112. The article was published in *Gerarchia* in the September 1928 issue. See *O.O.*, Vol. XXIII, pp. 209–216. On the relationship between Korherr and Himmler in January 1943 regarding the "final solution" then taking place, see Richard D. Breitman, *The Architect of Genocide. Himmler and the Final Solution* (New York: Alfred A. Knopf, 1991), p. 241–242.

editorial also failed to indicate any solutions. But it was obvious that the issue was very much alive.

The matter did not end there. During the same period and specifically between December 15, the date of the Spengler review, and December 22, 1933, the Duce wanted to read another book also published by Bompiani. It was about one of Mussolini's old "acquaintances," the racist ideologue Gobineau and was written by the journalist Lorenzo Gigli.[113] The book had been published several months before and was therefore not simply a casual reading. Also, this was before the Christmas season, a time when he would have more time to read. Except for an insignificant part, the sections of the book that he underlined once again all dealt with the issue of race.

Ever since he was a young man Mussolini had been quoting Gobineau often at length.[114] Now, however, he felt that Gobineau was confused or simply mistaken by his completely "feudal" views, as evidenced by his assigning the predominant role to the aristocracy—as Gigli (p. 97) had also pointed out. Mussolini forcefully underlined

---

113. Mussolini marked the dates on the title page. He wrote "1932-XII," but unquestionably this was a mistake for 1933. The printing date for the book Mussolini read by Lorenzo Gigli, *Vita di Gobineau*, is May 25, 1933 (he therefore read it six months after publication). Located in ACS, Biblioteca, Collezione Mussolini n. 38. The physical existence of this text has also been indicated in Renzo De Felice, *The Jews in Fascist Italy. A History* (New York: Enigma Books, 2001), p. 239. Mussolini underlined only chapter IV, "La Tragedia dell'Umanità" [The Tragedy of Humanity] (pp.77–115), which is totally dedicated to Gobineau's racist theories.

114. Mussolini had quoted his racist theories—in discussing "pangermanism"—in his book *Il Trentino visto da un socialista (note e notizie)*, published by Quattrini in 1911 (it was n. 8 in the "Quaderni della Voce"). *O.O.*, Vol. XXXIII, pp. IX–X, 152–154. On the

sentences both by Gigli and Gobineau, such as: "race is the only agent of history" (p. 82), or others about the "yellows" and the "blacks" as having no sense of "honor" (p. 85); that the Semites were the result of crossbreeding between "whites" and "blacks" (pp. 91, 93, 94), the "cunning" of the "Semite" Ulysses (p. 95) is an "illustration of Semitic infiltration" having "some serious consequences in the daily spectacle of capitalist society" (pp. 106–107), and finally a sentence that sounds like *Mein Kampf* such as: "Germany by now is emptied of Aryan elements" (p. 110). The topics were identical in many cases.

Another event of personal interest to the Duce that is more difficult to assess also took place at that time. Hoepli had just published, on October 28, the day commemorating the march on Rome,[115] the first two volumes of Mussolini's writings: *Scritti e discorsi* (Writings and Speeches), which had been agreed to at the end of July. The cover page stated that this was the "definitive" edition, which therefore included all the texts the author had approved for publication; the other texts were clearly excluded. The published volumes were one and seven of the complete works. The first volume contained many pieces written between 1914, when the future fascist leader became editor in chief of *Il Popolo d'Italia*, and the end of the First World War; the texts were naturally in favor of Italy's intervention

---

racism of the young Mussolini, now see Giorgio Fabre, *Mussolini razzista. Dal socialismo al fascismo: la formazione di un antisemita* (Milan: Garzanti, 2005).

115. The date is printed on the book's advertising wrapper. There is a telegram of thanks from Mussolini's secretary to Barella, for sending the two volumes and dated

in the war. The second volume contained articles concerning the Concordat and the Lateran Pacts, from 1929 to 1931. Mussolini clearly intended to supply the public and posterity with solid doctrinal content.

These events provide the background for Mussolini's "reading" of the mysterious and monumental book entitled *Mein Kampf*. And thanks to the detailed excerpts prepared by the translation office at the Ministry of Foreign Affairs, he was made aware of the book's most important points.

Judging from the amount of work that went into the writing of the "summaries," it is clear that those in charge at the Italian Ministry of Foreign Affairs viewed Hitler's *Mein Kampf* as politically extremely important. Ordinarily reports on important books prepared by the staff for both the upper echelon and Mussolini were no longer than three typed pages, and more often they were only on a single page. Books could be politically significant, but those receiving the summaries had very little time and the report had to be extremely succinct. In this case, however, for a single book they submitted six texts, each one between four to five and up to twelve pages long. Two or three employees were involved in the editing and writing of these reports.

Once Suvich returned from Germany the Ministry of Foreign Affairs received an initial extract, divided by topics, that was sent to the Duce and which he underlined. Then trustworthy translators at the ministry followed up with other summaries, also by topic and with

---

November 1, 1933. See in ACS, SPD, CO, b. 1042, f. 509.164. Hoepli, Ulrico. Casa editrice.

extensive quotations from the text.[116] The Duce underlined several parts and the sections he singled out prove significant. The markings correspond in every way, in style, and appearance to those made by Mussolini in other books and reports. Once again the fascist leader focused on a topic that had previously attracted the attention of the translators, even within chapters not specifically dedicated to the subject of race.

The section on "mongrelization" using France as an example of cross breeding with Africans from the colonies is revelatory, as it relates to the experience of the French occupation of Germany by the Army of the Rhine,[117] which included Moroccan and Senegalese troops;[118] the example of Central and South America, where the "Latins" were much more willing than the "Germanics" to mix with the "natives"; and Hitler's faulting the German people for failing to stick to the "animal unity" that held other peoples together—this passage must have convinced Mussolini that Hitler wasn't always referring to a "single" race and that he also had a race mixing problem in Germany; the reference to the racial mixing that had taken place in southern Italy; the attack on "modern pacifism" of "Jewish" origin that failed to provide the "Aryans" with the feeling of "loyalty" that alone could serve as the characteristics of race.[119]

---

116. These documents are reproduced in Appendix B.
117. Until 1923 [NDT].
118. Doc. B-III.
119. Doc. B -V.

Only one of these topics could be construed as hostile and truly offensive to the founder of Fascism: the mention of southern Italy as a geographic area that Hitler viewed as particularly mongrelized due to race mixing, which Germany would do well to avoid imitating.

It is impossible to take the interpretation of Mussolini's underlinings any further but it remains clear that the issue of race as handled in *Mein Kampf* was the one he was most interested in. While in other countries the pages revealing the Führer's politically aggressive and warmongering attitude captivated the readers' attention, the Duce showed completely different interests by focusing on his racist pronouncements. Curiously another important section did not appear to generate the same interest on the Duce's part. Although it was summarized by the ministry's translators, Hitler here admits that "Fascist Italy" had shouldered the "struggle" for a long time "against the three main weapons of Judaism."[120]

If there are many lingering doubts that prior to December 1933 the Italian leadership had no real knowledge of the content of *Mein Kampf*, it's clear that after that date the Duce and his entourage were well informed, if only thanks to those excellent summaries. According to some rather dubious memoirs[121] published later on, around mid-1934, Mussolini reportedly stated that he had "never succeeded in reading . . . that brick." This may be—and probably is—true: he was being candid

---

120. Doc. B-II.
121. The statement to the "fascists of Forlì" is in Paolo Monelli, *Mussolini piccolo borghese* (Milan: Vallardi, 1983), (first published in 1950), p. 155.

about not having given it a complete and thorough reading. It is also evident that by then he was well acquainted with large portions of the "brick" in question, portions that were of particular interest to him and that several months later he knew rather well.

Mussolini and his staff were fully aware that they were offering the Italian reading public a rabidly racist text which they found interesting for that specific reason and not, as in Great Britain, because it was a warmongering tract. The Duce favored Hitler's anti-Versailles demands and couldn't object to Tyrolean irredentism which never appeared in the book. He could in theory have rejected the racist aspects but he chose not to do so and in the end that was the section that was "closest" to his interests at the time.

The Duce was attempting to find his way and gather information towards a clear picture of "German-style" racism, an issue not new to him. Before 1914, as a young man he had spent some time reading and writing about German racial theories. Those texts however were not included in the new edition of *Scritti e discorsi*, where Mussolini had made some radical selections of his own writings, eliminating all those published before the First World War, including the articles on Gobineau. It is impossible to determine whether Mussolini did so to differentiate himself from Hitler. Hitler's "universal" approach— ethnic, geopolitical, sociological—in discussing race was very different from Mussolini's early writings. It may be altogether possible that the Italian dictator was gathering information about a type of racism that differed greatly from his own.

In other words the Duce was attempting to counter the challenge that was created by the force of German racist propaganda and specifically Hitler's theoretical *appeal*, because in the end this amounted to a clash between strongmen as well. Alternatively, even if it could mean watering down his own writings, Mussolini was offering his personal ideological vision but he was—as will be demonstrated further ahead—thinking of something much more tangible. For now, however, he studied looking at the big picture as to what this new racism that was challenging him meant with respect to his past intellectual baggage and Gobineau in particular. This was certainly not a simple path to follow.

There is a noteworthy coincidence that may not be as fortuitous as it appears. Even the imprisoned Italian Communist leader Antonio Gramsci, with far fewer resources at his disposal, was thinking along these lines[122] in discussing Gigli's book on Gobineau, which he knew only from reading a few book reviews. Gramsci felt that Gobineau's "aristocratic" idea was somehow related to the Nazi "political and military ideology of efficiency" and not "a bookish abstraction," concluding that nineteenth century aristocratic principles had led to Nazism. He was reflecting on history and the origins of racist movements. Compared to Gramsci Mussolini was instead trying—

---

122. See the note (end of 1933–beginning of 1934) in book 17. Antonio Gramsci, *Quaderni del carcere*, v. 3, edited by Valentino Gerratana (Turin: Einaudi, 1975), pp. 1943–1944 (and editorial note vol. 4, pp. 2976–2977). It doesn't appear that Gramsci had read the book itself but rather reviews of the book published in *Leonardo* or *Italia Letteraria*.

literally—to build a competing and tangible *theory* for himself because of the aggressive challenge represented by *Mein Kampf.*

Chapter X

The Translator

Valentino Bompiani was becoming increasingly worried by the innumerable delays of a text that was now ready to go to press; he was also footing the bill out of his own budget, and putting on as much pressure as he could through letters and telegrams to obtain the new preface he'd been promised.[123] Without the preface the book couldn't go to press. The Italian Ministry of Foreign Affairs and Mussolini's Press Office continued to help as much and as fast as they could. Acting at Rome's request, Italian ambassador to Berlin Vittorio Cerruti continued to contact the Chancellor, repeating his requests for a preface.[124] But Hitler procrastinated. In January 1934 he even came

---

123. Docs. A49, A55, A58, A62, A65, A67.
124. Doc. A52.

up with a new reason to delay everything: he had started to write a mysterious third volume as a response to the criticism of the first two coming from various countries.[125] It was best to wait for that book, he told the ambassador, and then publish the other two at the same time.

There is an explanation to the delay. *Mein Kampf*, the "book" of the Nazis, had become a considerable source of embarrassment for Germany worldwide. The Germans probably thought that the publication of an Italian edition with the well-known controversial passages available in translation would add fuel to the objections cropping up abroad. As for the "third volume" Hitler had in fact dictated some time before, to the same Max Amann, in fact, a new text that focused on foreign policy. This happened during the summer of 1928 but the book hadn't been published and very few people even knew it existed. It would be published for the first time only in 1961.[126] Occasionally, when it suited him, Hitler would come up with the idea of publishing the new book and this was one of those times. So much for his procrastination.

When queried directly by an alarmed Bompiani, Eher Verlag responded even more disappointingly,[127] saying that Hitler could not

125. Doc. A57.

126. I. Kershaw, *op. cit.*, pp. 291, 688. Amann typed it as Hitler dictated. See *Hitlers Zweites Buch. Ein Dokument aus dem Jahr 1928*, edited and with notes by Gerhard L. Weinberg and the introduction by Hans Rothfels (Stuttgart: Deutsche Verlags-Anstalt, 1961), p. 7. It was translated and published in Italy under the title *Il libro segreto di Hitler*, edited by Adriana Pellegrini (Milan: Longanesi, 1962). See the introduction by Telford Taylor on p. 24. The English edition has recently been published, again edited by Gerhard L. Weinberg, *Hitler's Second Book. The Unpublished Sequel to* Mein Kampf (New York: Enigma Books, 2003).

127. Doc. A63.

write prefaces for foreign editions. Furthermore, Eher Verlag was now making a new demand—thereby revealing the existence of the May 30, 1933, contract—by asking to review the translation. The contract contained no clause regarding any such change. The Italians had protected themselves from such a request by leaving the future publisher free to choose a translator. This was yet another example of German cunning in a story filled with more than one sly move by the protagonists.

The matter didn't end there. The date of Eher Verlag's answer, February 14, 1934, was crucial to another key issue that ran parallel but was still intimately connected to *Mein Kampf*. On that day the official Catholic newspaper *Osservatore Romano* published a news item announcing the reasons for placing the book, *Der Mythus des 20. Jahrhunderts* (The Myth of the Twentieth Century) by Alfred Rosenberg, on the Catholic church's list of forbidden books. First published in Munich in 1930, the Holy See banned the book seven days before, on February 7, 1934, for being anti-Christian and "calling for the establishment of a new religion."[128]

---

128. The book had already been heavily attacked by the *Osservatore Romano* on February 7, third page "A Book of Odious Falsehoods for German Youth". On the same day as Rosenberg's book was banned, a second book was also placed on the index by Ernst Bergmann, *Die deutsche National Kirche.* It should be noted that the Italian police were informed of this book but did not ban it. See ACS, MI, DGPS, DAGR, F4, b. 18, f. Chiesa Nazionale Tedesca, libro di Bergmann, Ernst. A note dated March 2, 1934, taken from a Reuters news item mentioned the book but without any further consequences. It stated that "all of Christian religion is a product of Semitism and Roman culture." For the Church's stand against Rosenberg, see Fritz Sandmann, *L'Osservatore Romano e il nazionalsocialismo 1929–1939* (Rome: Cinque Lune, 1976), pp. 73–74. R. De Felice, *The Jews, cit.*, p. 115.

Rosenberg had been given VIP treatment in the past by the Duce as the editor of the *Völkischer Beobachter* and later as head of the Nazi party's foreign department. He had been invited to Rome to speak at the well-known Volta Conference on Europe in November 1932 where the Fascist leader had introduced his German protégés to the world stage. On that occasion the Duce had even granted Rosenberg a private audience at the Palazzo Venezia.[129] During the months that followed the attitude of the Italians toward the theoretician of Germanic purity had changed,[130] but everyone was aware of those political gestures. The Catholic church had also signed a Concordat with Germany on July 20, 1933, while remaining hostile towards racism, especially of the Rosenberg variety. The spectacular ban of that important book was the culmination of those disagreements, since the book had been quite popular in Germany: some 70,000 copies had been sold in 1934.[131] Given their early relationship the Vatican's ban must have come as a major embarrassment to the Italians. Among the lay press it appears

---

129. Regarding Rosenberg addressing the Volta Convention, see Reale Accademia d'Italia. Fondazione Alessandro Volta, Convegno di Scienze morali e storiche. 14–20 novembre 1932-XI. *Tema: l'Europa. Vol. I, Atti preliminari—Processi verbali* (Reale Accademia d'Italia: Rome 1933), pp. 51 and 272–84. But see also the papers assembled in ACS, PCM, Gab. 1931–1933, b. 1663, f,. 14.3.5827. I. Roma. Convegno Volta (Novembre 1932-XII). For the audience of November 15 requested by Renzetti, which took place the day after the inauguration of the Convention, see ASDMAE, MAE, Gab. 1919–43, b. Gab. 88, f. Udienze S.E. Capo Governo, R.

130. See what Mussolini told Renzetti on May 9, 1933, as reported by Pompeo Aloisi, who was at the meeting: "He told him to tell Hitler not to send out people like Rosenberg; it seems that he received an icy reception in London." (Baron Aloisi, *Journal (25 juillet 1932–14 juin 1936)*, introduction and notes by Mario Toscano [Paris: Plon, 1957], p. 121).

131. The information about the sales of the book is in Henry Rollin, "Racisme et catholicisme. II. Vers une nouvelle réforme," *Le Temps*, March 4, 1934, p. 2.

that only *Il Tevere*,[132] edited by Telesio Interlandi published a very short news item on the matter.

The Catholic attack on Rosenberg's book was such a politically important piece of news that Hitler personally discussed it with the Duce[133] during his trip to Italy the following June.[134] Placing the book on the list would also have other direct consequences. An Italian translation of *The Myth of the Twentieth Century* had been ready since the beginning of 1934,[135] but following the decision of the Holy See publication was interrupted and would never be carried out. Years later, in 1939, the Ministry of Popular Culture actually blocked the entry of the original edition into Italy.[136] This problem therefore appeared just as Bompiani was negotiating to obtain Hitler's exclusive preface and

---

132. For the news announcing that only the books by Rosenberg and Bergmann were affected, see the Vatican news in the issue of February 14–15, 1934.

133. Meeting of June 14, 1934; see photo.

134. Mussolini summed up what Hitler said about Rosenberg in a report on his conversations of June 14–15, 1934, sent to De Vecchi, who at the time was the ambassador to the Holy See. Published in Benito Mussolini, *Corrispondenza inedita*, edited by Duilio Susmel (Milan: Ed. del Borghese, 1972), p. 142, and R. De Felice, *Mussolini il Duce*, I, cit., p. 495. Hitler recounted the conditions allowing the German concordat to "work": "that useless gestures such as the placing of Rosenberg's book in the index, a book that would have gone unnoticed without the Catholic racket; a book that in any case concerns only the author and not Nazism."

135. G. Sommi Picenardi, "Rosenberg, l'Anticristo," *La Vita Italiana*, May 15, 1934, p. 668.

136. The text was included in the list of publications "banned from the Kingdom" since January 26 to October 31, 1939 (ACS, MI, DGPS, DAGR, Massime, S4, b. S4 (provv.), S4 A, f. 6. "Elenco delle stampe sequestrate." There is also a report almost certainly written by Guido Landra addressed to Minister Dino Alfieri, dated November 17, 1938, that recommended against the translation offered by Giulio Cogni specifically in order to avoid irritating the Catholic hierarchy. ACS, MCP, Gab., 1 Versamento b. 151, f. Collaboratori Ufficio Razza, sf. Prof. Cogni Giulio.

amounted certainly to a serious setback for German-style racism in general.

Mein Kampf however was a very different story. Besides the fact that it was not anti-Catholic, the book was the work of a head of state and that made attacking it all the more difficult. Once Rosenberg's "Myth" was out of the way *Mein Kampf* would—and actually did—remain the only authoritative Nazi text that could be exported outside Germany. Even though Hitler complained, it's debatable whether he was truly so displeased by the ban on Rosenberg's book.[137] The entire matter was not a good omen for the publishing fortunes of *Mein Kampf* in Italy. In any case, besides the Rosenberg matter the Ministry of Foreign Affairs and the Press Office—both directly under Mussolini's personal supervision—didn't waver in their support for Bompiani and a speedy publication of *Mein Kampf*. Two examples will illustrate this point. Bompiani found out that a contract actually existed and it was confirmed—to reassure him—that he was under no obligation to have the translation reviewed by the Germans.[138] Further, Bompiani was allowed, after making a request to read the entire text, to find out about certain selected sections of the contract that he had preferred to ignore until then.[139] He wasn't even told the amount paid or the various other details, but was simply given those sections of interest to him. This was

---

137. In May 1933, during a conversation with a few Catholic church leaders, as the nunzio was to inform Rome, Hitler declared that he "rejected" Rosenberg's book, which was not "a Party book." See Giovanni Sale, *Hitler, la Santa Sede e gli ebrei. Con documenti dall'Archivio segreto vaticano* (Milan: Jaca Book, 2004), p. 363.
138. Doc. A64.
139. Doc. A62.

how Bompiani actually found out between February 23 and 26, 1934, that the contract placed his company under certain obligations he knew nothing about.

The Italian authorities must have been prompted to disclose what had been kept secret because then all publishing-related issues with the Germans—for example the delivery of the agreed copies, the identity of the translator, or the actual control of the copyright—would rest with Bompiani rather than government administrative offices. Some key responsibility was therefore transferred to the publisher, who was still kept in the dark about the agreements concerning the race and religion of the translator, nor was that issue brought up until the actual publication took place. Ironically, Bompiani was therefore free to choose the translator he liked best; the contract bore no mention of this issue in any of its sections.

Yet Angelo Treves,[140] the translator, was a "Jew," most certainly registered at the Jewish Community of Milan and at the time perhaps the most prolific of all Italian translators from German and other languages. He translated the works of some sixty-odd writers for many

---

140. Regarding biographical data, we have been able to find only that Angelo Samuele Treves was born in Vercelli on October 7, 1873, had married Gisella Pugliese and moved to Milan in September 1917. In August 1938 he appears on the list of the Jewish population of Milan (his wife was listed as the head of the family); in the 1942 census he was no longer a resident. Refer to the following for information: birth certificate from Vercelli sent to us by the Records office on May 4, 2001 (the date of his death is not mentioned); the "census" in ACS, MI, DGPS, DAGR, GI, b. 114, f. 414, sf. 73. ins. Provincia di Milano. Vestratto della poplazione della Comunitá Ebraica di Milano. Lettera P [Extract of the population of the Jewish Community of Milan. Letter P]; and to the "Rubrica degli ebrei residenti in Milano" ["Listing of the Jews residing in Milan"] of 1942 that is in the same envelope.

publishers, including books by Shalom Asch, Schnitzler, Unamuno, Essad Bey, Nietzsche, Suetonius, several Marxists, and even Spengler, whom Mussolini liked so much. Treves was a very important cultural figure during those years but, possibly because of this "cursed" translation of his, any traces of his existence were almost completely erased after the war.

Bompiani thought that it was in any case better to avoid placing Treves' name on the cover page or anywhere else in the book. The volume was published as number 23 in the series "Selected books, the overview of our times" and had no acknowledged translator since the real one, as a Jew, had to be kept hidden. Only some time later would the mention "Translated by Prof. A. Treves" appear in the book—not on the cover page but only in advertising copy promoting the titles in the series. This was to begin, as evidenced by copies of the book still extant, with the edition of *La mia battaglia* (My Struggle) published as of March 15, 1937, some three years after the initial printing. How or why this came to pass remains unknown.

The matter of Hitler's contribution finally came to a head. Once again pressed by Ambassador Cerruti (the prodding actually was coming from Rome) Hitler stopped procrastinating and delivered the text of the new preface, which he personally signed.[141] The banning of Rosenberg's book and its placement on the "index" list may well have contributed to this decision. Thanks to the Bompiani edition Nazi

---

141. See photo.

ideology had acquired a guaranteed pulpit that had been denied to the *Myth of the Twentieth Century*.

Hitler's delivery of the new preface came practically at the same time as the seizure—by the French police acting on the request of Eher Verlag, following the Paris trial mentioned previously—of the unauthorized French translation of *Mein Kampf* by les Nouvelles éditions latines.[142] This greatly enhanced the value and the friendly significance of a preface specifically tailored to Italian readers, who were going to discover an absolutely genuine and authorized translation.

The preface was at first sent to Rome, where the Duce read it[143] and then forwarded to the publisher in Milan, to be returned after being retranslated back, and to Hitler, who approved the text.[144] Bompiani then completed the printing[145] even before receiving final approval: the print date of the first edition of *La mia battaglia* was March 15, 1934, while Hitler's final okay reached Ambassador Cerruti only on March 23. The preface was a short and somewhat convoluted text,[146] wherein Hitler proudly indicated—and this was his old and often repeated slogan[147]—the close kinship that existed between

---

142. "Mein Kampf Seized in France," in the *Times*, March 6, 1934 (p. 13, col. c). For the announcement of the soon to published edition see Raymond Millet, "Mein Kampf et les Français," *Le Temps*, February 27, 1934. It was the interview of one of the two translators, Jean Gaudefroy-Demombynes.
143. Doc. A70.
144. Docs. A66–77.
145. See photo.
146. Doc. A74.
147. In the 1931 preface to the book by Vincenzo Meletti, *Die Revolution des Faschismus*, Hitler had written more modestly about the "affinity" between the two movements in

Fascism and National-Socialism, "intimately connected in their basic attitude and world view" and the policy of peace they would pursue together. Even though very succinct, this was after all a new text prepared exclusively for the Italian edition precisely as Valentino Bompiani had requested.

---

the "new idea of the State" (see Hans Woller, "I rapporti di Mussolini e Hitler prima del 1933. Politica del potere o affinità ideologica?", in *Italia contemporanea*, 196, September 1994, p. 494). On the other hand, in a thank-you letter of June 8, 1931, after receiving an autographed photo of Mussolini brought back by Göring, Hitler mentioned the "spiritual relations contained in many key points and principles of Fascism and the National Socialist movement which I lead" (copy of the letter in BAK, collection N. 1235 (Nachlass Renzeti), f. 3/Korrespondenz 1931).

Chapter XI

Anti-Nazi Censorship

With the benefit of Mussolini's secret backing, the Italian edition of *Mein Kampf* had a relatively simple publishing history, unlike some of Hitler's other writings or other Nazi propaganda books that encountered many, often insurmountable, obstacles in fascist Italy. One may therefore conclude that the Italian translation of *Mein Kampf* was driven exclusively by the top-level agreement that set it in motion and probably by the secrecy surrounding the entire enterprise.

Italy's dissatisfaction and the tension in relations between Italy and Germany worsened at the end of 1933 and the beginning of 1934. The aggressive German policy toward Austria was the main reason. Hitler had made it a point to avoid clashes with Italy—and had written as much in *Mein Kampf.* Nevertheless a movement in favor of *Anschluss* was rapidly snowballing both in Germany and Austria with his approval.[148] This situation caused serious diplomatic repercussions because of worrisome reports reaching Rome about the penetration of Nazi propaganda in the Alto Adige.[149]

One of the obvious consequences was the hardening attitude of Italian authorities, especially toward Nazi literature. For example, in March 1934, the date is not specified, a police directive to check Hitlerian propaganda in Italy and to seize the pieces targeting Austria was circulated.[150] On March 20, 1934, at more or less the same time as the publication of *La Mia Battaglia*, Fulvio Suvich signed an even more restrictive order for the Italian police to seize Nazi propaganda because it attempted to destabilize Austria by transiting through Italy.[151]

---

148. Jens Petersen, *Hitler e Mussolini. La difficile alleanza* (Bari: Laterza, 1975), pp. 177–180.

149. For the penetration in the school system, see ACS, PCM, Gab. 1934–1936, b. 1760, f. 1.1.13.680. Propaganda hitleriana in Alto Adige [Hitlerian propaganda in Alto Adige].

150. See the very confidential circular signed by Senise on March 4, 1934, to the prefects requesting checking on the "Hitlerian movement" in Italy and confirming the orders to seize and destroy Hitlerian propaganda material that had arrived for shipment into Austria. ACS, MI, DGPS, DAGR, 1934, b. 2, f. B5. Raccolta di circolari [Collection of circulars] 1934; but mostly: ACS, MI, DGPS, 1934, b. 2H, f. Manifestazioni di propaganda Hitleriana. [Hitlerian propaganda dissemination]. C1. Affari Gen. li.

151. ACS, MI, DGPS, DAGR, Massime, S4 b. 103 A (provv.), Stampa in genere f.4. "Stampa di propaganda hitleriana" ["Hitlerian propaganda press"]. This hostility affected mostly Nazi propaganda targeting Italians. In April 1934 Mussolini personally prevented—probably through a pro-tourism decision—the seizure of an English-language Nazi propaganda illustrated magazine "distributed free of charge in all the hotels" in the province of Bolzano. ACS, MI, DGPS. DAGR, F4, b. 4, f. [The] American Illustrated News. Rivista pubblicata in Berlino. The quoted sentence comes from a letter from the prefect of Bolzano dated April 18, 1934. On the letter a stamp

Following a general decision purposefully withheld from the German authorities, which would remain secret, Suvich requested a tough repression that would be felt in the neighboring country. "It is unacceptable from the political and police point of view," he wrote on that occasion, "that hostile propaganda towards a friendly country seeking results contrary to our general policy be allowed to continue."

As a consequence of that order, during the months that followed, in the second half of June 1934, the Duce personally forbid, in the two "German" provinces of Trent and Bolzano, at least two pamphlets of Hitler's speeches translated into Italian.[152] The texts did not contain territorial demands regarding the *Südtyrol* and were written by the German Chancellor, but they were banned because they could be construed as propaganda. It should be noted that this harsh proscription was enacted after Mussolini had met with Hitler for the first time (June 14 and 15, 1934).

"Discussed with H[is] E[xcellency] the Head of the Government" and the handwritten annotation by Bocchini: "Must not be seized."

152. ACS, MI, DGPS, DAGR, F4, b. 105, f. "Stampa di propaganda hitleriana," sf. Discorsi di Adolf Hitler al Reichstag ["Hitlerian Press Propaganda," sf. 2. Speeches by Adolf Hitler to the Reichstag]. These were speeches given on January 30 and March 31 of that same year. On the letter from the prefect of Turin dated June 21, 1934, handwritten note by Carmine Senise: "Seen by H[is] E[xcellency] the Head of the Government. Discussed with His Excellency. To be forbidden in the provinces of Trent and Bolzano." The telegrams with the ban went out on July 17, 1934. It must also be noted that in more conspicuous situations the positions taken were to be more flexible. See for example the permission granted by Ciano on April 26, 1934, acting therefore with Mussolini's approval, to EIAR (the Italian broadcasting organization) to broadcast Hitler's May 1 speech. (ACS, MI, UC, telegrams sent, 1934, n. 12694.)

Even more relevant was another order following the arrival in Italy of a relatively large number of copies, about sixty-eight, of a publication written in five languages containing "speeches by German professors in praise of Hitler on the occasion of the plebiscite for the election of the German Chancellor."[153] On September 12, 1934, the Duce issued an order to Police Chief Arturo Bocchini to "prevent its distribution and not deliver any other copies." Bocchini immediately prepared a telegram banning it throughout Italy.

This order issued by the head of the Italian government regarding the distribution of Hitler's speeches was to remain unchanged for the next two years. Two more speeches by Hitler, published in 1935 and 1936, were also seized at that time despite the greatly improved relations between the two countries. Some time later the Italian ambassador to Berlin simply recorded his opposition to the seizure of the second of the two texts: "What would we say if speeches by the Duce were banned over here?" It was only then that all the speeches were allowed back into Italy once again, but the booklet by the professors praising Hitler would remain on the banned list forever.

Even more revealing was the fate of the *Brown Book*, compiled and published by Willi Münzenberg denouncing Nazi responsibility in the Reichstag fire. At the end of 1933 several copies printed in German

---

153. ACS, MI, DGPS, DAGR, F4, b. 13, f. Bekenntnis der Professoren an den Deutschen Universitaten und Hochsschulen zu Adolf Hitler und dem Nationalsozialistichen Staat. Regarding the AGR notation of September 11, the stamp "Discussed with H[is] E[xcellency] the Head of the Government" and in Bocchini's hand the notation as quoted in the text.

and French were imported into Italy.[154] The central police authorities, starting in November of that year, refused to ban the book and beginning in February 1934 Rome would officially inform a few related administrative offices that distribution would be allowed in Italy. When a local police chief in Trieste, acting on his own, decided to confiscate the book, pressure from Rome quickly reversed the order.

Nazi propaganda during those years was therefore being thwarted in Italy: a one-party regime—such as that of Fascist Italy—simply could not allow propaganda to be distributed by another party on its territory, even though it was the Nazi party, however politically close or even affiliated it may have been. Furthermore, some books that the Nazis could certainly not approve of were being allowed into Italy in what had to be viewed as an annoyance deliberately carried out by the fascists. Even laudatory speeches or enthusiastic approval of the Führer could fall under the ax, which is particularly significant regarding the translation of *Mein Kampf*, and even though it came under heavy criticism for its idea of German racial superiority it continued to receive

---

154. ACS, MI, DGPS, DAGR, F4, b. 15, f. Braunbuch über Reichstagsbrand und Hitlerterror. Handwritten notation on the letter from the Prefect of Genoa dated November 14, 1933, that accompanied the book shipped to Rome: "The other copy is with H.E. the Chief [of Police]." The Trieste matter took place between April 13 and June 8, 1934. For editions of the *Braunbuch* edited by Willi Münzenberg and published by Éditions du Carrefour, see Jean-Michel Palmier, *Quelques remarques sur les techniques de propaganda de Willi Münzenberg*, in *Willi Münzenberg un homme contre. Colloque international 26–29 mars 92 Aix-en-Provence. Actes.* Organisé par la Bibliothèque Méjanes L'Institut de l'image, Aix-en-Provence 1993. It was forbidden because its communism, the "second Braunbuch" (prohibition dated June 21, 1934, requested by Mussolini's Press Office on the 19th.) ACS, MI, DGPS, DAGR, f4, b. 26, f. Dimitroff contre Göring. (Libro edito a Parigi).

favorable but cool treatment as a text protected by the regime's top leadership. It was a less than enthusiastic welcome with traces of touchy irritation, but it remained most certainly liberal enough, as will be demonstrated later on.

Chapter XII

The Welcoming Party

*L*a mia battaglia (*My Struggle*) was finally printed on March 15, 1934, and made ready for distribution. The flap copy mentioned that the London *Times* had dubbed the book as being the "Nazi Bible." As planned the text included only the second volume of the original German book but began with 37 additional pages rather than one hundred as originally forecast by Bompiani in September 1933 summarizing the first volume. This summary turned out to be shorter than expected because the chapter entitled "Nation and Race" was also condensed and not translated in its entirety as previously planned. In the end, the total number of pages was about seventy less than what had been envisioned (431 instead of 500).

The cuts on the other hand were clearly not intended as censorship at all. The translation was faithful, or at least attempted to be even when reproducing passages in italics or boldface, conforming exactly to the German edition. The book was unquestionably just as racist and anti-Semitic as the original: Hitler's words had not been diluted; nothing in the book—which literally reproduced the original—could be construed as being offensive to Italy, even in those passages, favorable to the Italians regarding the Alto Adige (South Tyrol). There was also the clear reference that the keen translators at the Ministry of Foreign Affairs had noticed to the anti-Semitism existing in Fascist Italy, which remained in the translated text and now appeared on pages 360–361.

In a "Note by the Italian Publisher"[155] Bompiani explained why there were fewer pages than in the original edition; what he wrote did not differ from his confidential justification to the Press Office in September that Mussolini had approved. The cuts made to almost half of the book were necessary because of the "size" of the original text, which would have "prevented the vast distribution" it deserved as "a work that portrays the thinking and the spirit of modern Germany." Furthermore, Bompiani continued, the first half of the book, which had been summarized, was of "predominantly German interest," while the second part, which was being published, was of "universal interest, since the importance and the worldview of National-Socialism are also universal." This in so many words amounted to a colossal faux pas. In

---

155. Adolf Hitler, *La mia battaglia* (Milan: Bompiani, 1934), pp. 1–2.

his long speech of March 18 three days after *La mia battaglia* was off the presses and with the knowledge that the book was about to be published and that it included the Chancellor's preface, Mussolini clearly stated that *Fascism* had been transformed from being "an Italian phenomenon" into "a universal phenomenon."[156] *Fascism* and not Nazism, which was a derivation of sorts.

The translation was harshly criticized some months later by Delio Cantimori, a brilliant young and important scholar[157] who may have been influenced by the news regarding the Italian edition coming from France. Cantimori was not satisfied with Bompiani's explanatory note and thought there was some kind of censorship at work in the cuts made to the text, which he viewed as a manipulation of the reader towards a distorted understanding of the book—for example, by reducing the sections dealing with Nazi propaganda that Cantimori viewed as being particularly important. In any case, those were totally baseless accusations. We now know that the reasons behind the cuts were rather mundane and tied to Bompiani's desire to make the book easier to read and to sell; Mussolini and his entourage had played no part whatsoever. Cantimori was correct with respect to other problems with the translation, for example the use of the word "Duce" to translate the term "Führer," which was an awkward form of flattery; but this did not justify such aggressive criticism, regarding the

---

156. *O.O.*, Vol. XXVI, p. 185.

translation of course and not the text itself. It was a complicated book to translate but Treves had been faithful to the original and was a good craftsman.

Very soon Bompiani received the regime's official reaction. As we have mentioned Italy and Germany were experiencing some tension, mainly regarding Austria. The truncated Italian version of *Mein Kampf* was therefore being released in a rather unfavorable climate.

There is another, rather unusual, "coincidence" worth noting. On March 23, 1934, the fifteenth anniversary of the rally at the Piazza San Sepolcro, a date enshrined in the fascist calendar, and exactly one week prior to the publication of *Mein Kampf,* Italian newspapers announced that two more volumes of Mussolini's works—the *Scritti e discorsi*—in a "definitive" edition were being released by Hoepli. These were the second and eighth volumes, the former covering the period preceding the march on Rome and the latter containing Mussolini's most recent texts and speeches. In this way two of the Duce's four volumes also contained texts that had been written long before the German book. These also provided an additional link in the "anti-*Mein Kampf*" chain: Mussolini at that point was competing in the Italian market with four volumes of his own complete works versus Hitler's single massive text. In all there were to be eight projected Mussolini volumes but these ended up growing to twelve. Even in sheer numbers there could be no

---

157. *Leonardo,* May 1935, pp. 224–227. Now in Delio Cantimori, *Politica e storia contemporanea. Scritti 1927–1942,* edited by Luisa Mangoni (Turin: Einaudi, 1991), pp. 306–311.

question as to which of the two weighed heavier, value and content notwithstanding. The Duce was even reprinting his *Doctrine of Fascism* written with Giovanni Gentile and originally published in 1932. *Il Popolo d'Italia* naturally immediately celebrated its publication with an effusive article by Ottavio Dinale,[158] who had been close to the Duce for many years and was one of the paper's most respected editorial commentators.

On March 30, prior to the publication of the Italian translation of *Mein Kampf*, the newspaper *Il Tevere* published a front page advanced passage of the new preface, which it termed "a political event of the greatest interest"; while on April 3 *Il Popolo d'Italia* (a newspaper Mussolini owned) published a review of the book[159] prior to its actual release.[160] The review was signed "Farinata," a pseudonym used by Ottavio Dinale, who had just reviewed the Duce's collected works. Dinale was also a staunch anti-Semite, who in October 1933 had denounced in that same paper an excessive Jewish presence in "decision-making jobs," meaning positions of power, in the city of Trieste and even requested that the prefect should "take action" on the issue.[161] Mussolini had received Dinale twice in his office, on March 27

158. Ottavio Dinale, "La Rivoluzione fascista, 25 marzo 1919–28 ottobre 1922," PDI, March 23, 1934.
159. Doc. A78.
160. The fact that the review had been written before publication was confirmed by Paul Gentizon, the Rome correspondent of *Le Temps*, who phoned the item into the newspaper. See "Italie. Une traduction italienne de Mein Kampf," *Le Temps*, April 6, 1934 (front page).
161. The article was published on October 4. See Michele Sarfatti, *Gli ebrei nell'Italia fascista. Vicende, identità, persecuzione* (Turin: Einaudi, 2000; translation by Wisconsin

and 28, five days before the review was published, and the press had mentioned those meetings. There could be no doubt about the fact that the review of *La mia battaglia* was thoroughly "inspired" and "authoritative."[162]

Dinale's article on *Mein Kampf* was at the same time courteous and diplomatic and even part enthusiastic about the structure and content of the book, except for criticism of the "theoretical" section, which he simply called "boring." He made only two specific negative comments regarding the message the book contained. The first one concerned the idea of the superiority of the German race and the "absolute mastery of one race over every other." This was a harsh and completely "self-servingly Italian" observation, yet it wasn't at all critical of Hitler's racism and anti-Semitism. Dinale's review mentioned nothing of Fascist anti-Semitism even though it could easily be located, thanks to an extremely detailed index, which had been reproduced from the original German, under the entry "Fascist Italy and Judaism."

After the initial criticism of the concept of German racial superiority there came Dinale's other position, which we may now

---

University Press in the spring of 2006), p. 87. On October 21, 1933, Dinale was received by Mussolini and requested that he be asked to contribute articles and items more often. Mussolini promised to do so and Ciano, the Press Officer, confirmed this in a letter dated October 29. ACS, MCP, Gab., b.8, f. 41. Dinale Ottavio. Farinata. For the audiences of March 1934, ACS, SPD, CO, b. 1313, f. Udienze. 1934. On the audience papers there is marked the date of March 27, 18:30 and on the 28th at 17:00 hours. The news that Dinale had been received by the Duce was published in *Il Popolo di Roma* of March 30 on page 2.

162. Hubert Lagardelle, for example, attributed it to Mussolini himself. See Hubert Lagardelle, *Mission à Rome. Mussolini* (Paris: Plon, 1955). p. 75.

analyze in a different light: a bitter critique of the preface that Hitler, as we now know, had written pursuant to the request of the Italian authorities and Mussolini himself. The preface was being attacked because it underscored the similarities that existed between Nazism and Fascism. According to Farinata (Dinale), all of *Mein Kampf* provided ample proof of the differences that existed between the two regimes and testified to the superiority of Fascism precisely because it didn't attempt to promote the dominance of one race over all others. "Free and flexible in its human realism and the strength of its universal ideas, Rome seeks to teach." According to *Il Popolo d'Italia* a comparison of Nazism and Fascism was unacceptable. This was not explicitly stated but the volumes of Mussolini's *Scritti e discorsi* stacked in every bookstore made the statement obvious.

Even when examined in the best light the Germans could only conclude that the review was only half favorable. The semi-official mouthpiece of the Italian regime failed to welcome the book with the same enthusiasm they showed for the publishing agreement that had produced the new edition. It was a cold welcome, and it was viewed that way abroad as well, in particular by an extremely well-informed observer, as journalist Paul Gentizon.[163] But it must be said that it wasn't cold because it rejected the book's racism but rather because it repudiated the idea of German racial dominance. In this sense it was only another episode in the bitter polemic between Germany and Italy

---

163. Art. cit., *Le Temps*, April 6, 1934 (front page).

at the time and perhaps the consequence of the shadow being cast over the Fascist leader, which he was beginning to feel. The piece in *Il Popolo d'Italia* confirmed that the racist slant was precisely what it found most interesting about the book.

Margherita Sarfatti.

Galeazzo Ciano as Head of the Prime Minister's Press Office, 1934.

Fascist leaders C.M. De Vecchi *(right)* and Emilio De Bono *(left)*.

Roberto Farinacci *(right)* during the Republic of Salò with C.A. Biggini.

Joseph Goebbels.

Giuseppe Bottai.

King Victor Emmanuel III.

Giuseppe Toeplitz, Managing Director of the Banca
Commerciale Italiana.

Guido Jung, Minister of Finance.

King Victor Emmanuel III and Mussolini in the early 1930s.

The first meeting between Hitler and Mussolini at the Venice airport, June 14, 1934.

The Munich headquarters of the Nazi daily
newspaper, *Völkischer Beobachter*.

Dino Grandi, Italian ambassador to London in 1936.

Enigma Books

Hitler with Rudolf Hess, c. 1934.

Philosopher Giovanni Gentile.

Valentino Bompiani around 1933 at the publishing company in Milan.

Chapter XIII

The Jews

There is more to the article in *Il Popolo d'Italia*. In the days that immediately preceded the book's release the newspaper published a few statements of a clearly racist nature that were significant because of their timing, headlines, and content.

The first completely unexpected piece was entitled *Razza ed impero* (Race and Empire) and appeared as a long front-page editorial on February 17, after the decision had been reached to move ahead with the publication of *Mein Kampf*.[164] Writer Icilio Petrone was the author and the occasion was probably the twenty-fifth anniversary of the death of Alfredo Oriani. The article outlined the history of Italian culture,

---

164. Doc. A59.

from Dante to Mazzini, Garibaldi and Alfredo Oriani, as the history of a race, with Mussolini and the Fascist revolution being the culmination of this long "racial journey." "Here we see the unmistakable originality of our revolution that produced a man who is one of our very own, laboriously prepared by thousands of years of pain; he is us; he is the being that each one of us carries inside and who can finally take the typical shape of the race through his blood, his character, and his ideals all rooted in history." The author even managed in passing to chide the "Nordic races" for having lost the contest against the "Latin peoples," who managed to give birth to the Renaissance in spite of the Protestant Reformation.

One month later, on March 18, in a speech during the regime's second five-year Congress at the conference of the entire Fascist leadership—an occasion important enough to be broadcast on radio throughout the country and abroad—Mussolini repeated once again the concept of an "Italian race"[165] and, resorting to some old expressions,

---

165. The text of the speech ("Il grande discorso del Duce alla II Assemblea quinquennale del regime e la sua profonda risonanza in Italia e nel mondo") was published on PDI on March 20, together with many news items surrounding the event. The article also had—and this was extremely rare—a few photos of the handwritten manuscript of the speech itself. Among them was the first page of the part of the speech that *Il Popolo d'Italia* entitled *La difesa della razza* [The Defense of the Race], which began with the sentence: "The military power of the State, the future and security of the nation are tied to the demographic issue…" In the manuscript text as printed, the beginning reads instead: "Must we preserve the race? Yes. The regime has tackled this problem since the early years…" The printed text is also in *O.O.*, vol. XXVI, pp. 185–193 (cited here starting at p. 190). For the hints about the African action in the speech, see also Esmonde M. Robertson, *Mussolini as Empire-Builder. Europe and Africa, 1932-36* (London, Basingstoke: Macmillan, 1977), p. 94. Among the telegrams sent out by the Cypher Office of the Ministry of the Interior during the

stated its greater value compared to other races. Very cautiously, the dictator began outlining his plan for the conquest of Ethiopia and probably more. "Italy is privileged to be the most clearly identifiable nation geographically. The most compactly homogenous from the ethnic, linguistic, and moral point of view. Religious unity is one of the greatest strengths of a nation."

The words were more or less identical (with the exception of the religious issue) to those published in *Il Popolo d'Italia* some fourteen years before in an article that was about to be reprinted in the second volume of *Scritti e discorsi*.[166] It also deeply and proudly differed with Hitler's writings, which Mussolini had read and even underlined about the German people and that Bompiani was preparing to publish. Hitler had written[167] of his anguish about the "poisoning of the blood by the penetration of the body" of the German people; of Germany's "open borders"; of the "infiltration of foreign blood reaching to the core of the Reich." The Duce, on the other hand, supported the unity and homogeneity of the Italian race. The volume of *Scritti e discorsi* would soon make it amply clear to everyone that Mussolini had authored those words as early as 1920.

We must, however, mention two other short articles published by *Il Popolo d'Italia* on the same subject. The positioning of the articles and

---

weeks preceding the event, several were sent to summon top regime figures to Rome specifically to listen to the speech.

166. Mussolini, *Per le frontiere di pace. Alle Alpi Giulie!*, PDI, February 22, 1920 (for vol. II of the *Scritti e discorsi* see p. 57).

167. Doc. B-V.

the style in which they were written were typical of the anonymous editorials Mussolini was known to publish at the top of the second page of his newspaper. The two articles do not appear in the Duce's *Opera Omnia*, edited by the Susmel father and son, or the collected articles[168] kept in the archives of the Duce's personal secretariat containing the lists of the handwritten originals. However, the style, the topics, and the use of quotations were all typical of Mussolini's writing and the articles can undoubtedly be attributed to him. Regardless of whether the Duce or someone else actually wrote the editorials, they remain extremely significant.

The editorial entitled *America Negra?* (A Negro America?) was published on March 24. It stressed the drop in births among whites and the high number of blacks in the United States: 11.5 million out of a total population of 123 million. "Half century or a century from now will we see Negroes in the White House?" was the conclusion reached by the anonymous editorial writer. A similar article was published the next day, the 25th, this time about France, a country, as we know, also discussed in *Mein Kampf,* on the same issue and that Mussolini had singled out.[169] The title of the article was *La nuova invasione* (The New Invasion) and it used official statistics to denounce the multiethnic mix of a French municipality of 5,000, half of whom belonged to non-French races and nationalities. What was being created was "a Polish, a

---

168. The lists are in ACS, SPD, CO, Zinc box, sc. 17. But see *Premessa ai volume di appendice all'opera "Opera Omnia di Benito Mussolini,"* in *O.O.*, vol. XXXVII, *Appendice I*, pp. XXVI–XXXI.

Czech, even a Moroccan France, but certainly not a French one," as the same "anonymous" writer pointed out.

On March 31, the day after the publication of Hitler's preface in *Il Tevere*, *Il Popolo d'Italia* published on its front page with a highlighted typeface another article about "The discovery and arrest of a group of anti-fascist Jews connected to the émigrés." A similar headline, over the same text minus the comments, also appeared in other newspapers. The arrest had taken place twenty days before, on March 11 at Ponte Tresa on the Swiss-Italian border but the press was announcing it only then.[170] The text was a communiqué prepared by the chief of police at Mussolini's request and sent to the newspapers through Ciano's Press Office the day before, March 30, with the request that they "give the communiqué enhanced positioning."[171] This came as the first spectacular public signal that in Italy Jews could be considered as enemies because they were Jews.[172] The article also pointed out an outrageously hostile and anti-national (as well as false) detail: one of the

---

169. Doc. B-III.

170. Michele Sarfatti, *Gli ebrei, cit.*, pp. 92–93. *L'Osservatore Romano* published the news on April 1 (p. 10) under the title "L'arresto dei membri di un'organizzazione antifascista" [Arrest of the members of an anti-fascist organization] without ever noting even in the copy that these were "Jews."

171. ACS, Agenzia Stefani. Morgagni Papers, box 69, f. Rapporti quotidiani del Capo dell'Ufficio stampa di S.E. il Capo del Governo. sf 2. Dal Gennaio 1934 al Dicembre 1935 [Daily reports of the head of the Press Office to H.E. the Head of the Government. sf. 2. From January 1934 to December 1935].

172. Regarding the first displays of Mussolini's anti-Semitism, see now G. Fabre, *Mussolini razzista*, cit. and G. Fabre, "Mussolini and the Jews on the Eve of the March on Rome," in Joshua D. Zimmerman (ed.), *Jews in Italy under Fascist and Nazi Rule 1922–1945*, (Cambridge and New York: Cambridge University Press, 2005) pp. 55–68.

people under arrest had cried out as he escaped: "Cowards! Italian dogs!"

These accusations were published at random in the newspapers and were not only directed at individuals who just happened to be Jewish. Explicit official orders of an anti-Semitic nature were also issued to the press. On that same day, March 30, immediately following the order to publish the communiqué, Ciano issued another directive to the newsmen: "A Jewish theater group that produces plays in Hebrew is about to visit Italy. Do not write about it." Ten days later, on April 10, the order was modified in a more jocular vein: "We wrote to ignore it but now we can simply announce the play's schedule at the Manzoni Theater [in Rome] and someone trying to be funny may also add that they went to see the play but did not understand a single word." The local Rome daily, *Il Messaggero*, kept on ignoring the theater group despite that authorization.[173] Other newspapers took the same position, according to the available record.

On April 5, 1934, Ciano's press report stated that it, which naturally meant Mussolini, "considered" that an article by Liliana Scalero[174] about Heinrich Heine published the same day by *Il Popolo di Roma*, another Rome daily, was "inappropriate." The article was a review of

---

173. Until April 20—the program for the Manzoni Theater reads "Alfredo Bambi con la sua compagnia" [Alfredo Bambi and his players]—the program remained unchanged and anonymous: "Eccezionali spettacoli cinematografici di prima visione" [Quality exclusive first-run films]. In *Il Popolo di Roma* the theater program for the Manzoni was completely eliminated.

174. Liliana Scalero, "Il carteggio di un ironista," *Il Popolo di Roma*, April 5, 1934 (third page).

the letters written by the German and Jewish poet as published by Treves in a book. The author of the review was a highly respected German scholar, she was to win a prize from the Italian Academy for her translation of *Faust*. It is difficult to see what could possibly be "inappropriate" in that article, other than its praise for a Jewish and German poet who was rather eloquent and that the Germans considered one of their best. Scalero had written statements to the effect that: "The rationalist Jew was perhaps thinking back to the prophetic words written in 1823 to Emmanuel Wohwill: 'We are no longer strong enough to wear a beard, to fast, to hate or to suffer because of hate.'" It is worth pointing out that the inordinately violent so-called "Anti-Heine-Kampagne" launched in Germany against the poet actually began some two years later, in late December 1935.[175]

There was more. On April 9 Ciano told newsmen that a "recommendation" was going to the Stefani Agency[176] to "avoid writing about the festivities for the end of the Passover in Tripoli"; all newspapers should therefore ignore that event as well. It should be pointed out that public festivities for the "Pesach" in Tripoli were organized by the tourist office of the new governor of Libya, Italo Balbo.[177]

---

175. Volker Dahm, *Das jüdische Buch im Dritten Reich* (Munich: Beck, 1993), (2nd ed.) pp. 161–162.

176. Italian official news agency during the fascist period.

177. The news was in two articles in *Il Popolo di Roma* of March 29 ("Manifestazioni folcloristiche in Libia. La festa ebraica di "Pesah"") and on the 30th (Renato La Valle, "Itinerari turistici in Tripolitania").

All Italian national, local, and even Fascist party newspapers were accredited with the Head of the Government's Press Office in Rome. This impressive series of orders, issued while the Italian translation of *Mein Kampf* was being published, was imparted across the board without exceptions to the entire Italian press. It was therefore no accident that from April 7 to 9 *Il Tevere* published a few articles attacking active German-Jewish intellectuals only because they were Jews.[178] In this context we should finally mention an incident that remained largely unknown at the time but that was subsequently very much discussed, namely, Mussolini's decision to enact complete and preemptive censorship of all books about to be published. The matter has now been brought to light,[179] and was set in motion either on April 2 or 3 when the Duce decided to stop the distribution of a romance novel by Mura, a well-known woman novelist, that described a sentimental and sexual affair between a white Italian woman and a black man. To make sure that such a situation would not recur and, in his own words, to protect the "dignity of the race," Mussolini decreed that all manuscripts were to be submitted prior to publication for approval by the authorities and by his office as a last recourse. A ministerial circular was sent to all the prefects in Italy.

---

178. This was "Non abbiamo bisogno di registi ebrei" [We don't need Jewish film directors] of April 7–8 (quoted in R. De Felice, *The Jews, cit.*, p. 131) and also "Cronache dello schermo. 'Liebeler' od il caso Ophüls," of April 9–10 that also mentioned the author of the subject of the film, Schnitzler ("here we go back to the Jewish novelist").
179. G. Fabre, *L'elenco, cit.*, pp. 22–28.

Italian book publishers naturally found out about the decision and who had made it. The publishers—who were part of the country's publishing elite—were naturally better informed than anyone else as to what was really happening in the country.[180] Following the initial "signal" given to Bompiani and Mondadori about *Mein Kampf,* all Italian publishers—of both books and periodicals—were now being put on notice on the issue of racism.

At this stage the regime's public pronouncements on racism were of various types: either positive, in that they praised racism by simply placing the Italic race on a pedestal; or negative, by being race repressive, anti-black, and anti-Semitic. Naturally, there is no direct link to the Italian translation of *Mein Kampf* and even less to indicate that something happened as a *consequence* of that publishing event. We may, however, state that while the book was being published following Mussolini's decision, new and unusual positions taken by organizations under his direct control became public knowledge while at the same time a whole set of secret decisions, both racist and anti-Semitic, were also made, as the next chapter will show.

The positions taken in public were somewhat cautious, mainly because of the way the Catholic church was reacting to German racism, but they were nonetheless unmistakable. Just as *Mein Kampf* showed the

---

180. Alberto Carocci discussed it with Carlo Emilio Gadda when he complained about the delays in publishing his *Il castello di Udine,* which had been blocked by the censors. See the letter of May 16, 1934, in *Lettere a Solaria,* edited by Giuliano Manacorda (Rome: Editori Riuniti, 1979), p. 508. "For the historical record," Carocci

way toward a multifaceted racism that was both anti-Semitic and anti-black but also anti-Slav, which was less interesting to fascism at that point, Italian fascism was also cautiously building up its positions. Never before had there been a time in Italy where all forms of racism could be rolled into a single policy, especially the two "main" twentieth century tendencies: the anti-Jewish and anti-black strains. There is no evidence that the publication of *Mein Kampf* actually led to the merging of the two, but, as far as Italy was concerned, this was the first time there was a broadly "integrated" and blatant form of racism. *Mein Kampf* undoubtedly played a role in the process.

Mussolini, furthermore, had publicly placed his own much older racism up before Nazi racism, and Hitler confirmed this in specific pages of *Mein Kampf*. But with the exception of the key issue asserting Germanic racial superiority, there had been no Italian attack against German racism. So the Chancellor's book made little noise in the Italian market during the months that followed. Despite some cool criticism the book met with moderate success: one month after the first printing on April 25, 1934, Bompiani went back to press, reaching the third printing by September 30.[181] The "Bible of Nazism," which we

---

wrote, "it seems that this regulation originated in the Head of the Government's anger over a romance by Mura."

181. For reasons unknown the listing of editions that later appeared in the copyright page of the Italian edition never included the third edition. Starting with the edition printed on March 15, 1937, the third edition was considered as such. We have no information as to print runs or sales quantities. The last edition found was the XVIIIth in 1942.

might add was also the "Bible of racism," was carving out its own niche in the Italian book market.

Chapter XIV

The First "Purges"

The founder of Fascism was therefore reading and publishing racist books; he was writing anonymously on the subject, using racially slanted language; his Press Office was issuing directives to newspapers targeting the Jews; and he inaugurated preventive censorship by singling out a book that allegedly offended "racial dignity." This all took place in the course of the first quarter of 1934 and appeared to be part of the racist-discriminatory variety of propaganda decisions within the publishing industry.

Yet while the Duce was following the publication of *Mein Kampf* at the beginning of 1934 he did not limit his action to propaganda and public opinion. He also made some very practical decisions.

In 1933 Mussolini had suggested to Hitler that he, Hitler, exercise caution in expressing his anti-Jewish ideas by applying pressure to the "top" Jewish leaders instead, gradually eliminating them just as he was doing in Italy.[182] In a quiet but not completely secret way, Mussolini proceeded to "purge" his former collaborator and possibly also his lover, Margherita Sarfatti; she was forbidden from publishing in *Il Popolo d'Italia*; her friend Carlo Foà resigned as dean of the faculty at the University of Milan; and the man who was probably most criticized as being the quintessential "Jew"[183] in Italy, Giuseppe Toeplitz, was fired from his position as managing director of the Banca Commerciale. These actions help clarify a comment that Mussolini made in September 1938 regarding Margherita Sarfatti, as reported by Giuseppe Bottai: "I understood five years ago that the Jewish issue would be thrust upon us and I wanted to free myself of it. I had her fired from *Il Popolo d'Italia* and from the editorial board of *Gerarchia* . . . obviously she was given her regular separation pay... "[184] The "Jewish issue" was not being "thrust upon" upon him at all, since Mussolini himself was the one setting it up.

By 1933 the Duce had already disposed of the Jewish members of his staff: Press Officer Guido Artom and Giacomo Beer, head of the Prime Minister's cabinet. Invariably these measures were taken quietly and came with small "consolation prizes," but nevertheless they did take place and their anti-Jewish character became obvious. It is also noteworthy that other "Jewish" persons holding important positions at the time were not affected, especially among the financial decision

---

182. For later data see G. Fabre, *Mussolini e gli ebrei, cit.*, pp. 204–218.
183. When the words *Jew* and *census* are used, either singular or plural in quotes, it denotes racist policy intent.

makers. Among these was Minister of Finance Guido Jung, whom Mussolini still considered as being untouchable, perhaps because he felt that a Jew could best facilitate relations with high finance in Italy and abroad.[185]

While this was the situation during the first half of the year, by the end of 1933 Italy was engaged in a truly vigorous and secret policy of destabilizing the Jews. On November 20, 1933, the Ministry of National Education placed restrictions on foreign Jewish university students, and in particular those coming from Germany to study in Italy. These restrictions, as stated in an official announcement, were to avoid "harming the very friendly relations" that Italy had with some countries, one of them obviously being Nazi Germany.[186] From then on, Italian consuls overseas were expected to approve the entry of students and weed out the "undesirables," meaning those unwelcome to the German authorities. The document never specifically referred to the "Jews," but they were undoubtedly considered a major issue at that time.

---

184. Giuseppe Bottai, *Diario 1935–1944*, edited by Giordano Bruno Guerri (Milan: Rizzoli, 1989), p. 134. See date of September 23, 1938.

185. R. De Felice (*The Jews, cit.*, p. 493), in citing the memoir of one of Mussolini's inner circle (perhaps Margherita Sarfatti), wrote that this person said, regarding Minister Jung, that at the time Mussolini had said "a Jew was what was needed at Finance."

186. The text of circular n. 18596 is in the Ministero dell'Educazione Nazionale, Direzione Generale dell'Istruzione Superiore, *Raccolta delle leggi, dei decreti, dei regolamenti e delle circolari sulla Istruzione Superiore dall'anno 1933 al 1938.* (Rome: Istituto Poligrafico dello Stato, 1939), pp. 1020–1021 (on pages 1021–1022 is the ministerial order of November 18). I thank Luciano Canfora for having pointed out the volume. Quoted in part in Elisa Signori, "Una *peregrinatio academia* in età contemporanea. Gli studenti ebrei stranieri nelle università italiane tra le due guerre," in *Annali di storia delle università italiane*, 4, 2000, p. 155.

The leaders of the Italian Jewish community, were well aware of this problem; they were also worried about overtly anti-Semitic demonstrations that were, as we know, instigated by Mussolini himself. A letter addressed to the dictator was to be sent by the leaders of the Union of the Communities (including its president, Felice Ravenna),[187] voicing their grave concern. The letter complained of "episodes are not rare in various walks of life in Italy showing how the Jews were not always being treated like other Italian citizens, and how their circumstances sometimes feel the effects of old prejudices." Because of their extremely cautious attitude, the letter was never sent and we now have a copy, but the knowledge and awareness of what was happening was certainly very palpable.

Using the same mindful stealth as before, the elimination of high level "Jewish" personalities progressed during the following months, albeit in a limited and irregular way, but nevertheless without interruptions.

In January 1934, as previously mentioned, Margherita Sarfatti had therefore been "fired" from her last official position as the editor of *Gerarchia*; her Jewish secretary, Isa Foà, was dismissed at the same time.[188] On January 1, 1934, Gino Jacopo Olivetti resigned as secretary of the Confederazione Generale Fascista dell'Industria, the equivalent of today's Confindustria.[189] The resignation came at the same time as

---

187. AUCEI, UCII, Attività dell'UCII fino al 1933, b. 43, f. 115. The note was sent to various persons, Rabbi Angelo Sacerdoti among them (on December 1). I thank A. Capristo for drawing my attention to this document.
188. G. Fabre, *Mussolini e gli ebrei, cit.*, p. 209.
189. The date of resignation is mentioned in the circular sent by Pirelli and given to the press two weeks later. See "Il saluto del Commissario della Confederazione alle

the appointment of Alberto Pirelli as the new commissioner, who according to his diaries pressured Mussolini to retain Olivetti in his position, but the Duce refused to budge. Pirelli's appointment—he was to remain as head of several minor industrial associations—came with a whole list of appointments of new national commissioners in every area of the corporative organizations. One of Olivetti's friends was later quoted by Felice Guarnieri as saying: "To get rid of one Jew, they knocked off ten Christians!"[190]

In March and April 1934 another important "Jew" in Italian finance and economics, Camillo Ara would lose his top management job.[191] Ara was president of Sofindit, a company that in the early 1930s was rescuing many firms caught up in the financial difficulties created by the Comit [Banca Commerciale Italiana] at that time. Since March 1933 IRI, which was managed by Alberto Beneduce, had acquired all the common stock of Sofindit. On March 13, 1934 it was decided to shut down the company, with the closing actually taking place on April 25, 1934, when Ara became one of Beneduce's deputies but was denied

---

organizzazioni nazionali e provinciali," in *L'Organizzazione industriale*, January 20, 1934. The "salutation" was dated the 13th. On December 29 Mussolini had named the commissioners to the thirteen confederations (Stefani communiqué of December 30). See *L'Organizzazione industriale*, of December 31. For Mussolini's refusal see Alberto Pirelli, *Taccuini 1922–1943*, edited by Donato Barbone (Bologna: il Mulino, 1984), p. 121.

190. Felice Guarnieri, *Battaglie economiche fra le due guerre*, edited by Luciano Zani (Bologna: il Mulino, 1988) (first ed. 1953), p. 163. Guarnieri is obviously mistaken in dating the event in 1931. See Franklin Hugh Adler, *Italian Industrialists from Liberalism to Fascism. The political development of the industrial bourgeoisie, 1906–1934* (Cambridge: Cambridge University Press, 1995), p. 434.

191. See [Guido Montanari,] *Introduzione*, Banca Commerciale Italiana. Archivio storico. Collana inventari. Serie VI, vol. 3, *Società finanziaria industriale italiana (Sofindit)*, s.e., Milan, 1991, pp. XXV–XXVI and XXXVIII. For the speech to the Senate, *O.O.*, vol. XXVI, pp. 148–149.

any important missions. On January 13, Mussolini, speaking in the Senate, mentioned Sofindit, made some derisive remarks, such as it being "a word with a somewhat Ostrogothic sound" and a company that was "in a convalescent mode." By the end of April the situation prompted Edgardo Morpurgo, president of the Assicurazioni Generali, to withdraw his candidacy to the board's management council, where according to him and given the existing climate, there were already too many Jewish board members.[192]

However it is also interesting to note that during this period in 1933 two "appointments" of "Jews"* were made where the Duce did take a position: the podestà (mayor) of Trieste in October and that of Senator Isaia Levi in December.

In Trieste there was very strong pressure to block the appointment of Enrico Paolo Salem as mayor: he was a Catholic but had a Jewish father and a Jewish name. Rumors hostile to Salem began to surface during the summer.[193] The article by "Farinata" Ottavio Dinale in *Il Popolo d'Italia* previously mentioned showed no evidence of being inspired from higher up.[194] On October 4, 1933, Dinale wrote in an article commenting on a letter he had received that "in a certain city where the Israelites represent two percent of the population" (a rather cryptic remark but he was referring to Trieste) the Israelites "control

---

192. Anna Millo, *Trieste, le assicurazioni, l'Europa. Arnoldo Frigessi di Rattalma e la Ras* (Milan: Franco Angeli, 2004), p. 167.

193. A.S.Ts, Prefettura, Gab., b. 505, f. Salem Enrico Paolo. Podestà Trieste, where one also finds informant reports against Salem dated July 1933.

194. Farinata, "Discussioni," PDI, October 4, 1933 (see Michele Sarfatti, *Gli ebrei, cit.*, p. 87).

everything, positions, decision making jobs and important command posts." He also requested that the local prefect take action.

The prefect, Carlo Tiengo, answered by taking a firm stand in the opposite direction. The same day the article was published in *Il Popolo d'Italia* the prefect was supporting Salem's formal candidacy.[195] He may have been prompted by economic reasons because at the beginning of 1932 he had entrusted Salem with the task of rescuing the Popolare Triestina bank that was filing for bankruptcy. Salem completed the task in August 1933 and also made large contributions to the PNF.[196] We should add however that on the same day he filed Salem's candidacy Tiengo made another unusual proposal: the new podestà of Trieste would have not one but two deputies, both of them loyal fascists. The prefect could then insure that his candidate would be secure. The Ministry of the Interior approved this strange proposal.

In the second case, the appointment of Isaia Levi, an industrialist from Turin, as senator—which was confirmed by a Royal decree of

195. ACS, MI, DGAC, Podestà e Consulte municipali, b. 293, f. Trieste. Vicepodestà. The file on the podestà is missing in the Trieste section. But from the letter of October 4 on the vicepodestà, cited after, it appears that Tiengo had sent his proposal on Salem that same day.

196. A.S.Ts, Prefettura, Gab., b. 505, f. Salem, Enrico Paolo. Podestà Trieste. Information on Salem's "merits" are in a long report by Tiengo dated June 11, 1934, when the prefect proposed that he be awarded a title of nobility by Rome (and it is possible that with what was going on this constituted a form of extreme defense). But Mussolini rejected the proposal on June 19. The documentation in Mussolini's secretariat is in ACS, SPD, CO, b. 394, f. 144.914. Salem, Enrico Paolo. Trieste. The amount Salem donated for the summer camps of the PNF was 200,000 lire. The appointment to podestà was made on October 12, 1933 (see Silva Bon, *Gli ebrei a Trieste 1930–1945. Identità, persecuzione, risposte* [Gorizia: Istituto regionale per la storia del movimento di liberazione nel Friuli-Venezia Giulia, Libreria Editrice Goriziana, 2000], p. 39).

December 9, 1933[197]—stirred up rumors claiming it was a promise made by the Duce after Levi had agreed to shore up Zanichelli, Carducci's publishing house, which was in financial trouble, and perhaps, as a reward for other help he had provided to the PNF.[198] The appointment was highly unusual in any case and one for which the Duce showed a personal interest, since he didn't even pause when the prefect of Turin voiced several warnings.[199] It is possible on the other hand that he was misled at least in part about the matter. His police had informed him of some past "legal" problems that had plagued Levi a few years before, only after the appointment.[200] Finally, there is no record of the role played by the King.

---

197. For the entire appointment file see ACS, PCM, Gab., Senatori del Regno, b.6, f. 346. Aspirante. Levi Gr. Uff. Isaia.

198. We refer to reports by informers of the Political Police. The frist one regarding the "laticlave" of July 19, 1930, and the last one regarding the financing of Zanichelli publishing was dated December 4, 1933 (ACS, MI, DGPS, DPP, f. personali, b. 717, f. Levi Grand'Uff. Isaia). The rumors about the appointment as senator as compensation for bailing out Zanichelli publishing were repeated in Brunella Dalla Casa, but without any further documentation (Brunella Dalla Chiesa, *La società anonima Nicola Zanichelli: un'impresa editoriale fra le due guerre,* in *Editoria e Università a Bologna tra Ottocento e Novecento. Atti del 5° Convegno, Bologna 26–27 gennaio 1990,* edited by Aldo Berselli, Comune di Bologna e Istituto per la Storia di Bologna [Bologna, 1991], p. 107). Umberto Ricci, then prefect of Turin, in a notation that must have been made before the beginning of September 1933, wrote: "H.E. the Head of the Government would have already formally promised to Grand Officer Levi an appointment as senator." (ACS, PCM, Gab., Senatori del Regno, b. 6, f. 346. Aspirante. Levi Gr. Uff. Isaia.)

199. The new prefect of Turin, Agostino Iraci (former head of the Cabinet of the Ministry of the Interior), voiced doubts about Levi in a letter dated November 1, 1933. See ACS, PCM, Gab., Senatori del Regno, b. 6, f. 346. Aspirante. Levi Gr. Uff. Isaia).

200. During and immediately following the First World War Levi had been investigated and even arrested twice for supplying war material to the enemy. See ACS, MI, DGPS, DPP, f. personali, b. 717, f. Levi Grand'Uff. Isaia. The news became public only the day after his appointment, probably due to the rumors that were circulating. On that day, December 10, the chief of police asked for the file on one of those matters (for the notation that shows the "taking" of the file by the chief

There were therefore two appointments of "Jews," Salem and Isaia Levi, made while the purges were being enacted. Mussolini had a dual attitude regarding the "Jews" at that time. In both of these cases, however, it appears that there were some unavoidable economic "requirements" at work, and possibly corruption.

Very soon, during the first few months of 1934, both plans for the actual purging of Jews from positions of "responsibility" or "decision making" were being systematically implemented, with a broadening of the targeted individuals. At first the Duce and his staff began using detailed "census" information to ascertain the religion of those involved. Then blanket orders were issued, no longer aimed simply at removing *individual* Jews from high positions—better identified by their religious affiliation as "Israelites"—but rather targeting them across the board and identifying them as Jews in specific areas—this being naturally either political or economic but certainly national in scope.

Four of these "census" operations and the subsequent "orders" issued, involving hundreds of well-known personalities in politics and business, both local and national, have been identified so far.

The first "religious census" taken among stockbrokers was ordered by the Ministry of the Interior and carried out by the prefects on

---

of police on December 10, 1933, see ACS, MI, DGPS, UCI, b. 98, f. 2990). The file in question is the same as the one now in ACS, MI, DGPS, DAGR, Atti speciali, b.3, f. 9. Esportazione di panno grigio effettuata da Curti, Colombo, Levi e Toscano (1918) [Exportation of grey cloth by Curti, Colombo, Levi, and Toscano (1918)]. From that file and other items on the 16th a new and very critical report was written about Levi (even though the police were unable to confirm whether Levi had in fact been condemned at the time, since all documents relating to the case had disappeared).

February 12, 1934, with initial results delivered on March 3.[201] It covered all nine Italian stock exchanges—Rome, Milan, Turin, Genoa, Bologna, Naples, Trieste, Florence, and Venice. The "census" asked ethical and political questions, basically about the degree of support given to fascism, along with the "possibility of belonging to the Jewish faith." There was a clear and threatening potential for associating "Jews" and "anti-fascists." This was a very broad investigation to be carried out in such a short time, which created problems for the prefects since this kind of information had never been collected by their services before. Milan, the largest stock exchange, had ninety-nine brokers, while about two hundred had been identified nationally.

Interestingly, on the same day that the final data on the "census" was compiled (March 3, 1934), Mussolini asked the ISTAT (Italian Central Institute of Statistics) to "find out the figures regarding the Jews in Italy."[202] The president of ISTAT immediately provided the Duce with numbers from the 1931 census. It is not known if the request was connected to the stockbroker census or if it was to be used to prepare future "orders," or other unidentified estimates. In any case, it was part of an intensive exercise in demographic and quantitative analysis.

---

201. See the outgoing telegrams issued by the Cypher Office, n. 3940 of February 12, 1934, signed by Buffarini Guidi and then numbers 5501 of February 28 and 5720 and 5721 of March 3 all signed by Mormino. And then incoming numbers 11346 and 11178 of March 1 (ACS, MI, UC).
202. ACS, SPD, CR, cat. 169/R, b. 140, f. 14 Statistica degli ebrei residenti in Italia. See Giuseppe Leti, *L'Istat e il Consiglio Superiore di Statistica dal 1926 al 1945* (Rome: Istituto nazionale di statistica, 1996), p. 201.

The second episode happened two months later. The big mess regarding the arrest of the Jewish "conspirators" had just quieted down after the newspapers had published several sensational articles. The story of those arrests, which took place between March 11 and 31, and the write-up in the press were given a strong anti-Semitic slant by the Duce and the administrative offices reporting directly to him.[203]

Another less sensational episode had taken place that failed to reach the front pages of the dailies but was nonetheless significant. Two brothers, Mario and Manfredo Segre, sons of a former Milan Jewish stockbroker, Michele Segre, who were also stockbrokers themselves, were arrested on April 2. This was followed by the seizure of their magazine *Borsa* (stock market), which they both edited and published.[204] According to documents in the archives the Segre

---

203. We refer to a few reports by policemen that followed the "conspirators" for several months before they were arrested in part on March 11. See in particular the report by Renzo Mambrini of December 19, 1933, and that of March 6, 1934, by Francesco Nudi. See ACS, MI, DGPS, DPP, f. material, b. 114, f. 3. sf. Giustizia e libertà in Italia e Sevizio Togo n. 1; e sf. Arresto dei responsabili 12–13 marzo, 34. But see Joel Blatt, "The Battle of Turin, 1933–1936: Carlo Rosselli, Giustizia e libertà, OVRA and the Origins of Mussolini's Anti-Semitic Campaign," in *Journal of Modern Italian Studies*, I, 1 (Fall 1995), pp. 22–57, in particular p. 28. But also see, for more complete information and mostly for Mussolini's personal input, Michele Sarfatti, *Gli ebrei, cit.*, pp. 90–94.

204. ACS, MI, DGPS, DPP, fasc. Pers., b. 89/A, f. Segré Sergio e Silvio [*sic*, instead of Manfredo]. At first, on March 24, a phone call was intercepted from Segre's office recommending to the other speaker to not go to vote in the referendum and the voting for the Chamber of Deputies taking place the next day. On probable orders coming from Mussolini a search of the office followed, with no arrests. On March 31, on the other hand, another phone call was intercepted discussing with irritation the titles on the front pages of newspapers that day regarding the "arrests of the Jews." It was only then, on April 2, that Bocchini gave the order for an immediate arrest. After their father, Michele Segre, intervened, Mussolini rescinded the arrest on April 11; and then on June 2, maintaining the seizure in force and effect he also withdrew the administrative sanctions. In the same file there are items concerning the effect of the arrests on the Milan stock exchange.

brothers had been caught twice through telephone wiretaps under the direct control of the Presidency of the Council of Ministers, i.e., Mussolini. In the first instance it was about a request they made to an individual to refrain from voting the following day (March 25) in a national referendum sponsored by the regime. The Segre brothers were only gently threatened in that instance. The second case took place just six days later: a phone call made from their office was tapped, recording their comments on the press campaign against the Jews at the end of March in which they were saying: "It's disgusting!" This led to their arrest, and made a strong impression among stockbrokers by spreading the suspicion that a "Jewish" financial plot existed against Italy and that it was being manipulated to intimidate a key sector of Italian national life.

By the beginning of April there were many anti-Semitic irons in the fire. Then came the second "census." On April 9 Chief of Police Arturo Bocchini, acting on behalf of the Duce's Press Office, sent a request to the prefectures of a few major cities, Venice, Trieste, Milan, Florence, Turin, and to the chief of police in Rome, to identify the "Jews" working at major newspapers, representing the bulk of the large circulation Italian dailies.[205] The Press Office took the initiative because—as someone had pointed out—"Italian journalism is very

---

205. A.S. Ts, Prefettura, Gab., b. 363. For this investigation we only have the answer provided by Trieste (same file, written on April 27) and perhaps a report on the journalist Enrico Rocca sent to Rome police headquarters on May 18. (ACS, MI, DGPS, DPP, fasc. pers., b. 1138, f. Rocca, Enrico Lino di Ettore giornalista.) As for the information to the Press Office, it originated with a mysterious "inside source" (and therefore had somehow been manipulated at the Press Office). Two copies of the information item (indicating a few newspapers that should receive it) are in ACS, MPC, Gab., 2 vers., b. 4, f. Gli ebrei e il regime.

much under the control of the Jews," and therefore an investigation had become necessary. The letter to the prefects was to remain "strictly personal" and requested that these investigations be kept secret. The memorandum also pointed out the high percentage of "Jews" in the universities, implying that the investigation could be extended to that area as well.

The third episode began at the very same time as the preceding one. On April 9 and 10, 1934, Giuseppe Mormino, head of the Cabinet of the Minister of the Interior (therefore Mussolini) transmitted to the general directorate of civil administration (municipalities and provinces) a double order issued to all prefects on the 11th and stamped "extremely confidential and personal."[206] First came the requirement that for *future* recommendations for appointments to podestà and deputy podestà or presidents and deputy presidents of the provinces (in other words, the mayors and deputy mayors of cities and towns and the heads of provinces and their deputies) it would be necessary to specify the candidates' religion; the second order was a demand to disclose the religion of those persons *currently* heading local administrations.

Under Secretary of the Interior Guido Buffarini Guidi, who issued the April 11 order to the prefects, also added something new: this request now applied to low-ranking political appointees, municipal, and

---

206. Copies of both telegrams (ACS, MI, UC, telegr. in partenza nn. 10806 and 10807) and the orders of the Cabinet are in ACS, MI, DGAC, Podestà e Consulte municipali, b. 27, f. 239. Amministratori degli Enti Autarchici. Religione. But already as of the 8th a decision seems to have been made. A telegram sent on the 7th from Venice at 8:15 p.m. arrived in Rome at 1 a.m. regarding the renewal of the deputy dean that was placed in the "action taken for now" on the 8th. ACS, MI, DGAC, Podestà e Consulte municipali, b. 19, f. Venezia.

provincial managers and consultants (the equivalent of today's municipal and provincial council members), and he also added to this list all those in charge of charitable and public assistance offices. In a matter of days the order to disclose the religion of these individuals was extended from the local leadership to include those in very subordinate positions. This could be viewed in part as the consequence of a recent law having a provision whereby municipalities and provinces could be governed in certain circumstances by managers and consultants,[207] who could also have access to the top layer of the local administration. What remains unclear and is not explained to this day is the extension of the regulation to charitable and social institutions.

The fourth episode came on April 16, 1934, just five days after Buffarini Guidi's telegram on local political positions. Buffarini Guidi explained to the prefects[208] that "following the instructions for the appointments of administrators of the Towns and Provinces we warn Your Excellencies that even for those persons to be appointed to corporative and labor-related positions subject to the approval of the Ministry of Corporations and the Ministry of the Interior, the religion of all the appointees shall always be stated."

The new requests for information were related to the previous "census" of political administrators. The April 16 telegram was meant to inform the Ministry of the religion of the local corporative council leaders and the heads of local workers' and entrepreneurial associations.

---

207. Article 48 of the law established that "in the municipalities where there is no deputy podestà, the Podestà [mayor] may appoint a consultant as a replacement." Article 112 established that the vice president of the province, who could become president, had to "chosen among the rectors."

Within five days the Ministry of the Interior had issued orders to identify the religious affiliation of the entire Italian local, political, economic, social, and charitable administrations, present and future. The prefectures would continue providing this kind of information to Rome in the years to come as a matter of course.[209]

208. ACS, MI, UC, telegr. in partenza n. 11534.
209. See the circular from Buffarini Guidi of June 5, 1936, requesting that the prefects keep up to date all information regarding four kinds of administrative entities (communes, provinces, corporations, charitable institutions), including those on religion. The circular is in A.S.Ba., Prefettura, Gab., 2 vers., b. 96, f. 1. Cat. 5.1. Amm.ni comunali. Varie.

Chapter XV

More Census Investigations and Further "Purges"

What did these "census" activities actually consist of? They certainly represent a tangible slice of Italian history at a time of deep changes, and must be viewed in the broader context of other vast institutional changes, often similar to earthquakes that were rocking Italian society at the time.

For the sake of accuracy it must be said that in three out of four instances the "census" initiatives came either together with or in expectation of some sweeping government initiatives or the introduction of laws through which Mussolini intended to alter the structures and the chain of command throughout the entire country. The fourth case, involving the census of the press, was undoubtedly meant as the investigation of an "institutionally" dangerous profession having a great deal of influence on society.

The decision to target stockbrokers came following an initiative by the Council of Ministers on February 3 when it launched an ambitious plan to convert an old loan into a new one, called the "redeemable at 3.5 percent."[210] This amounted to a new public issue to line the state's coffers. The bond issue took place amid draconian police measures to avoid any possible exodus of capital overseas, as well as limiting reimbursements on the old loan as much as possible. Stockbrokers played a key role in the operation since they were allowed to issue redemptions.

The "census" began on the day immediately following the "redeemable" bond operation, on the 10th, since the 11th was a Sunday. There is no available information as to why the "census" was requested on February 12. We can only speculate that some confidential information reaching the Ministry of the Interior may have been directed against a specific "Jewish" stockbroker or targeting "Jewish" stockbrokers in general. This was in any case a broad-based

---

210. For both the legal decree on the bond issue and the ministerial enactment decree see ACS, PCM, Atti, 1934, Ministero delle Finanze, b. 214, f. 35. Draft of an R.D. on the redeemable bond issue at 3.50% in exchange to the fulfillment of consolidated interest at 5 percent. The problems relating to the placement of state bonds at the beginning of 1934 were explained by Mussolini in his speech made at the Chamber on May 26, 1934. See *O.O.*, vol. XXVI, p. 235. For a complete picture of the seesaw effect at the Milan stock exchange in 1934, see the diagrams by Mario Segre, *La borsa. Operazioni, prezzi e dati statistici* (Turin: Einaudi, 1935), p. 133 (the author was one of those arrested mentioned earlier). A reconstruction by Stefano Baia Curioni, *Regolazione e competizione. Storia del mercato azionario in Italia (1808–1938)* (Bologna: il Mulino, 1995), pp. 351–357. For a critique of the operation see F. Guarnieri, *op. cit.*, pp. 438–439. See also Gabriella Raitano, *I provvedimenti sui cambi in Italia nel periodo 1919–36*, in *Ricerche per la storia della Banca d'Italia*, vol. VI (Bari: Laterza, 1995), pp. 320–323.

financial operation aimed at securing the "structural" control of Italy's economy.

Regarding the heads of local administrative offices, the "census" came after a recent and extremely important piece of legislation signed by King Victor Emmanuel III barely one month before, on March 3, 1934, and published in the *Gazzetta Ufficiale* on March 17. This was the new important text of the law reorganizing the municipalities and the provinces with the accompanying criteria for appointments and management functions.[211] As the law was enacted the elimination of all unmarried podestà and provincial leaders was in taking place.[212] There was also a need to "fill" certain positions that had been previously frozen while the new legislation was being drafted; for example, the vice presidents or deputy heads of provinces. There was also a specific request from the Ministry of the Interior to the prefects requesting recommendations for the position of vice president.[213]

Regarding the corporative positions in the provinces the new "uniform text" of the law on provincial councils of the corporative

---

211. R. D. "Approvazione del testo unico della legge comunale e provinciale." G. U. March 17, 1934, n. 65.
212. ACS, MI, DGAC, Presidi e Rettorati provinciali, b. 5, Amministrazioni Provinciali Presidi. Sostituzioni celibi. The first telegram calling for the exclusion of unmarried persons was dated February 5. Many others were to follow that addressed either municipal or regional positions.
213. The request was sent by Buffarini Guidi by telegram to the prefects on April 3, 1934, asking for "relevant proposals" for nominations of vice presidents selected among the rectors on the basis of Art. 112 of the new single text. ACS, MI, DGAC, Presidi e Rettorati provinciali, b. 5, f. telegram for distribution to all the Prefects of the Kingdom of April 3, 1934.

economy was enacted[214] by a decree dated September 20.[215] This followed an extremely long discussion involving some strong-arm tactics starting in February between the Ministry of the Interior (Mussolini was the minister) and the Ministry of Corporations (where Mussolini was also the minister). The dispute centered on which of the two ministries would have the final say in picking the top names (in this case the vice presidents, since the prefect was also the president) of the provincial corporations.[216] The conflict had gone all the way up to the Council of State, which handed down its informed opinion in March, accepting the "concerted" decision by both ministries, not so much on the identities of the men but rather the functions that were involved. The founder of fascism himself would resolve the dispute by approving the opinion issued by the Council of State but bending it somewhat to allow the Ministry of the Interior to also have a say in the

214. See Bruno Biagi, *Lineamenti dell'ordine corporativo fascista* (2nd ed.), (Bologna: Zanichelli, 1939), pp. 240–244.

215. The decree for the "Approval of the single text on the laws governing the provincial councils of the corporative economy and the provincial offices of the corporative economy," signed on September 20, 1934, n. 2011 was published in the *Gazzetta Ufficiale* (G.U.) on December 21, 1934, n. 299. Art. 8 stated that the vice presidents, who were in effect the true heads, the prefect being the president, appointed by the Minister of Corporations "in harmony" with the Minister of the Interior. The preceding law (June 18, 1910, n. 875, G.U. July 14, 1931, n. 160) set up in art. 2 that presidents and vice presidents were appointed by the Minister of Corporations "in harmony" with the Minister of Agriculture.

216. For the discussion relating to the decree see ACS, PCM, Atti, Ministero delle Corporazioni, 1934, b. 238, f. Schema di R. decreto che approva il Testo Unico delle leggi sui Consigli e sugli Uffici Provinciali dell'Economia Corporativa. [Draft of the R. decree approving the Uniform Text of the laws on the Councils and Provincial Offices of the corporative economy.] From a letter from Buffarini Guidi himself dated July 29, 1934, it can be verified that at that date the Minister of Corporations had not accepted the principle of "harmonizing" the appointments. As for the Council of State: ACS, Consiglio di Stato, Processi verbali delle Adunanze generali 1934/2. Adunanza generale dell'8 marzo, 1934.

appointments. When Buffarini Guidi began the "religious" census of local corporative positions on April 16, he mentioned the "appointments to be approved by the Ministry of Corporations in harmony with the Ministry of the Interior"; he was referring to a law that had not yet been enacted and he was also bending the recent opinion issued by the Council of State to suit his purpose.

The record offers no absolute certainty that the conflict originated with the Ministry of the Interior's wish to control the "census," with the possibility of handling sensitive matters such as "race" and "religion". However, given the harshness of the institutional conflict and the discriminatory context, the result could also come from the ongoing competition between two bureaucracies to manage data so sensitive that it also was itself "political" in nature.

There is no doubt in any case that "eliminations" did take place based upon religion. This was not the case with the first census that centered on stockbrokers, which did not include any "elimination" orders; but there is also no absolute certainty that none took place or that there were no consequences.[217] No information as to the consequences of the census taken in the press could be located. The third and fourth "censuses," on the other hand, were followed by

_____

217. As of today we only know that in 1938, with the racist laws, the resignations of 36 "Jewish" stockbrokers were accepted along with an equal number of "floor representatives" of the same that were not all "Jews." See R. D. of November 7, 1938, n. 4382 and Ministerial Decree of November 10, 1938, n. 4383 (G.U. of November 17, 1938, n. 262, pp. 4758–4760). Later on the operation was repeated for three more floor representatives (Ministerial Decree of November 23, 1938, nn. 4570, 4571, 4572, G.U. November 29, 1938, n. 272, p. 4929).

"eliminations" of candidates for appointment based on their belonging to the Israelite faith.[218]

Information about the selection of the heads of local administrations is available in the extensive files of the Rome central archives that are replete with data on the issue. For example, the Ministry of the Interior barred the confirmation of Giacomo Beer, a Jew, as vice president of the province of Ancona "because of the new instructions received."[219] In Ferrara the situation was more complicated, since the prefect, Amerigo Festa, put up an all-out defense of the podestà Renzo Ravenna, who was very close to the powerful fascist leader Italo Balbo.

The Ferrara episode began just before the "census," confirming that its purpose was in fact to immediately eliminate individuals from consideration. On April 4, 1934, the Ministry of the Interior requested that Ravenna be replaced because, according to information received, the "citizens" of Ferrara would have been displeased to have a mayor of the Jewish faith."[220] But Festa, as we have seen, rejected the idea, answering that Balbo, who was the "chief" in Ferrara, had complete confidence in Ravenna as someone who would never create any

---

218. In the province of Forlì there was the case of a vice president of the evangelical religion, Paolo Maria Guarini. The Cabinet issued an immediate approval. ACS, MI, DGAC, Presidi e Rettorati provinciali, b. 10, f. Forlì.

219. ACS, MI, DGAC, Presidi e Rettorati provinciali, b. 6, f. 15803. Ancona. The letter by Mormino we quote is dated April 16, 1934.

220. Michele Sarfatti, *Gli ebrei, cit.*, p. 94 and all pages 93–95. For the following correspondence see ACS, MI, DGAC. Podestà e consulte municipali, b. 150, f. Ferrara. Podestà. The Ferrara-Rome correspondence was already identified by Paolo Ravenna, *L'arcivescovo e il podestà ebreo*, in *L'Arcivescovo Ruggero Bovelli e la Resistenza ferrarese* (Ferrara: Corbo, 1997), pp. 62–63. Festa's answer was dated April 10.

problems with Church authorities. He put up a fight, but faced with renewed pressure in June on other Jewish candidates, decided to withdraw two names he had placed on the list as consultants, while holding fast on a third Jewish candidate for the corporative council.[221] Festa was involved in a real power struggle, perhaps with Balbo's support, and pointed out that the Jews accounted for "most of the economic activity in the provincial capital" and therefore needed some sort of political representation.

Serious objections also surfaced later on, this time from the prefect of Varese, about the renewal of the appointment of Giacomo Cohen as podestà of the town of Vedano Olona.[222] Following the statement issued in the newspapers about the Jews arrested at Ponte Tresa, Cohen had resigned from the Jewish Community of Milan by writing a very harsh letter and transferred the funds earmarked for the Community treasury to fascist organizations instead. Having thus proved his "fascist faith," the prefect recommended Cohen once again on May 6 to Rome as a candidate for appointment.

Mussolini and his functionaries were thus facing multiple forms of resistance and a host of negative attitudes. There was also the danger of causing turmoil within institutions that had too many "Jews" who therefore had to be eliminated. Such was the case of Giacomo Beer,

---

221. ACS, MI, DGAC. Podestà e consulte municipali, b. 150, f. Ferrara. Consulta municipale. The letter by which Festa was confirming the choice of a Jew was dated June 17, 1934.
222. ACS, MI, DGAC. Podestà e rettorati provinciali, Podestà, b. 302, f. Vedano Olona. There is an item on Giacomo Cohen in Alberto Gagliardo, *Ebrei in provincia di Varese. Dalle leggi razziali all'emigrazione verso Israele. Tradate 1938–1947* (Varese: Anpi Arterigere, 1999), p. 102.

former head of the prime minister's Cabinet, who had been serving as prefect of Venice for the past eight months; but this was not to last and on September 14, 1934 he was transferred to Catania, a lesser posting.[223] Beer pointed out that Venice had twelve Jewish administrators and that they filled sixteen different positions among them.[224]

Therefore, by the middle of May Mussolini ordered a different approach. The Duce's cabinet, based on "higher authority,"[225] meaning Mussolini himself, ordered that those involved should proceed "to examine carefully on a case-by-case basis" the relevant situations. The order also specifically stated that "belonging to the Jewish religion must not be considered a sufficient reason for being unsuitable to hold public office."

There could be no further doubt about what was being discussed: "Jews" were henceforth to be considered on a "case-by-case" basis. The formula by which they were "not always" to be eliminated limited the original intent to a certain extent and certainly the interpretations that had been provided. But at the same time the generic reference to "public office," coming from the Cabinet of the Ministry of the Interior (therefore from Mussolini), could be understood in the broadest manner possible.

---

223. Mario Missori, *Governi, alte cariche dello stato, alti magistrati e prefetti del Regno d'Italia* (Rome: Ministero per i beni culturali e ambientali, 1989), p. 623.
224. The letter with the list was dated April 17, 1934. ACS, MI, DGAC, Podestà e Consulte municipali, b. 27, f. 239. Amministratori degli Enti Autarchici. Religione. In Ferrara there were 9, in Vercelli 5, Verona 7, and so on.
225. Mormino's letter to the DGAC was dated May 19. ACS, MI, DGAC, Podestà e Consulte municipali, b.27, f. 239. Amministratori degli Enti Autarchici. Religione.

What were the consequences therefore? For the local administrations there is the comprehensive statistical data compiled by the Ministry of the Interior. The April 1934 census indicated that "Israelites" were to be found in "decision-making positions" in some twenty-nine local administrative offices. When the same census was undertaken some four years later, on March 29, 1938 (before the fascist racial laws), only six local administrations still had any Jews, two of them about to be replaced and two others close to being changed; of the two remaining, one was Gino Olivetti, a consultant in Turin.[226] The "selection" process had been rigidly slow, cautious, and carried out in fits and starts.

Only incomplete and fragmented data exists regarding the other "census" of the local corporative councils and any orders resulting. One case of elimination took place in Genoa: in October 1934, following the prefect's reply, an agricultural labor organizer named Romano Munari was considered as practicing the "Jewish faith," according to the local police chief, whose sources cannot be verified. The man was promptly excluded.[227] We may safely conclude that such eliminations must have also occurred elsewhere.

---

226. ACS, MI, DGAC, Podestà e Consulte municipali, b. 27, f. 239. Amministratori degli Enti Autarchici. Religione.

227. The correspondence regarding this matter is in A.S. Ge., Prefettura (1879–1945), Gabinetto, b. 107 [Atti riferentesi all'economia corporativa] at prot. 2380/1934. The designation by the Confederazione Nazionale dei Sindacati dell' Agricoltura e Foreste took place on September 28, 1934. On October 2 Albini, the prefect of Genoa, informed the Ministry of Corporations in Rome of the recommendation, because as far he was concerned Munari possessed the required "qualifications" and was giving his "go ahead" in the case. The head of the Cabinet at the Ministry of the Interior, Mormino (who among other things was the former prefect of Genoa) telegraphed Albini on October 25 to find out which was the "religion practiced" by Munari. After

As we have noted, this was a time of vast structural change. The fascist dictator was creating completely new institutions throughout the country, not limited only to local entities, but also involving the prefects. The institutions were to emerge as very strongly "fascistized" because those in charge had to provide credentials of loyalty to the regime more than ever before. At the same time using the laws, confidential circulars, and organizations under his direct control, and in particular the Ministry of the Interior, the Duce was shaping those institutions politically, making them "Judenfrei" oriented with no Jews in any top positions—or at best staffed only with loyal "Jews" and as such not that much different from the Nazi project.

Thanks mostly to attrition, changes in society, the end of various mandates, and institutional turnover, Mussolini was slowly picking off those "prominent" Jews through a deliberate but continuous selection among local leadership cadres with many fits and starts. A political set of pincers was at work from top to bottom and Mussolini's allusion to religion during his speech of March 18, 1934, now becomes much clearer. Referring to the "Italian race" Mussolini had said: "Religious

---

about a half a day of investigation by the local chief of police, the prefect answered the Ministry of the Interior on October 27 that Munari, "according to confidential information practices the Jewish religion." On November 30—one month later—the Ministry of Corporations informed the prefect that the Ministry of the Interior "does not deem it appropriate, for reasons of political expediency, to support the nomination" and requested a new candidate. We don't know whether this is the matter discussed by Danilo Veneruso in *Gentile e il primato della tradizione culturale italiana. Il dibattito politico all'interno del fascismo* (Rome: Studium, 1984), pp. 233–234. Veneruso cites a folder in the archives of the Cabinet of the prefecture of Genoa (n. 54) where the documentation he brings up now cannot be found; yet "the collection in question has not been touched since it was assembled" (communication of the director of the A.S. Ge, Paola Caroli, January 14, 2004).

unity is one of the people's greatest strengths." In applying that principle he was slowly proceeding with key eliminations.

Two of the most glaring anomalies regarding the removals still require an explanation: the election on March 25, 1934, to the new Chamber of Deputies of four "Jewish" deputies, including Gino Olivetti and Guido Jung,[228] and the appointment of other Jews to the corporative councils in November. Especially in the latter case, the institutions were totally deprived of any kind of decision-making power.

The election to the Chamber was actually an appointment made on the recommendation of the Grand Council, and in this case it came late enough with respect to the "eliminations" of Jews from positions of national prominence. The Chamber was dissolved on January 19 and requests for candidates were sent to the Fascist party, the prefects, and local corporations on the following day.[229] The first known "census"

---

228. See also Michele Sarfatti, *Gli ebrei, cit.*, pp. 89 and 168–169. The deputies were Gino Arias, Guido Jung, Gino Jacopo Olivetti, and Riccardo Luzzatti. On the other hand the telegram that Mussolini sent to the prefect of Trieste on March 8, 1934, requesting information on Edgardo Morpurgo for his possible nomination as senator is not really meaningful (ACS, MI, UC, outbound telegr. n. 6248). This may have in fact been in response to a real intention to nominate him. As for Prefect Tiengo's answer, he could, in the midst of much praise, write on March 12: "some say he is egotistical and hungry for money" (A.S. Ts, Prefettura, Gab. B. 505, f. Morpurgo, Edgardo). This correspondence is also quoted in A. Millo, *op. cit.*, p. 168.
229. The first telegram dated January 20 (ACS, MI, UC, telegr. outgoing n. 1701), signed by Duffarini Guidi centered on the outgoing deputies. For the new candidates a request for information to the prefects to be circulated to the federal Party secretaries and signed by Buffarini Guidi went out in telegram n. 2195 of January 26. The telegram of the 27th signed by Mormino was n. 2322. The religion of the candidates was never asked, not even regarding the obviously "Jewish" names. The request for information on Riccardo Luzzatti signed by Cabinet Chief Mormino went out with telegram n. 3663 of February 10. The answer from the prefect of Milan with

went out three weeks later, as previously indicated. In any case, the procedure for the elections to the new Chamber began *before* the new "census" started.

The election procedure also started before *Il Tevere* began its new press campaign against Zionism and also against Jews in general on January 30, 1934, which found its way to the pages of other Italian daily newspapers.[230] These cast a heavy shadow of suspicion over the entire Italian Jewish community. By then the selection mechanism of the candidacies to the Chamber was already forging ahead following its unstoppable course.

A second important explanation is inherent to the institutional changes at work. For a variety of reasons the actual project to revise the Constitution by the Chamber of Deputies and the Senate had been postponed. In November 1933 Mussolini stated there had not been enough time to enact the reforms but that "very soon" the old Chamber would be modified in a corporative mold, meaning that it would be dissolved and the deputies sent home.[231] This could explain why Ettore Ovazza was informed in January 1934 that Mussolini himself had decided to place five "Jews"[232] among the deputies, who

the information, which was all positive and made no mention of religion, went out on February 12 (ACS, MI, UC, telegr. incoming n. 8035).

230. The first article was "Specola. Ebrei," *Il Tevere*, January 30–31, 1934. For the other articles in the campaign see R. De Felice, *The Jews, cit.*, pp.131–135.

231. He stated it in his speech to the general assembly of the national council of the corporations on November 14, 1933. See *O.O.*, vol. XXVI, p. 94. He reiterated it in the speech to the Senate on January 13, 1934, where he said that the "the destiny [of the Chamber] was to be decided: after the the start of the actual functioning of the corporations. See *O.O.*, vol. XXVI, p. 151.

232. The item appears in a letter from the president of the Jewish Community of Turin to Felice Ravenna, president of the Union, dated January 23, 1934, in ACDEC,

were later reduced to four. These Jewish deputies were to have a very short "tenure" in any case. The current Chamber was actually replaced by the elected Chamber of Fasces and Corporations, formally convened in 1939, which included no Jews since the racial laws had been enacted in the meantime.

The makeup of the new Councils of the Corporations that were to include worker's representatives and management was announced by the press on November 9, 1934.[233] There were a few "Jews" or persons with Jewish names among the hundreds of names listed and only one, Gino Olivetti, as head of his section for textile products of which he was the vice president. There is virtually no information about these appointments other than they followed the usual "census" that included information about the person's religion and that it was organized by the Political Police;[234] it is uncertain whether there were any preventive eliminations due to religion or "race." The inclusion of those names is not stranger than that of the deputies since the newspapers immediately pointed out that this institution was also in

---

Leone and Felice Ravenna Collection, b. 9, f. 1. I thank Michele Sarfatti for providing me with a copy of the letter. The information was said to come from Ettore Ovazza. The letter is cited in Michele Sarfatti, *Gli ebrei, cit.*, p. 89.

233. See *I membri dei Consigli delle ventidue Corporazioni*, PDI, November 9, 1934.

234. The law setting up the Corporations was dated February 2, 1934, n. 164. Other laws and regulatory decrees were to follow (see Alberto Aquarone, *L'organizzazione dello Stato totalitario* (Turin: Einaudi, 1965), pp. 203–206.) At the beginning of August the Ministry of Corporations requested of the Ministry of the Interior information on the various candidates. The information is now collected in the personal files of the Political Police that was in charge of requesting news from the prefectures and local police headquarters. The important point is that the prefectures and the police headquarters did provide information on the religion of the candidates while the Ministry of Corporations did not ask for it in its standard files.

need of reform.[235] Since all substantive decisions were being made by the Ministry of Corporations, this was at best only an advisory body.[236] In the end, only Gino Olivetti could be said to have any real important role.

Another episode may have had some bearing in this context. Tiengo, the prefect of Trieste, whom we have already encountered, was informed in advance of the barring of Guido Segre, a "Jewish" candidate who was also an industrial entrepreneur in minerals and other areas. On October 25 Tiengo wrote to the Under Secretary at the Ministry of Corporations to support Segre's inclusion on the list.[237] "His exclusion from the corporations would create nervousness and turmoil in the industry and as a politician, I feel it is my duty to inform you that I am confident that a solution can be obtained." The request was considered but Segre was not nominated. In the absence of other documents many questions remain unanswered. The presence of those names could also be attributed to extreme caution on a murky and difficult issue, such as that of the nominations and the purges, especially concerning the professions.

These problems were even more apparent in another case with no economic ramifications that took place at the same time (end of November 1934) regarding the cancellation of the appointment of

---

235. See "La riforma dell'assemblea del Consiglio delle Corporazioni," *Il lavoro fascista*, November 10, 1934.
236. Alfredo Cioffi, *Istituzioni di diritto corporativo* (2nd ed.), (Milan: Hoepli, 1935), pp. 197–207.
237. A.S. Ts. Prefettura, Gab., b. 506, f. Segrè, dott. Guido. For the trust Segre continued to have in Mussolini even after the enactment of the racial laws see the

Guido Finzi as dean of the veterinary school at the University of Milan.[238] The incident caused a clash between Roberto Farinacci, who was Finzi's protector, and Francesco Ercole the Minister of National Education. The year before Ercole acting on orders from Mussolini had demanded the resignation of Carlo Foà, a Jew, from his position as dean of the College of Medicine and Surgery.[239] As Farinacci pointed out in a letter to Mussolini's secretariat, Ercole "told him [Farinacci] that Prof. Finzi was not to be appointed, since the Duce forbid it because he was a Jew." The matter reached back to Mussolini himself. The bone of contention was not the fact that Finzi had been excluded because he was a Jew—which was clear to everyone involved—but that Ercole had communicated confidential decisions taken by the dictator to third parties. Thus by the time of the new appointments on January 24, Ercole was fired as minister.

Mussolini wanted to keep his actions secret. However, these had become so broad in scope, involving so many people, that discrimination against the Jews was surfacing in many parts of Italian life and the racist choices being made could no longer remain hidden. Both the prefects and the police commissioners in charge of the investigations, the various functionaries in the prefectures and the

---

memoirs of his nephew, Vittorio Segre, *Storia di un ebreo fortunato* (Milan: Bompiani, 2000), (first ed. 1985), p. 32.

238. The correspondence in ACS, SPD, CO, b. 6, f. D. 201. Milano. Laboratorio per la preparazione di vaccine e sieri. The correspondence with the recommendations in ACS, MPI, DGIS, Miscellaneous of various divisions. Div. I-II-II (1929–45) b. 27, f. 23.4. Milano. R. Università. Presidi di Facoltà. A letter from Guido Finzi himself to Farinacci dated January 24, 1935, in ACS, Farinacci collection, b. 21, f. 1224. Finzi, Guido.

239. G. Fabre, *Mussolini e gli ebrei, cit.*, pp. 207–209.

carabinieri were aware of what was going on; the "corporations" at the local and central levels, as well as the civil servants at many ministries, were also very much in the know. To these one must add people aware of isolated episodes, such as a few journalists and intellectuals who knew of the purges at the Academy of Italy[240] and some at the Ministry of National Education and at the universities.[241] The entourage of Margherita Sarfatti was almost certainly "in the know" as well. Very few persons were aware of the full picture and even fewer knew where things were headed, but the initiative was so broad that many people knew something was happening.

Information had clearly filtered down to Fascist party circles. The events in question may best explain the harsh article published on April 10, 1934, by Farinacci's newspaper, *Regime Fascista* attacking the Zionists who expected to "hold on to positions of power, honors, and sinecures in our country."[242] *Regime Fascista*—it should be pointed out—

---

240. We refer to the eliminations recorded since 1932–1933 that important figures such as Guglielmo Marconi, Ugo Ojetti, the mathematician Francesco Severi, and Giovanni Gentile. See the two essays by Annalisa Capristo, "L'esclusione degli Ebrei dall'Accademia d'Italia" and "Tullio Levi-Civita e l'Accademia d'Italia," in *La rassegna mensile di Israel*, respectively September–December 2001, pp. 1–36 and (for G. Gentile) January–April 2003, in particular p. 253.

241. The prefect of Perugia informed the Ministry of National Education of the Jewish religion of a doctor who was a candidate as "libero docente" at the university on June 11, 1934. ACS, MPI, DGIS, Liberi docenti, 3a s. (1930–1950), b. 87, f. Calef, Carlo. We do not know if this was an excessively zealous decision by the prefect or whether it was done for other reasons. I thank A. Capristo for having provided the document.

242. "Decidersi," in *Regime fascista*, April 10, 1934. Cited also in R. De Felice, *The Jews, cit.*, p. 136. The article as the consul at Jerusalem said was reprinted in the Zionist daily *Doar Hayom* in Jerusalem on April 19, 1934. According to the consul, the Zionist paper had written that *Regime Fascista* had "published an article where he stated that the Jews were not loyal toward the countries they live in and therefore they should not be given important positions." ASDMAE, MAE, DGAP, 1931–43, Palestina, b.

after the initial "quiet" expulsions that Mussolini carried out in May 1933, had suggested that "positions of responsibility are being given to Jews" using the proportional criteria.[243] The screaming press headlines about Jews plotting against Italy were clearly only the visible part of an immense iceberg covering the entire country.

As previously shown, caution took many forms. The fascist dictator was understandably fearful that the abrupt and final elimination of the Jews from "important positions" could cause serious institutional damage, especially to the economy. This may have been on Mussolini's mind when he refused to accept the resignation of Minister Jung in April 1934 that it was rumored he had handed in immediately following the publication of newspaper articles about the plot hatched by the "Jews."[244] Jung was in any case replaced on January 24, 1935, at the same time as Francesco Ercole and, according to a person who spoke

---

8, f. Sionismo (2° semestre 1934). But as of the 8th the same *Regime Fascista* ("Troppo tardi") had anonymously attacked the industrialist Jarach because he had not denounced in the past "the action of some Jews who have messed up the finances and the national economy," referring probably to Toeplitz.

243. "Che Jehova ci giudichi" [May Jehovah Be Our Judge], in *Regime Fascista*, May 26, 1933. See G. Fabre, *Mussolini e gli ebrei, cit.*, pp. 215–217.

244. The matter was described by the Political Police in eleven reports coming from different sources, from the Vatican to Montecitorio, attributing the resignation in part on the communiqué regarding the arrests and also to existing problems in economic policy. ACS, MI, DGPS, Polizia Politica, fascicoli personali, b. 679, f. Jung. On Guido. One of these reports is part of the collection of Mussolini's secretariat and there is a sentence underlined in blue pencil about the "Jewish origin" (while in an information bulletin dated December 11, 1928, the word "Israelite" is underlined). ACS, SPD, CR, cat. 480/R, b. 142, f. 157. Jung, Guido. Finally some of the same information bulletins report on Mussolini's refusal to accept the resignation. According to one informer this happened "not so much because [Mussolini] would like to keep Jung, but because of his custom to be the one to impose resignations rather than have others offer them to him."

with him in confidence, was dismissed because he "was Jewish."[245] One month later (on February 27, 1935) Jung converted to Catholicism—it is unknown whether the two events were connected or not but it is possible that they could have been. On March 18 Oscar Sinigaglia, another "Jew," saw his resignation accepted. He was president of ILVA, a large public steel company, and a friend and relative of Jung's.[246]

At that point Teodoro Mayer remained the only "Jew" left in an important position at a large public finance company. Mayer was also on the board of directors of the Assicurazioni Generali, as well as president of several other corporate boards; he was a Senator since 1920 and Minister of State since 1931, when he became president of IMI (Istituto Mobiliare Italiano). There is no available information as to whether this imposing set of positions, that even Jung did not have,

---

245. The statement belongs to Antonio Pesenti and seems to originate in a conversation between him and Jung. See Antonio Pesenti, *La cattedra e il bugliolo* (Milan: La Pietra, 1972), p. 249. Regarding the conversion see Annalisa Capristo, *L'espulsione degli ebrei dale accademie italiane* (Turin: Zamorani, 2002), p. 271. In his own handwriting Mussolini in a private letter dated October 25, 1935, answering a question asked by "a Jew" as to why Italy undertook the war in Ethiopia and the sanctions with a deflationary policy, noted "it actually was a Jew: Jung." ACS, SPD, CR, cat. 480/R, b. 142, f. 157. Jung, Guido.

246. Lucio Villari, *Le avventure di un capitano d'industria* (Turin: Einaudi, 1991), pp. 128, 176. A few days before March 3, 1935, on the other hand, the governor of Somalia, Maurizio Rava, was replaced officially for military reasons (the coming Ethiopian campaign). The item comes from a private letter by Rava written that day, in ACS, MAI (1937–45), b. 1866 (Governo della Somalia. Segreteria del Governatore. Corrispondenza 1931–1935), f. senza titolo. The "Jewish" origin of Rava was rather uncertain and was not investigated even during later years, yet the Rome police department had ascertained as of November 19, 1938, that both parents "belonged to the Jewish religion and practiced the Jewish faith." ACS, MI, DGPS, DPP, f. pers., b. 1097, f. Rava, Maurizio S.E.

were of any help, or whether something had happened inside the IMI. Mayer in any case resigned the presidency of IMI on March 14, 1936.[247]

---

247. Giorgio Lombardo, *L'Istituto Mobiliare Italiano. Modello istituzionale e indirizzi operativi: 1931–1936* (Bologna: il Mulino, 1998), p. 43.

Chapter XVI

Not Even a Single Jew

This was the context, unknown until now, in which the Italian edition of *Mein Kampf* was published. The translation represented much more than just an odd episode, if only because it was at the core of the relationship between Hitler and Mussolini. What remains nebulous is the project or political idea on Mussolini's mind regarding the issue of racism when he encountered Hitler's ideas on the subject.

Mussolini expressed his "anxiety" regarding the "racial" situation in Italy on various occasions at that time. In several articles, some of them anonymous,[248] he expressed serious concern about Italy's declining

---

248. As for the editorials regarding the low birth rate in Italy, see "La realtà" published by the PDI on October 1, 1933. It was then reprinted on December 20 in the PDI once again ("Cifre"). Others followed: January 25, 1934 ("Ancora cifre"), on

birth rate. This drop would have threatened the entire Fascist project, since it was based on the vaunted strength and steady demographic increase of the "Italian race." This was happening just as Mussolini found out about a reversal of that same trend due to a demographic increase in Nazi Germany.[249] On the other hand, we have seen what was "troubling" the Duce at that time regarding the "European" and the "white race" in general. As Mussolini wrote on August 11, 1934, in the foreword to a racist book by one of the staff writers of his newspaper, the issue of the survival of the white race compared to the others was "in all its dramatic essence . . . the most urgent among 'the problems of our time.'"[250]

Mussolini was in the midst of planning his war of aggression against Ethiopia and such pronouncements must be placed in that context. By

---

February 6 ("Ancora cifre") on February 27, 1934 ("Ancora cifre"), on May 5, 1934 ("Regresso bianco e progresso giallo") [White Regression and Yellow Progress]. Reprinted in *O.O.*, vol. XXVI, pp. 64–65, 124–125, 159–160, 167, 173–174, 218–219. But see mostly Mussolini, "La razza bianca muore?" [Is the White Race Dying?] PDI, September 4, 1934 (*O.O.*, vol. XXVI, pp. 312–315). This particular article was also given to the American newspapers of the Universal Service.

249. "Demografia tedesca" [German Demographics] January 21, 1934. As for Mussolini's interest in German demographic data showing a continuous downward slide, we know for example that on November 14, 1931, he had asked the embassy in Berlin for German statistics. The information on "the impressive reduction of the German population" was shown to him on December 23. ASDMAE, MCP, DGSE, b. 110, f. 1931. Popolazione tedesca. On the downward German numbers see also Mussolini's articles already cited, dated August 18 and 20, 1933, in PDI (*O.O.*, Vol. XXVI, pp. 41–43.)

250. See *O.O.*, Vol. XXVI, p. 297. The book was by Guglielmo Danzi, *Europa senza europei?* [Europe Without Europeans?] (Rome: Ed. Roma, 1934). As for Danzi, as Duilio Susmel noted in his *Conclusione Dinale-Susmel* (*O.O.*, Vol. XXVI, p. VI), he was together with Ottavio Dinale and Mussolini himself, one of the anonymous editorial writers for the PDI during this period.

then Fascism was already gearing up with its "anti-black" mindset and rhetoric, at least in terms of colonial ventures. Following the signing of the Four Power Pact in July 1933, which became effective one year later, a new Italian law had been approved, known as the "Structural Rules for Eritrea and Somalia," which for the first time set limits for categories of "mixed race" persons to acquire Italian citizenship and consequently work permits and other opportunities.[251] There is no other data on anti-black racism at that time.

The dictator's various "statements" in 1934 were doubtless much broader in scope, at least regarding his constant "attention" to the falling birth rate and a non-African "race" such as the "Jews." These issues surfaced at the time of the occupation of Ethiopia and required more fine-tuning. The pace of these "eliminations" through institutional changes indicates that it would have taken many years to be completed, as it actually did happen. It was a very long-term project

---

251. The law of July 6, 1933, n. 999. See mostly file ACS, PCM, Atti, 1933, Ministero delle Colonie, 1933, b. 174, f. 7. Disegno di legge organica per l'Eritrea e la Somalia. For discussion and bibliography on this law see Michele Sarfatti, *Gli ebrei, cit.*, p. 96, and Giulia Barrera, "Particolarità, razza e identità: l'educazione degli italo-eritrei durante il colonialismo italiano (1885–1934)" in *Quaderni storici*, n. 109, April 2002, pp. 42–44. See also the confirming document from Minister of Colonies Emilio De Bono to the Presidency of the Council (March 2, 1934) regarding the cases of three "mixed race" persons. They had been hired by the Italian colonial administration but not recognized by their Italian father and therefore were not to be considered as being Italians and especially not members of the PNF. De Bono was proposing to rehire them anyway. But given the enactment of the ruling for Eritrea and Somalia this would have been the last such case, as De Bono pointed out. See ACS, PCM, Gab., 1934–36, b. 2039, f. Obbligo di iscrizione al P.N.F. per i meticci che stipulano o rinnovano il contratto d'impiego. For some of the barriers already placed since 1930 to the entry of "Negroes" from the colonies into Italy, see Gianluca Gabrieli, *Africani*

with many pauses and reassessments. When it began exactly or how detailed the advance planning was remains unknown but we may now assume that there was a definite timetable, as for example in the case of the changes in the Chamber of Deputies.

Without a doubt the Duce was searching for a tangible form of racism that would be "Italian," or better still "Mussolinian," in content. This was all being worked out at the same time as the new institutions—what has been triumphantly described elsewhere as the Italy of the "consensus". It is possible that the "reforms" were being introduced as a vehicle for the various racist-eliminationist actions. But perhaps the opposite was the case and the reforms were merely the institutional veil of a racism that Mussolini and his closest advisers had been thinking about many years before is in itself an idea requiring future investigation.

Based on the facts Mussolini was building what appears to be a country increasingly and *fundamentally* devoid of any Jews in top national or local decision-making positions.[252] This fits into his obsession as an

---

in Italia negli anni del razzismo di stato, in *Nel nome della razza. Il razzismo nella storia d'Italia 1870–1945,* edited by Alberto Burgio (Bologna: il Mulino, 1999), pp. 202–203.

252. The note from Ciano to Renzetti of April 19, 1934 (the marked date of March 19 is wrong), should also be read with this in mind concerning a newspaper Renzetti sent, the anti-Semitic newsletter *Weltdienst (Service Mondial),* published in Erfurt, edited by Ulrich Fleishhaure. The newsletter had identified a few "Jews" as leaders in Italy (Salem and Isaia Levi among them). Ciano pointed out the mistakes, such as indentifying Alfredo Rocco and Giuseppe Pavoncelli as Jews, and requested that Fleishhaure be informed. ACS, MCP, Gab., Reports (1922–1945), b.3, f. Report, n. 20. "Giuseppe Renzetti maggiore: relazioni sulla situazione politica in Germania e sul contenuto dei suoi abboccamenti con Hitler, Göring ed altri ufficiali nazisti." The matter is cited in M. Michaelis, *Mussolini,* cit., p. 76.

old "professional politician," to create a leadership cadre required to launch a tough, aggressive, and broadly defensive pro-European and white racist policy. These were major choices, not window dressing, intended to remain as secret as possible. As far as the rest of the world was concerned Mussolini did not look like an anti-Semite. The tolerant image he cultivated during his interview with Emil Ludwig was upheld and he even claimed to be the defender of the Jews in Palestine.

There was also an unavoidable social consequence. Mussolini was himself not simply the engine behind the slow elimination of Jews from public "decision-making positions" at various levels—all the way down to the "second tier"—but was also driving their equally slow exclusion from other positions and from having any viable presence at all. We have mentioned the orders given to the press in April on various "Jewish" issues published at the time. In September 1934 Mussolini ordered that an old fascist journalist and contributor to *Il Popolo d'Italia*, Anita Levi Carpi, not be sent to Japan as Italy's representative, and penciled a note: "We don't send a Jewish woman around."[253]

During the same month the censorship office banned the theatrical production of *The Wandering Jew*, based on the Ernest Temple Thurston film by the same title. It was the story of a Jew who had offended Christ and had been condemned to eternal life until the Inquisition

---

253. The annotation is in a letter by Levi Carpi to Mussolini dated September 10, 1934. The newswoman requested being sent as correspondent for *Il Popolo d'Italia* and the Ministry of National Education. ACS, SPD, CO, b. 414, f. 156.158. Levi Carpi, Anita. Rome.

burned him at the stake. The censor, Leopoldo Zurlo,[254] commented that the play "could have led to unwelcome discussions." Many years later Zurlo explained, however, that he was rejecting the "obvious glorification of the Jew." In this case there is no evidence of Mussolini's direct involvement but the selective hostility toward the Jews and the "Jewish question" was increasing.[255] All this doesn't mean that Mussolini was about to side with Nazi racial theories. The review of *Mein Kampf* in *Il Popolo d'Italia* had underscored this fact and the Duce would repeat it many times in his newspaper columns. He didn't accept the Nazi principle of German superiority or the existence of such a thing as "Aryan" racial "purity," while he held that the "Italian race" was in fact pure.[256]

In Italy the real issue concerned those Jews who believed in fascism and appeared to have been spared. The various "census" operations and eliminations favored the emergence of the "fascist Jews" but they

---

254. The script with the letter dated September 2, 1934, is in ACS, MCP, DG Teatro e Musica. Ufficio censura teatrale, b. 161, f. 2943 (ex 4139) *L'Ebreo errante*. See also Leopoldo Zurlo, *Memorie inutili. La censura teatrale nel ventennio* (Rome: Ed. dell'Ateneo, 1952), pp. 206–207.

255. Also in May 1934, following an anonymous letter that accused the Scala theater in Milan of having produced a "Jewish concert," with a Jewish conductor, Bloch, and financed by "the Jewish community" (something that was denied by the Milan prefect), Mussolini had the matter investigated and commented: "Where is the harm if the Scala gives a concert of Jewish music? As long as Semitic activity finds an outlet in art and spends money for it there's nothing to fear!" The annotation is just after March 17, 1934. ACS, SPD, CO, b. 2495, f. 555.902/2 Milano Teatro alla Scala. The folder is cited by Antonio Barbon, *Aspetti della privacy di un dittatore. Mussolini e i musicisti del suo tempo* (Milan: Angeli, 2000), pp. 13–14. Barbon did not cite the pencil annotation that was half erased, probably to maintain confidentiality.

only created problems for the authorities later on once contradictions began to surface. The magazine *Nostra Bandiera*—that represented those Jews who considered themselves fascists—was based in Turin and began publication on May 1, 1934, possibly with support from the local PNF and the prefecture.[257] By September it was taking issue with no less than *Il Popolo d'Italia*,[258] which had published an anonymous editorial accusing the Jews of failing to assimilate with the population

---

256. For this last one see for example "Teutonica" and "Fallacia ariana," PDI respectively May 16 and August 14, 1934 (*O.O.*, vol. XXVI, pp. 232–233 and 298). But mostly "Razza e razzismo" on September 8 (*O.O.*, vol. XXVI, pp. 327–328).

257. In his request for discrimination of December 22, 1938, the editor, Deodato Foà, stated that he had received the support of the federal secretary of the PNF and later of the prefecture for his Zionist project. In the same letter he said that he later had a few "conversations" with Ciano, then Under Secretary for Press and Propaganda, one of them requesting the closing of the magazine *Israel*. ACS, MI, DGDR, f. personali, b. 69, f. 5038 Dis. Foà, Deodato di Giacobbe. But also see his memoir of April 7, 1940, in ACS, MI, DGPS, DPP, f. pers., b. 512, f. Foà, Deodato. Giornalista. His relationship to the Ciano office is confirmed. See his request for approval at the beginning of 1936 regarding a supposed declaration by Mussolini (later found not to exist) to a delegation of Jewish-American students. Foà asked the Ciano ministry (he had been promoted to minister), who in turn asked Foreign Affairs (ASDMAE, MAE, Gabinetto 1919–43, b. Gab. 129, f. Ufficio Stampa 1936, sf. Foà, Deodato). Unfortunately Michaelis thought the declaration by Mussolini to be authentic: M. Michaelis, *Mussolini, cit.*, p. 83.

258. "Fantasie," PDI, September 11, 1934. It was the only second page column of this period that was not attributed to Mussolini in *O.O.* The piece was inspired by an article by Kadmi Cohen in the *Mercure de France* supporting the idea of the historical non-"assimilation" of the Jews. The anonymous writer shared the same opinion. The answer came in "Le panzane del signor Kadmi Cohen," in *La Nostra Bandiera*, September 18, 1934 (mentioned in Luca Ventura, *Ebrei con il Duce. La Nostra Bandiera (1934–1938)* (Turin: Zamorani, 2002). The same Cohen wrote a letter to *Il Popolo d'Italia* that was published on September 26 ("Gli ebrei e l'arco di Tito"), to correct a few details. Kadmi Cohen was also quoted by Mussolini in his well-known speech to the national council of the PNF on October 25, 1938, as an example of how the Jews viewed themselves as "unable to assimilate" (Michele Sarfatti, *Mussolini contro gli ebrei* (Turin: Zamorani, 1994), p. 48).

of the countries in which they lived. No one could doubt that Mussolini himself was the author of the piece.

There is no indication that the dictator was inclined to favor the "fascist Jews" unless it was in his immediate interest. In July 1935 during an interview with a German newsman he explained in no uncertain terms: "He [Mussolini] thinks that the Jews cannot be fascists and therefore he eliminated them [entfernt] from important positions [wichtigen Aemtern]. The Academy [of Italy] doesn't include any Jews."[259] Mussolini was therefore signaling to Hitler, who had read the interview that he was (secretly) moving ahead as he had described on various occasions. All Jews had therefore been already "eliminated" from "decision-making" positions by that date—which was not completely true, as previously shown.[260]

All this did not lead to the unleashing of mass and public racism or anti-Semitism; on the contrary, the fascist leader was careful to not copy the German model. Mussolini occasionally gave anti-Semitic or

---

259. The interview of Sven von Müller was given on July 9, 1935, and does not appear to have been published but the text was shown to Hitler and von Neurath, who annotated it. See BAK, Reichskanzelei, R43 II/1448 fol. 251. M. Michaelis, *Mussolini, cit.*, p. 95.

260. It appears that the case of Guido Segre was different as Mussolini wanted to request that he become president of the ACAI, Azienda carboni italiani [Italian Coal Company], which was a government-controlled enterprise (see the announcement in *Il Messaggero* of July 27, 1935). ACAI was the result of a merger of two companies, ARSA, owned by Segre himself, and BACU-ABIS. Segre was therefore appointed to head a company of which he was part owner. For the telegrams from Mussolini requesting information on Segre see ACS, SPD, CO, b. 2212, f. 534.163 Segre Gr. Uff. Guido. Trieste. For the company see ACS, PCM, Gab., 1937–1939, b. 2279, f. 3.1.10.6627.2 Azienda Carboni Italiani (ACAI). Consiglio di Amministrazione e Nomine del presidente.

racist signals. These were difficult to recognize because they were occasional and covert. Yet several foreign newspapers, and not just Jewish ones, were aware that something was happening in Italy.[261] It is possible that Mussolini thought that a "low key" and secret type of discrimination was the only way to seize the leadership of European racism from Nazi Germany. Nazism had been trailblazing showing that what was unthinkable until then, namely, that a racist political group could take over a large European country and run it with a racist agenda; Fascism, operating on a broader scale, would find even greater "opportunities" internationally. The relationship Fascism had established with religion and the Catholic church was one of those "opportunities." Mussolini wrote as much in the preface to a book[262] published in December 1934 that was reproduced in the foreign newspapers. He stated that the relationship with religion was fundamental "in modern times and on the continents occupied by white civilization" and that Fascism, as he had said in March at a political rally, had solved the problem best by defending and promoting the "religious unity" of the Italian people, actually excluding other

---

261. We have already mentioned the statements by some "Jewish" newspapers in Palestine. In Poland, Italian ambassador Bastianini reported some negative comments on June 6, 1934 (ASDMAE, MAE, DGAP 1931–45, Germania, b. 21, f.3. Germania, 1. 1934, Antisemitismo Tedesco). The newspapers expressing doubts about fascist anti-Semitism were *Hajint* (Hebrew), *Nowiny Codzienne,* and *A.B.C.*

262. Mussolini, *Stato e Chiesa,* preface (dated December 2, 1934) to G. De Rossi Dell'Arno, *La Conciliazione e il Risorgimento* (Rome: Italia e Fede, 1935), in *O.O.,* XXVI, pp. 399–401, in particular 400–401. Published in *Le Figaro* on December 18, 1934. A reference to this text is also in Giovanni Miccoli, "L'Italia cattolica e il fascismo," in *La rassegna mensile di Israel,* January–April 2003 (Vol. LXIX, n. 1) p. 172.

religions. Fascism therefore benefited from this added feature by serving as a guide to a "white" and "European" racism.

Even the Four Power Pact, the grand alliance that Mussolini was able to forge during this period, could have gone beyond its immediate political requirements, to become an enduring agreement favoring a white European race.[263] Once the policies of the Four Power Pact failed, Mussolini attempted something different at the end of 1934 and the beginning of 1935 with the CAUR (Comitati d'Azione per l'Universalità di Roma), which was originally a veteran's organization recast to handle new kinds of issues. In December 1934 the presidency of the Council of Ministers financed an international CAUR convention in Montreux, Switzerland, where many pro-fascist European organizations convened, excluding the Nazis since it was directed against them.[264] One of the issues on the agenda later discussed and approved and where the Italians had certainly been active was precisely the "Jewish question," whereby each country would be asked to make its own decisions without resorting to a "universal hate campaign

---

263. Suvich recalled in his memoirs how much Mussolini appreciated ("he had been favorably impressed") the talk by the theoretician of Aryanism, Alfred Rosenberg, to the Volta Convention in 1932 just as he was setting up his Four Power Pact (F. Suvich, *Memorie, cit.*, p. 140). For Rosenberg's presentation, Reale Accademia d'Italia. Fondazione Alessandro Volta, Convegno, *cit.*, pp. 272–284.
264. For the complete financing of the Montreux convention (December 16–17, 1934) and of the various delegations by the Italian Presidency of the Council, see ACS, PCM, Gab. 1937–1939, b. 2122, f. 1.1.8.3.2967/3. Comitati d'Azione per l'Universalità di Roma. Contributi. For a first reconstruction of the CAUR matter see: "I tentativi per la costituzione di un' internazionale fascista: gli incontri di Amsterdam e di Montreux attraverso i verbali delle riunioni," edited by Gisella Longo, in *Storia contemporanea*, June 1996, pp. 475–567.

against the Jews," but rather "since some Jewish groups have settled in many places as though these were a conquered territory while secretly exercising an influence that is detrimental to the moral and material interests of the homeland," CAUR members were committing themselves to "fighting" against "those elements."[265] It was the usual selective policy secretly adopted by Mussolini. Through the CAUR Fascism was attempting to go in a well-traveled direction in absolute secrecy and in its own way take the lead in European anti-Semitism.

One additional detail: at Montreux it was proclaimed that when framing its policies "each country" was to take into account "the rules of natural law and morality," meaning that these would go beyond existing national regulations and legislation. This was a very serious point that the Jewish and Fascist *Nostra Bandiera* immediately singled out while otherwise interpreting the communiqué as being both anti-Nazi and anti-racist.[266]

The government-sponsored translation and publication of *Mein Kampf* had only casually dwelt on the book's content. But as months passed and Hitler's power grew as he settled in office, Mussolini was carefully examining the racist message the book contained as it was being enacted by the Nazis. Mussolini's actions were very broad and

---

265. For the text of the final resolutions we quote from the mimeographed report in ASDMAE, MAE, Gab. 1931–43, b. Gab. 493, f. [CAUR] Parte generale. For the active participation by the Italians, specifically on the "Jewish question," see the letter of February 5, 1935, by one of the participants, the Romanian Ion Motza, *Corrispondenza col Welt-Dienst (1934–1936)* [Parma: All'insegna del Veltro, 1996], p. 44; I thank Mauro Raspanti for bringing this book to my attention.

the discriminations we mentioned in 1933-1934 were only a portion of the actual racist actions being considered and taken in Fascist Italy at the time. In actual terms, since 1933 they signaled the tortuous beginnings of racial persecution in Italy.

266. Ettore Ovazza, "Il 1° congresso europeo fascista e la questione antisemita," in *La Nostra Bandiera,* December 27, 1934.

Chapter XVII

"Nobody reads it"

Back to *Mein Kampf* and to Mussolini's further reactions after the publication of the Italian translation. During 1934 the Duce cited the book on at least two occasions in *Il Popolo d'Italia* in anonymous editorials, on August 29 and September 5.[267] The comments were polemical in tone in both instances, neither favorable nor hostile. The text quoted in some detail was that of the Bompiani edition. The first editorial reference came at the section where "that sort of interesting New Testament of National Socialism"—as Mussolini wrote—turned into an accusation leveled at Germany for not knowing how to preserve a pure German race. "The German people lack the deep instinct for struggle based on the unity of the blood," as the Duce

---

267. *O.O.*, vol. XXVI, pp. 309–10, 315–316. These were "Alla fonte" e "Sempre alla fonte." Cited also by J. Petersen, *op. cit.*, p. 309. The first one on August 29 was the inspiration for the attack by M. Rivoire, *La razza contro la storia*, in *Popolo di Lombardia*, September 1, 1934, cit. by R. De Felice, *The Jews, cit.* pp. 114.

quoted Hitler in the Bompiani translation. On the same occasion Mussolini repeated a remark he had made on Gobineau during his interview with Emil Ludwig,[268] when he scathingly noted that "the theoretician of racism is absolutely one hundred percent French."

The issue of the nonexistent "integrity of the blood" of the German people was an idea that Mussolini had been mentioning for some time: in the copy of the German edition of *Mein Kampf* he had received from the Ministry of Foreign Affairs[269] and in the book about Gobineau he had underlined that same idea. The "Nazi Bible" description came from the flap copy of the Bompiani edition and Mussolini was probably being sarcastic in repeating it. The word "interesting" may have however been used at face value.

The second editorial was a rather bland attack on German policy based on the Bompiani translation, *La mia battaglia*. Mussolini quoted a passage from the "New Testament of National Socialism," where it was written that every European government, Italy included, had always been thinking in its own narrow self-interest. This was in Mussolini's words a simple truism. The article ironically concluded that "*Mein Kampf* will possibly follow in the footsteps of many other more or less famous books. Everyone talks about them but nobody reads them." Italy was in a rather heated political clash with Germany at the time and the Fascist leader had no difficulty in sounding aggressive.

The same dense brand of irony targeted *Mein Kampf* once again without referring to it by name, the readers would immediately grasp

---

268. Emil Ludwig, *Colloqui con Mussolini. Riproduzione delle bozze della prima edizione con le correzioni autografe del Duce* (Milan: Mondadori, 1950), p. 71.
269. Doc. BV.

who was involved since Mussolini was quoting himself, and came during an important and famous speech to the PNF when the Duce commented on the enactment of racist regulations.[270] On October 25, 1938 Mussolini made a reference to *Mein Kampf* since he claimed to have also created, at the same time, a racist ideology of his own: "Now, long after I have always talked about race, the bourgeoisie suddenly wakes up repeating 'Race?' I then asked myself: 'Could I possibly be like that writer who is more often quoted than he is read?'" Mussolini was not entirely wrong in proclaiming himself, at least in theory, as the initiator of the issue ("...I have always talked about race"). But at the same time he felt he had somehow missed the racist bandwagon. In spite of his secret attempts he had not been understood correctly and was rather bitter about it. He was a failed Hitler. Clearly, Mussolini had not written a *Mein Kampf* of his own having that kind of publishing success, however strenuously he attempted to prove the contrary by publishing volume upon volume of his complete works. Actually, he had in fact contributed to the success of Hitler's book.

---

270. Michele Sarfatti, *Mussolini contro gli ebrei, cit.*, p.47.

Chapter XVIII

Erased

There is a coda to the episode of the translation and publication of *Mein Kampf* in Italy with the translation and publication of a second and final volume that included the first part of the German original, omitted in the 1934 translation. The publisher was obviously Bompiani, using the title *La mia vita* (My Life), and it was published on April 28, 1938, just a few days before and in honor of the Führer's second visit to Italy, from May 3 to 10, 1938.[271] The book was published as number 48 in the same series as the previous volume. This time the translator's name did appear but was that of Bruno Revel of

---

271. G. Fabre, *L'elenco, cit.*, p. 411.

Bocconi University. There is no assurance that this was in fact an entirely new translation, or at least that it had been edited by A. Treves.

There is almost no information about the book's publishing history other than the fact that it followed the usual approval process at the Ministry of Popular Culture. In any case, there were no particular problems tied to its publication. The name of Angelo Treves had also disappeared in subsequent reprints of *La mia battaglia,* and from any promotional literature. Once Bompiani decided to publish a single volume, Bruno Revel was named as the translator on the front page of the thick tome, thereby becoming the de facto translator of the entire work. In 1942 "A. Treves" was, as a Jew, placed on a list of writers that were "unwelcome" in Italy.[272] In theory, therefore, all his books and translations would have been banned.

Valentino Bompiani rarely spoke of his edition of *Mein Kampf* after the war. But he did so once in 1949 in a letter to Curzio Malaparte when he voiced his displeasure as a publisher "that every Italian had not read the book because perhaps in that case many things would have turned out differently and many catastrophes could have been avoided."[273] One can only smile at the thought of Bompiani's desire to sell and have "every Italian" read his book. There is naturally no way to read the publisher's mind at the time he was publishing the Italian translation of *Mein Kampf.* But he did write in the book: "the universal

---

272. Ibid., p. 480.
273. *Caro Bompiani. Lettere con l'editore,* edited by Gabriella D'Ina and Giuseppe Zaccaria (Milan: Bompiani, 1988), pp. 428–429.

interest generated by the National Socialist mindset and phenomenon is universal." We don't know whether he later changed his mind or not, but those were the words he published in the first pages of the book in 1934 that were reprinted in subsequent years as well.

On another occasion in his memoirs published in 1972, Bompiani[274] almost certainly offered a false version of the facts when he wrote:

> One day Professor Angelo Treves came to me with a proposal to publish his translation of Hitler's *La mia battaglia*. I was surprised and couldn't understand how as a Jew he could be proposing what was the Bible of Nazism. We had just published a biography of Hitler by his opponent Theodor Heuss, who was to become the first president of Germany after the war. Treves kept on insisting stubbornly.
> "But why?" I asked.
> "We must show who Hitler really is."
> "We just published the book by Heuss."
> "Heuss doesn't say what Hitler will do."
> "Fascist censorship will ban the book."
> "Let's ask the Führer for an introduction to the Italian edition," he suggested undeterred.
> Hitler sent us the introduction. The book was published without making much noise.

Some forty years later Bompiani was still referring to the *Bible of Nazism*, the 1934 term coined by the *Times* of London, but in truth he had already used the same words in 1933 when he wrote to the Duce's Press Office.[275] The facts were actually very different and he was perhaps offering only a portion of the truth. Maybe Angelo Treves

---

274. Valentino Bompiani, *Via privata* (Milan: Mondadori, 1992), (first ed. 1972), p. 58.

really did think of translating the book on his own. There is simply no way to know and it cannot be flatly denied. When Bompiani published his memoir Treves had been dead for some thirty years[276] and his memory was and still remains completely erased. One thing is certain, however, that Treves, a Jew, was not the originator of the translation. That decision belonged to Mussolini. Now that we know how events really unfolded, Bompiani's reference to "Fascist censorship" during his conversation is truly off the wall. It was just one more episode of a very long and collective hidden agenda.

---

275. Doc. A 31.

276. In a listing of Jews provided by the Municipality to the Prefecture of the Republic in Vercelli on February 21, 1944, is listed his daughter Wanda, "daughter of the late Angelo." As of that date her father was probably deceased. See Domenico Roccia, *Il Giellismo Vercellese* (Vercelli, tip. Ed. La Siesa, 1949), p. 155. I thank Michele Sarfatti for bringing the book to my attention.

Documents

In Appendix A are documents relating to the political and publishing history of the Italian translation of *Mein Kampf*.[277] The first is dated February 3, 1933, and the last March 23, 1934. We also added a book review from *Il Popolo d'Italia* dated April 3, 1934.

In Appendix B are the texts prepared by the Cabinet of the Ministry of Foreign Affairs detailing the book's content regarding selected specific topics.[278] These reached the Cabinet starting December 16, 1933, until the end of the year or at the most during the first few days of 1934. These were the texts read by Under Secretary Suvich and Mussolini.

We have attempted as much as possible to reproduce the layout of the texts in both Appendices.

---

277. These are all filed as originals or copies in ASDMAE, MCP, DGSE, b. 368, f. Mein Kampf (Amann, Max). Some copies are also on file elsewhere. See documents A1, A8, and A15.
278. ASDMAE, MAE, Gabinetto, 1931–45, b. 354, f. Pubblicazioni di Adolfo Hitler (includes also rough copies and duplicates).

Appendix A

A1[279]

Berlin February 3, 1933 XI

Hitler's private secretary informed me today that the Director of the Munich National Socialist publishing company, Mr. Hamann [*sic*] is traveling to Italy in order to sell the translation and sales rights of the book by Hitler, Main Kampf [*sic*] to an Italian publisher. The purpose of the sale is to secure funding for the electoral struggle that as you know shall begin in a few days.

Dr. Hess in telling me this requested that I inform the interested Top Leadership to assist Hamman in his task. They would be very grateful to the Head of the Italian Government if **He could extend to the designated Italian publisher or to Hamann himself an amount to be determined.**

Hitler doesn't want to petition bankers and industrialists to assemble the funds required for the fight. However he is mobilizing everything he can through book sales, etc., to secure [funding.]

Since I feel that the results of the elections should be favorable to the Nazis and given the friendship they show toward Italy, I pass along their request respectfully asking that it be given favorable consideration.

Hamann is leaving for Italy today and he will be staying at the Albergo Flora in Rome where he shall wait for the persons he is to negotiate with that should be designated by the Top Leadership. He does not wish to remain in Rome more than two or three days since he must attend to the election campaign here due to begin in a few days.

(G. Renzetti)

---

279. The letter was heavily underlined by Mussolini, in particular the passage that is between asterisks above. It has his notation in the margin: "Call him today. M." A strong underlined passage is indicated here and Mussolini also corrected the error in "Main" by adding an "e" to replace the "a." See photograph. A copy is found in BAK, collection N.1235 (Nachlass Renzetti) f.12 Bezrichte 1934.

A2

Rome, February 9, 1933-XI

Mr. Max AMANN visited the Press Office accompanied by an associate of his. He is the director of the Nazi Party's publishing company, which has some 170 branch offices covering the entire Reich. The many party publications with a very large distribution as well as books on Fascism translated into German etc., along with numerous party newspapers that are printed at over one million copies per day during the electoral battles.

He brought a letter from Hitler giving him full power of attorney to negotiate a license of the copyright of the book Mein Kampf written by Hitler.[280]

On March 5 there will be a decisive election in Germany and a need for significant amounts of funds.

He compared the conditions of the struggle in Germany to those of Fascism in Italy and stated that in any case they will not relinquish power even if the election results should turn out to be unfavorable.

Hindenburg is old. The reds are very strong and there are daily clashes in the streets. Youth is for the Nazis; many students have joined the movement with a lot of enthusiasm. The workers assembled in many red labor unions (Gewerkschaften), will be compelled to come to their side. The Jewish financed press appears somewhat subdued.

Hitler recently declared that there shall be press freedom ...but only for those papers that tow the line!

Mr. Amann and his associate stated that they gathered an excellent impression from their visit to Italy.

---

280. See Document A3.

A3

Adolf HITLER
Office
Munich 2, Briennerstr. 45

POWER OF ATTORNEY

The director of the Heirs of Franz Eher Publishing Company, Ltd., Munich, Thierschstrasse 11
Mr. MAX AMANN
acting on my behalf is authorized[281] to sell the right to print my work Mein Kampf (My Struggle) to foreign newspapers, which right I had exclusively reserved to myself in the publishing contract with Franz Eher Ltd.

Munich, October 1, 1931

Signed: Adolf Hitler

This Power of Attorney is still in full force and effect.
Berlin, January 27, 1933

Signed: Adolf Hitler

A4

Ministry of Foreign Affairs
PRESS OFFICE

Telexpress n. 995/63
Addressed to:
R. CONSULATE GENERAL OF ITALY
MUNICH, BAVARIA
Rome, 2/13/33

(Re) Mr. AMANN MAX

(Ref.) Confidential

---

281. For Hitler's signed original see photo.

(Text) I would be grateful if your Y.E. would contact Mr. Amann, the publishing representative of the National Socialist Party in that city and give him the enclosed check n. 372547 of February 10, from the Banco di Napoli in the amount of L. 250,000.

Upon delivery Y.E. will obtain a receipt from Mr. Amann prepared as in the enclosed sample.

Given the sensitive nature of the matter, it goes without saying that we recommend to Y.E. to use every precaution so that the entire transaction shall remain completely confidential.

Y.E. shall also make sure that the total amount of the check enclosed is cashed and deposited in cash.[282]

(Polverelli)

A5

STATEMENT

I declare on behalf of Mr. Adolf Hitler to be his representative specifically authorized by a special[283] power of attorney to sell to Mr...........all rights that may belong to the author Mr. Hitler for any translation, publication and sale in the Italian language of his work "Mein Kampf," based upon the 1932 Munich edition.

---

282. The two closing paragraphs of an earlier version read: "Given the sensitive nature of the matter, it is obvious that we recommend to Y. E. the need to take every precaution so that the entire transaction remains entirely confidential. Y. E. will also make sure that the amount in the enclosed check is handed to this gentleman or other persons that may in any way trace the final destination of the amount."
283. The minuted version uses the term "regular" that was changed in the final version.

A6[284]

INCOMING TELEGRAM
N. 2150 P.R.

From: R. Consulate	Munich Bav., 3/3/33 XI 21:50 hours
Munich Bav.	Rome, 3/4/33 XI 1 hour

Destination: Press
Re: Message for Hon. Polverelli

12- With reference to the express telex 996/63 of the 13th of this month from Y.E. and following my telephone conversation with the Hon. Polverelli, I inform you that Amann has already left Berlin and is expected here at any moment.

I shall retelegraph as soon as I am in receipt.

Pittalis

A7[285]

INCOMING TELEGRAM
N. 2352 P.R.

From: R. Consulate	Munich Bav. 3/9/XI 13:10 hours
Munich B.	Rome, same 17:00 hours

Destination: Press
Re: Communication to Hon. Polverelli: Mr. Aman [*sic*]
14 – Ref. my tel. 12

Following many hesitations and excuses to delay the meeting, it was finally possible to have a conversation with Aman [sic] this morning. He said that he wishes to sell the rights based upon a regular contract for the edition of Mein Kampf in Italy not (I say not) wishing to accept the text of the receipt with the amount sent by the Ministry since it appears to be a political matter rather than a publisher's contract.

---

284. The telegram is stamped "seen" by Mussolini; Polverelli then filed it in the "record" section.
285. The telegram is stamped "read" by Polverelli who placed it in the "record" file.

Mr. Aman promised to send a draft contract tomorrow morning that I shall transmit for examination to Rome with the Cabinet pouch leaving the same evening.

Pittalis

A8[286]

Ministry of Foreign Affairs   Rome, March 1933-XI
Press Office
<u>MEMO FOR COMM. JACOMONI</u>

We are honored to inform Y.E. that due to high level decisions the Office has transmitted through the R. Minister in Munich and in a completely confidential manner to Mr. Amann, Max, the publishing representative of the National Socialist Party in that city, a check drawn on the Banco di Napoli in the amount of L. 250,000.

The said amount is meant to purchase the rights for the translation of the Italian edition of the biography of Hitler entitled Mein Kampf.

Mr. Amann who has been contacted by the R. Minister, has said that upon receiving the amount rather than signing the receipt sent by this ministry he prefers to draft a regular contract in order to avoid having the entire matter take on a political character and giving it a purely commercial aspect instead.

The R. Minister in Munich who is still in possession of the amount is negotiating with Amann at this time on the text of the contract in question.

---

286. The original is in ASDMAE, MAE, Cabinet 1919–43, b. Gab. 125, f. Documenti sottratti dai fascicoli originali dal Prof. Enrico Serra. Pietro Pastorelli 30.1.1982. Documents removed from the original files by Prof. Enrico Serra. Francesco Jacomoni was deputy head of the MAE cabinet.

A9

Consulate General of Italy   TELEXPRESS N. 35/28 R.
Munich Bavaria   R. Ministry of Foreign Affairs Press Office
                                                 Rome
Confidential   Munich (Bavaria) 10 March 1933 XI
Re: Mr. Max Amann
Ref: My telegram of yesterday n. 14

As of this evening, despite many phone calls, Mr. Amann has not yet sent the promised draft of the publishing contract due to the events[287] of yesterday and today in Munich that took up a lot of his time.

I shall continue to contact him and as soon as I receive the promised draft shall send it to the R. Ministry.

Pittalis

A10[288]

INCOMING TELEGRAM
In code N. 2428 P.R.
From: R. Consulate General
Munich Bavaria   Munich, Bavaria 3.11.1933-XI 13:10 hours
                                    Rome id. 17:30 hours
Destination: Press
Re: Communication for Hon. Polverelli: Mr. Aman [*sic*]
16 – Following my telegram n. 14.

Just received the text of the contract. Since I cannot use a courier until next Friday, please let me know by cable if I may send it by mail.

Pittalis

---

287. A probable reference to the recent political elections.
288. The telegram is stamped "seen" by Polverelli.

A11

Consulate General of Italy
Munich Bavaria

TELEXPRESS N. 36/29.
R. Ministry of Foreign Affairs—Press
Office

Rome

Confidential
Re: Mr. Max Amann
Ref: My telegram n. 16 of the 11th.

Munich (Bavaria) March 17, 1933 XI

I herewith enclosed transmit the two drafts of publishing contract as received from Mr. Amann.

I inform you that following the first conversation I had with Mr. Amann and in accordance with his request, rather than cashing the check in Italian lire I have converted the amount into marks for a total of RM 53,625. Since the contract is still in the negotiating stage I have deposited the amount in the bank account belonging to this R. Consulate General at the Deutsche Bank.

Pittalis

2 enc.

A12

PUBLISHING CONTRACT

First Copy

The ....
....

And the publishing company Fr. Eher Successors, a limited liability company at Munich, Bavaria, have agreed to the following publishing contract drawn up in two identical copies, signed with the agreement of both parties.

1. Fr. Eher Successors publishing company has the exclusive rights to the literary property of the work "Mein Kampf" by Reich Chancellor Adolf Hitler. The author has authorized the company to negotiate the sale of rights to foreign countries.

2. The ....

....

is purchasing from Fr. Eher Successors publishing company at Munich all Italian rights to the book Mein Kampf by Reich Chancellor Adolf Hitler. The Italian Publishing Company has the right to translate the work and publish the Italian text through Italian booksellers and in newspapers that are published in the Kingdom and in the Italian colonies. It therefore has the exclusive right to decide the editions and the appearance for publication.

3. The Italian publishing company is not authorized to translate the Italian text into other languages or into Italian dialects.

4. The text used for the Italian translation of the book "Mein Kampf" will be the 17th edition of the book itself. The Italian publishing company agrees to undertake to print in the inside page behind the title page or facing it, next to the Copyright notice the following sentence translated into Italian: "This edition is authorized by the original publisher Fr. Eher Successors, a limited liability company located at Munich, Bavaria, Germany."

5. As a single remittance for the acquisition of all rights for Italy the Publisher... shall pay to Fr. Eher Suc. publishing company at Munich upon signature of this contract the amount of RM.. (in letters...…..).

6. The translation expenses from German to Italian will be incurred by the Italian publisher. The translator must be an Italian citizen and cannot be of the Jewish (Israelite) religion or race.

In order to ensure that the Italian text conforms to the original German edition, Fr. Eher Suc. publishing company agrees to provide to the Italian publisher a German speaker to examine the Italian manuscript and ascertain that it corresponds to the original. The expenses incurred will be borne by the Italian publisher.

7. The Italian publisher agrees to provide free to the publisher and the original Publishing Company 15 bound copies of the first edition unless the entire production is printed with a paper cover (brochure). For every new edition the author will receive 5 free samples for every 1000 printed up to a maximum of 15 copies. These volumes should be shipped to the publishing company Fr. Eher Successors.

8. The publishing company Fr. Eher Successors agrees that the Italian publisher will sell to it copies of Mein Kampf at a discount of 50% off the cover price.

9. The rights sold on the basis of the present contract with the publisher... may be assigned to other Italian publishers. Eher publishing company must be informed by registered mail about any such assignment of copyright. The successor shall have the same rights and obligations contained in the present contract with the Publishing Company.............. ....

Munich, Date_____1933

The original German publisher   The Italian Publishing Company
                                         Fr. Eher Nachf. G.m.b.H.

A13

MEMO TO THE PRESS OFFICE
Contract to be negotiated with Fr. Eher –Succ. Publishing Company in Munich, Bavaria

Having examined the projected contract sent to this Ministry by Fr. Eher – Successors Publishing Company of Munich, for the sale of translation and publication rights in Italy of the book "Mein Kampf" written by Reich Chancellor Adolf Hitler, we are privileged to draw the attention of this office to the following points contained in said draft contract:

Article 1

The power of attorney letter dated October 1, 1931 that is in the file indicates that the author of the book had reserved his rights of ownership for foreign countries and that later by the same letter had generally authorized Publishing Company Fr. Eher Successors to sell such rights to <u>foreign newspapers.</u> The publication of a work in the foreign press is different from the publication of the work itself in book form. Therefore the letter-power of attorney appears to be insufficient in its present form or content to authorize the Publishing Company to enter into a contract as it is offering to do.

It would be necessary for the author to give the Publishing Company a regular authorization prepared by a notary public or at least with the signature verified by a notary public whereby he authorizes the publisher to sell his rights for Italy for the translation and publication of his work both to newspapers and in book form. The Publishing Company should also be authorized to negotiate the terms of sale, the price, receive funds and be able to issue a good and valid receipt.

It would therefore appear that Article 1 of the contract should be modified to read as follows: "The Publishing Company of Fr. Eher Successors has the exclusive literary property rights for Germany to the work "Mein Kampf" by Reich Chancellor Adolf Hitler. On the basis of a power of attorney dated ……………………….. validated by the Notary Public per the attached original form (or as an authenticated copy) has been authorized by the author to sell the translation and publishing rights for Italy of said work.

Article 2

For the sake of clarity it would seem appropriate to modify proposed text of Article 2 as follows:

"Fr. Eher –Successors Publishing Company of Munich, agrees by the present document to sell all rights to translation and publication for Italy to the book "Mein Kampf" by Reich Chancellor Adolf Hitler. The Publisher . . . . has therefore the exclusive right to translate and publish the text of the aforementioned book in Italy in the Italian language by Italian publishers of its choice as well as newspapers published in the Kingdom and in the Italian Colonies.

It also has the exclusive right for all matters regarding publication and the appearance of the book that will be published in Italy."

Articles 3 and 4

No comments.

Article 5

It appears that the proposed text would best be modified in article 5 as follows:

"The Company .... as the total cost for the acquisition of the exclusive rights for Italy for the book mentioned above from the Publishing Company Fr. Eher Successors of Munich, pays the Publisher upon signature of the present contract the amount of RM............ that the Publisher declares having received and for which it issues a receipt as being fully and completely paid upon signature of this document.

Article 6

Due to the freedom of religion that exists in Italy and the equal rights recognized to those belonging to various religious groups authorized within the Kingdom, it would appear advisable to possibly cancel the clause that forbids having the book translated by a person of the Jewish religion or race. Should Fr. Eher Publishing Company wish to keep such a clause the publisher acquiring the book could offer assurances by a separate letter that the translation would not be given to an Israelite. To cover potential complaints it would be best to add at the end of Article 6 the following paragraph:

"It is agreed that the Publisher............... may use the services, should it deem it necessary, of the person recommended and provided by Fr. Eher Publishing Company and that it remains free to accept or not the corrections or modifications that such person may propose."

Articles 7, 8, and 9

No comments.

A14

TELE EXPRESS n. 2378/127

Ministry of Foreign Affairs   To: R. Consulate General of Italy
PRESS OFFICE   Munich, Bavaria

Rome, APR. 10, 1933 Year XI

Re: Mr. Max AMANN
Ref: Your Express Telegram 36/29 of March 17.

(Text) Having carefully examined the two drafts of the publishing contract given to you by Mr. Amann, we are honored to enclose a copy of the contract with a few counterproposals as received from the ministry's legal department.

In asking you to inform Mr. Amann of the new draft we await their answer as the amount of RM 53,625 remains in the account of the R. Consulate General with Deutsche Bank until this matter is resolved.

Polverelli

A15[289]

Ministry of Foreign Affairs   Rome, April 27, 1933-XI
Press Office
MEMORANDUM FOR THE CABINET OF H.E. THE MINISTER

Further to the preceding memorandum, copy enclosed,[290] we are privileged to point out the following concerning the acquisition of the copyright for the Italian translation of the biography of Hitler, "Mein Kampf."

Having examined the draft of the publishing agreement that Mr. Amann had provided to this Ministry through the R. Consulate General

---

289. The original is in ASDMAE, MAE, Cabinet 1919–43, b. Gab. 125, f. Documenti sottratti dai fascicoli originali dal Prof. Enrico Serra. Pietro Pastorelli 30.1.1982. Documents removed from the original files by Prof. Enrico Serra. With the mark "seen" by Mussolini on the document. Then "Atti Gab[inetto] [to the files of the Cabinet]."
290. Refers to Doc. A8.

in Munich, this Office has drafted—in agreement with the Legal Section of the Ministry—a counterproposal with a few changes.

This counterproposal was sent to the R. Consulate General for Mr. Amann's approval.

In expectation of finalizing the contract itself the amount of RM 53, 625—equal to the check in Italian lire of 250,000—was deposited into the checking account belonging to the R. Consulate General in Munich at the Deutsche Bank.

A16[291]

Ministry of Foreign Affairs   Rome, May 10, 1933-XI
Press Office

MEMO FOR H.E. THE HEAD OF THE GOVERNMENT

This Office transmitted some time ago through the R. Minister at Munich and most confidentially for Mr. Amann Max, publishing representative of the National Socialist Party in that city a check drawn on the Banco di Napoli in the amount of Lire 250, 000 for the purchase of the rights to the Italian translation of the Biography of Hitler entitled "Mein Kampf."

Mr. Amann who was contacted by the R. Minister pointed out that upon receipt of the amount rather than signing the receipt sent by this Ministry he preferred to draft a regular contract in order to remove any political flavor from the matter turning it instead into a commercial venture.

The R. Minister in Munich is now negotiating an agreement with Amann regarding the contract itself.

After examination of the draft prepared by Mr. Amann, this Ministry sent to the R. Consulate General a counter project—in agreement with the Legal Section of the Ministry—containing some changes for Mr. Amann's approval.

---

291. The note bears the mark "seen" by Mussolini.

In expectation of the final draft of the contract itself –which has been recently pressed for—the amount of RM 53, 625—equivalent to the check in Italian Lire of 250,000—was deposited into the checking account of the R. Consulate General in Munich at the Deutsche Bank.

Since the counter project sent to Munich, Bavaria, on April 10 has not elicited any kind of response an urgent follow up request was sent some days ago to the R. Representative.

A17

	TELE EXPRESS n. 2820/150

Ministry of Foreign Affairs

PRESS OFFICE

TELE EXPRESS n. 2820/150

Addressed to

R. CONSULATE GENERAL OF ITALY

Munich, Bav.

Rome, May 11, 1933 Year XI

(Re) <u>Confidential</u>

(Reference) following telexpress Min. n. 2378/127 of April 10

(Text) In view of the need to define the note regarding the purchase of the translation rights for the Italian translation of the Biography of Hitler "Mein Kampf," we ask Y.E. to please indicate, as quickly as possible, if the publishing contract with Mr. Amann was completed and under which terms.

Polverelli

A18

INCOMING TELEGRAM
N. 4904 P.R.
From: R. Consulate   Munich, Bav. 5/24/33-XI 21:23 hours
Munich Bavaria   Rome   " " "   23:45 hours
Destination: Press
Re: Message for Hon. Polverelli

25- Hamann [sic] declares that he accepts the draft sent with Y.E. pouch N. 2378 of April 10.

Y.E. will kindly inform us whether we may sign the contract and when to make the related payment.

Pittalis

A19

OUTGOING TELEGRAM
N. 5199/30
Press Office
To: ITALCONSUL
MUNICH BAVARIA
IN CODE
Rome 5-27-1933-24:00 hours
(Text) Your telegram n. 25

Y.E. may proceed with signature of contract and related payment. It is understood that the text of the contract to be signed is the one containing our changes.

Polverelli

A20

INCOMING TELEGRAM
N. 5093 P.R.
From: R. Consulate   Munich, Bav. 5/30/33-XI 18:55 hours
Munich B.   Rome " " "   20:30 hours
Destination: Press
Re: Message for Hon. Polverelli

28 – Y.E. telegram n. 30. Signature put, Aman [*sic*] now points out in Art. 1 of the contract that he is unable to provide the Power of Attorney from Hitler (?) and proposes to replace it with a declaration of his own as to the exclusivity of the rights to "Mein Kampf."

He assured us that he has proceeded in the same manner with a contract in England.

Kindly send a telegram with your answer.

Pittalis

A21

OUTGOING TELEGRAM
N. 5343/31
Press Office
To: ITALCONSUL
MUNICH BAVARIA
IN CODE
Rome 5-31-1933-24:00 hours
(Text) Your telegram n. 78

Declaration by Amann is sufficient.

Polverelli

A22

MEMO FROM POLVERELLI TO MUSSOLINI
June 1, 1933-XI

The contract with Hitler's representative for the sale of the rights on the book Mein Kampf is taking place at the Italian Consulate General in Munich, Bavaria.

G.P.

A23

INCOMING TELEGRAM
N. 5342 P.R.
From: R. Consulate   Munich, Bav. 6/6/33-XI 13:39 hours
Munich B.   Rome " " "   16:00 hours
Destination: Press Foreign Office Rome
Re: Signature publishing contract
30 – Y.E. telegram 30 of the 1st.

Amann has signed the publishing contract which I will transmit in the next pouch of the 9th. I have proceeded to make the payment.

Pittalis

A24[292]

Consulate General of Italy	TELEXPRESS N. 5049/499
Munich Bavaria	R. Ministry of Foreign Affairs—Press Office
	<u>Rome</u>

Re: Max Amann
Ref: ministerial telegram n. 31 of the 1st.

Following my telegram n. 30 dated the 6th I transmit enclosed herewith the publishing contract signed by Mr. Amann in two copies as well as a separate receipt for the payment made of 53,625 marks with the relevant foreign exchange coupon.

Pittalis

A25[293]

PUBLISHING CONTRACT

The ....
And Fr. Eher Successors Publishing Company, a limited liability Company located in Munich have agreed today on the following publishing contract made in two identical signed copies indicating the agreement of both contracting parties.

I.

Fr. Eher Successors Publishing Company has exclusive literary property rights to the work "Mein Kampf" by Reich Chancellor Adolf Hitler. The Company is authorized by the author to negotiate the sale to foreign countries.

---

292. A note on the letter reads: "Com. Bruno Mondadori. Has no news from Milan. As soon as he knows he shall inform us. 4-VII-33-XI. Sapuppo. Records."
293. As shown in the photo there was a dual language version of the contact in German and Italian. We are not reproducing the German version in this book.

II.

Fr. Eher Successors Publishing Company of Munich sells through the present contract all translation and publishing rights for Italy of the book "Mein Kampf" by Reich Chancellor Adolf Hitler. The.................Publishing Company therefore has exclusive rights to publish the text in Italy in the Italian language of the aforementioned book by Italian publishers of its choice as well as newspapers published in the Kingdom and in all the Italian Colonies.

It also has exclusive rights for all editorial matters and the layout of the book that will be published in Italy.

III.

The Italian Publishing Company is not authorized to translate the Italian language version of the book into other languages or into dialects.

IV.

The text to be used for the translation of "Mein Kampf" will be the 17th edition of the work. The Italian Publishing Company undertakes to print on the inside of the title page or facing it besides the copyright notice also the following sentence translated into the Italian language: "Publication authorized by the original publisher Fr. Eher Successors, a limited liability company, Munich-Germany."

V.

The Company .... as the total acquisition cost of the rights it is purchasing on an exclusive basis for Italy on the above mentioned book by Fr. Eher Successors Publishing Company of Munich pays to the Publishing Company upon signature of the present contract the amount of RM. 53,625.- (fifty three thousand six hundred twenty five) that the Publishing Company agrees it has received and hereby gives full and final receipt by signing the present contract.

VI.

The translation expenses from German to Italian shall be borne by the Italian Publishing Company. The translator must be an Italian citizen.

To ensure that the Italian text corresponds in its meaning to the original German Fr. Eher Suc., declares that it is willing to place a German speaker at the disposal of the Italian publisher to examine the Italian manuscript to ascertain that the meaning of the translation coincides with the original. The related expenses shall be incurred by the Italian publisher.

In any case the Publisher.................................... may use the services of this person offered by Fr. Eher Publishing Company only if it is deemed necessary and convenient and it shall be free to accept or reject the corrections that are proposed.

VII.

The Italian Publisher agrees to provide to the author and the original publisher 15 bound copies of the first edition unless all the copies are printed with paper covers (brochure.) For every new edition the author shall receive 5 copies for every 1000 copies printed up to a maximum of 15 copies. These volumes must be shipped each time to Fr. Eher Successors Publishing Company.

VIII.

Fr. Eher Successors Publishing Company agrees with the Italian Publisher that copies of the book "Mein Kampf" will be sold for resale to Fz. Eher Succesors Publ. Co. at a 50% discount off the cover price.

IX.

The rights that are part of the present contract with ....Publishing Company may be assigned to other Italian Publishers. Eher Publishing Company will be informed by letter of any assignment of editorial rights. The assignee shall have the same rights and duties contained in the present contract belonging to ....Publishing Company.

Munich, Bavaria May 30, 1933/XI
The Original German Publisher   The Italian Publisher
Frz. Eher Nachf., G.m.b.H.
Verlagsbuchhandlung
(signed and stamped) Amann

A26

A. MONDADORI
PUBLISHING COMPANY
The CHIEF EXECUTIVE OFFICER
And GENERAL MANAGER

Milan, July 4, 1933 XI

Excellency,

The Director of our Rome office informed me of the conversation he had with Your Excellency regarding the book by Hitler "Mein Kampf."

As Your Excellency may well imagine this book had not escaped notice by our company since it has been on the market for several years and has had recent new editions. The only reason that held us back from making an Italian edition had to do with the book's size and the fact that part of it is of specific internal German interest.

We should add that shorter studies have recently appeared about Hitler also by Italian publishers.

If we had not been so fully engaged in publishing commitments we would have certainly examined the possibility of publishing the Italian edition of this work, however, Your Excellency should take into account that the series Panoramas of Fascist Culture that the Party has given us to publish and that will include some forty short volumes, plus the very extensive publications we are involved in for the Ministry of the Colonies regarding the ten years of activity by the Fascist Government (this publication has become a veritable encyclopedia of the Italian Colonies), besides many other publications of current political events have completely absorbed all out resources and driven us to a reduced program.

In any case I deeply thank Your Excellency for think of our company as the possible publisher of this work and my main regret is to not be able at this time to accept to publish it. On the other hand I would not want a delay on our part to jeopardize the success of the book itself which is obviously connected to current events.

Sincerely yours

Mondadori

To: H.E. SAPUPPO[294]
Press Office Ministry of Foreign Affairs
ROME

A27

TELEXPRESS N. 3973/119

Ministry of Foreign Affairs	Addressed to:
PRESS OFFICE	R. PREFECTURE
	MILAN

Confidential   Rome, July 22, 1933 Year XI

(Re) Communication with Bompiani publishing company

(Text) We would be grateful to Y.E. to communicate verbally[295] with the publisher Bompiani that this Ministry of Foreign Affairs has secured the rights to translate and publish in Italy the well known book "Mein Kampf" by Hitler, and is thinking of giving the Bompiani publishing company the task of publishing an Italian edition.

Your Excellency will tell Bompiani that the book is about 700 pages long in its original edition (Eher Publishing, Munich) and that his only expense would be the translation and publication costs while it may be

---

294. Giuseppe Sapuppo Minister Plenipotentiary was Deputy Head of the Press Office.

295. The word is added by hand. The original of the Telexpress is in the State Archives in Milan, Prefecture, Gabinetto, 2° versamento, b. 153. f. 044. Bompiani. Casa Editrice. Pubblicazioni. On the sheet there is also the word "noted" and the signature of Bompiani.

possible to forecast wide distribution in Italy given the timeliness of the topic and the notoriety of the author.

Kindly point out to Mr., Bompiani that he may inform the Press Office of the Ministry of Foreign Affairs directly regarding his decision.

Polverelli

A28[296]

VALENTINO BOMPIANI
PUBLISHING COMPANY S.A.

<u>Express mail Registered</u>   Milan 7/27/33
Illustrious Honorable Gaetano Polverelli
Head of the Press Office Ministry of Foreign Affairs
<u>ROME</u>

The Press Office of this Prefecture gave me Y.E.'s letter regarding the publication of the Italian edition of the book "Mein Kampf" by Adolf Hitler. My company is honored to be chosen and is ready to publish the book taking on the entire cost of translation and printing.

Could Y.E. be so kind as to inform me if I should request the original text from the German publisher or if it will be sent to me by the Ministry.

Since I leave next Friday for a long trip abroad I would be pleased to receive some information in advance to issue directives before I leave and therefore gain time during the month of August.

Allow me to thank you as I send my sincere salutations.

Your devoted
Valentino Bompiani

---

296. Handwritten note by Polverelli: "Spoke to Bompiani. Send him Hitler book with a note."

A29

PREFECTURE OF MILAN
Cabinet

N. 7074 Gab.   Milan July 29, 1933

Answ. Telexpress 7-22-33 N. 3973-119

Re: Bompiani publishing company

Hon. Ministry of Foreign Affairs

(Press Office)

ROME

Count Valentino Bompiani, to whom I communicated the content of your telexpress which I am answering, will write directly to your office regarding the proposal he received.

THE PREFECT
Fornaciari

A30[297]

Ministry of Foreign Affairs

PRESS OFFICE   Rome, July 29, 1933- XI

MEMO

Following the agreement reached over the phone this morning between Minister Sapuppo and Comm. Bompiani, the Press Office is pleased to send the Valentino Bompiani publishing company the book "Mein Kampf" by Adolf Hitler.

---

297. On the letter there is a handwritten notation: "Sent to Milan by registered express July 29, 17:00 hours."

A31[298]

CONSULATE GENERAL   Telexpress N. 7746/769
OF ITALY
MUNICH, BAVARIA   R. MINISTRY OF FOREIGN AFFAIRS
                          PRESS OFFICE
                          ROME
           Munich, Bavaria, September 6, 1933 XI

Re: Hitler's book "Mein Kampf"

The publisher "Franz Eher Nachf." informs me that the Marburg Institute for the Blind has obtained the right to publish an edition of 1000 copies of Hitler's book "Mein Kampf" written for the blind.

The management of the Institute has now asked the publisher "Eher Nachf" for permission to print foreign language editions including the Italian language.

The above-mentioned publisher has asked this R. Office whether an Italian edition of a maximum of 50 to 100 copies would be approved.

I ask the Ministry to please let me know the answer I should give to "Eher Nachf" company.

                                           Pittalis

A32[299]

Ministry of Foreign Affairs
PRESS OFFICE   Rome, September 14, 1933-XI
     MEMORANDUM FOR H.E. THE HEAD OF THE
                  GOVERNMENT

The Franz Eher publishing company has informed the R. Consul General in Munich, Bavaria that the Institute for the Blind in Marburg

---

298. On the letter there is a handwritten notation: "memo for the Chief."
299. On the note there is the "Nihil obstat, yes" written by Mussolini.

has obtained from that publisher the right to publish an edition of 1000 copies of the book *Mein Kampf* by Hitler written for the blind.

The Institute's management has asked Eher Nacf. Publishing for authorization to publish foreign language editions which would including the Italian language having a maximum printing of 50 to 100 copies.

Would Y.E. kindly advise us regarding the answer we may give to the R. Consulate in Munich for Eher Nacf.

A33[300]

Valentino Bompiani
Publishing Company   [Milan, September 8, 1933]

Excellency!

I believe I must offer Y.E. a few brief thoughts regarding the planned publication of Hitler's "Mein Kampf" in an Italian edition. These thoughts are motivated by the desire to best attain the goal of publication which is to bring to the attention of a <u>vast</u> Italian readership a work that the London "Times" has recently called "the lay Bible of the German people."

In its 1932 edition (Franz Eher publishing company Munich) this book is almost 800 densely printed pages divided in two parts: the first ("eine Abrechhung [*sic*]") contains the author's biography and the history of the birth and development of the National Socialist movement until 1926; the second "Die nationalsozialistische Beidegung [*sic*]" explains the philosophical, ethical, political and historical foundations of the Hitler movement.

Eight hundred thickly printed pages in a compact language such as German become over one thousand in Italian translation. A one thousand page book is not very attractive for our readers. Of course we will find an <u>elite</u> group of educated people or who are just curious about spiritual matters that will read it with interest, but the masses will not easily be persuaded to buy and read such a huge volume.

---

300. The underlined parts are in the text.

On the other hand a number of items relating to the author's life in general before he entered politics (which took place only after the end of the war) and pages explaining the inroads made by his ideas and the National Socialist Party during the initial years of its existence in one German Land or another; other parts that analyze the reasons for Germany's defeat in 1918 and the need to transform the Reich from a federal to a unified state (which has now become a reality) are of greater interest to the German than the foreign reader. The Italian reader in particular is more interested in discovering the spiritual underpinnings, the historical justification, and the complete program of National Socialism: almost all material that is to be found in the second half of the book.

Therefore in order to best reach the proposed objective of giving the book a broad distribution I think it would be best to reduce the size to no more than 500 pages and publish in its entirety, without abbreviations or cuts, the second half of the work, explaining the Hitlerian concepts of the state, the political organization, the struggle against Marxism and Jewish cosmopolitanism, the trade union problem and the course of foreign policy. The first half, which includes the author's biography and the origins of the movement, could easily be abbreviated in an introductory section of about one hundred pages where the pages of chapter XI, where the author explains the topic "People and Race" and examines the reasons for the superiority of the Aryan race, could be printed in their entirety.

Then we could have a book of about five hundred pages that can be sold to everyone at that price and with that page count illustrating the author's thinking, his plans and underscoring the analogies and derivations of the Hitlerian program and doctrine from fascism without boring the Italian reader with details belonging to the past that are of purely local interest.

More importantly <u>a preface dictated by the Author himself would add value and distribution to the work</u> in the Italian edition giving it an original character making stand out among all other non German editions; the pages that the author gives us will no doubt provide a new and very authoritative justification to the entire enterprise we are about to engage in.

I offer all this to Y.E.'s attention to find the best way to submit my proposals for the Author's approval and I remain dutifully in the expectation of the answers that Y.E. will decide to give me.
With respectful salutations

Your devoted
Valentino Bompiani

H.E. Minister L. [sic] Sapuppo
Ministry of Foreign Affairs
ROME

A34[301]

Wednesday 13 Sept. XI

Dear Ciano,

I am sending you the enclosed letter from Bompiani publishing regarding an office matter.

We have assigned to Bompiani the right to publish the translation of Hitler's *Mein Kampf.* Those rights were purchased for <u>political expediency.</u>

Bompiani is now requesting:

1. to abridge the first part of the book so that it doesn't end up being too long.
2. to secure a preface by Hitler.

The first point will probably require authorizations from the German publisher and we could write to the Consulate in Munich.

For the second point the Embassy in Berlin could act.
Cordially yours,

G. Sapuppo

---

301. Handwritten on the letterhead of "La Pace—Grand Hotel—Montecatini Terme." The underlined words are part of the text.

A35[302]

Ministry of Foreign Affairs
PRESS OFFICE   Rome, September 19, 1933-XI

MEMORANDUM FOR H.E. THE HEAD OF THE GOVERNMENT

The Bompiani publishing company which as Y.E. knows has been assigned the right to publish the translation of Hitler's *Mein Kampf* has pointed out the following to this Press Office:

The 1932 edition of Mein Kampf is a book of about 800 dense pages divided into two parts: the first part includes a biography of the author and the history of the development of the National Socialist Party up to 1926; the second part explains the philosophical, ethnic, political and historical foundations of the Hitler movement.

800 pages of densely printed pages in a compact language such as German would translate into more than 1000 pages in the Italian translation making it an unattractive book for our readership. It would be best therefore to abridge the first part into a one hundred page introduction at the most and instead publish the second part of the work in its entirety since it is in effect the more interesting of the two.

A preface dictated by the Author himself for the Italian edition would greatly increase the value and distribution of the work.

If Y.E. agrees with the observations made by Bompiani publishing we could first proceed by asking the German publisher's authorization through the Consulate in Munich and at the same time the R. Embassy in Berlin could request a preface by Hitler.

This Office awaits instructions that Y.E. will judge appropriate to send.

---

302. The note is underlined several times and has Mussolini's "yes" next to the sentence: "completely for the second part that is really the most interesting."

A36

Telexpress n. 5020/297

Ministry of Foreign Affairs   Addressed to:
PRESS OFFICE   R. CONSULATE OF ITALY
Munich, Bavaria
Rome, Sept. 20, 1933-Year XI

(Re) Book by Hitler *Mein Kampf*
(Ref)   Your telexpress 7746/769 dated September 6

(Text) We kindly ask that you tell the publisher Eher Nacf that there is no objection from this Press Office of the Head of the Government to the publication of the Italian edition for the blind of Hitler's book *Mein Kampf* for a maximum of 50 copies.

Ciano

A37

Telexpress n. 5095/302

Ministry of Foreign Affairs   Addressed to:
PRESS OFFICE   R. CONSULATE OF ITALY
Munich, Bavaria
Rome, Sept. 25, 1933-Year XI

(Re) "Mein Kampf"

(Text) Valentino Bompiani publishing company in Milan which has been assigned the right to publish the translation of "Mein Kampf" by Hitler has pointed out to this Press Office on the need to abridge the first part of the work that includes the biography of the author and the development of the National Socialist movement until 1926 into no more than a one hundred page introduction, while the second half which is actually the most interesting part would be published in its entirety.

We therefore kindly request that Y.E. approach the Publisher Aman [*sic*] Max to obtain an authorization for such a modification and reminding him that the 800 pages that make up the book translated into Italian would become about 1000 and therefore too thick a book for a broad audience. Furthermore the first part of "Mein Kampf" contains a lot of information about the author's private life preceding his political activity and the gradual progress of the idea and the National Socialist program. It is obvious that it contains information of greater interest to the foreign rather than the Italian reader.

We await your kind reply regarding the above.

Ciano

A38

Ministry of Foreign Affairs
PRESS OFFICE

Telexpress n. 5092/215
Addressed to:
R. ITALIAN EMBASSY
BERLIN
Rome, Sept. 25, 1933-Year XI

(Re) "Mein Kampf"

(Text) The Valentino Bompiani publishing company that was assigned the right to publish the translation of "Mein Kampf" by Hitler has pointed out the problems relating to the publication of the 800 pages in compact German language that become 1000 in the Italian translation; this would therefore make it a large and perhaps unattractive book for our reading public.

It would be preferable to summarize in an introduction of not more than about one hundred pages all of the first part of the book that includes the biography of the author and the development of the National socialist movement up to 1926 and to publish instead in its entirety the second half that contains the philosophical, ethical, political and historical foundations of the Hitler movement.

We have therefore asked permission from the German publisher Max Aman in Munich through the R. Consulate General.

It would also increase the prestige and distribution of the work to have a preface to the Italian edition dictated by the Chancellor himself. This would give the work an original character distinguishing it from other editions in languages other than German and in all probability the pages that Hitler would be willing to write would provide a new and authoritative justification to the edition itself.

I would be grateful to Y.E. to present this to the Author in the form and manner you judge best in order to satisfy the request from the Bompiani publishing company.

We await your kind response to the above.

Ciano

A39

R. ITALIAN EMBASSY
BERLIN

Telexpress n. 5297/1902
Addressed to the
Royal Ministry of Foreign Affairs
ROME

(Position) Press 6
(Re) "Mein Kampf"
(Ref) Telexpress from Y.E. n. 5092/215 of September 25.

Berlin, October 17, 1933-Year XI

I am honored to communicate to Y.E. that I have communicated personally to Chancellor Hitler the desire on the part of the Valentino Bompiani publishing company in Milan to obtain a preface dictated by him expressly for the Italian edition of "Mein Kampf."

The Chancellor told me that he would gladly accede to such a request.

I took the necessary steps to receive the said preface in order to transmit it to Y.E.

V. Cerruti

A40

VALENTINO BOMPIANI
PUBLISHING COMPANY S.A.

Milan, October 19, 1933-XI

To His Excellency Minister SAPUPPO
Ministry of Foreign Affairs
ROME

By the letter dated September 8, 1933 my company took the liberty of requesting some information from the Honorable Minister regarding the book by Adolf Hitler "Mein Kampf" without which it is impossible to continue in the preparatory work for the Italian edition of the volume.

We now are requesting your kind answer. With sincere regards.

VALENTINO BOMPIANI and Co.
The Managing Director[303]

A 41

5473/1304   Rome, October 21, 1933-XI
Dear Mr. Bompiani,

Your letter dated September 8 arrived while I was on vacation. I forwarded it to Count Ciano who immediately gave orders to accommodate your requests by writing to the Embassy in Berlin on one hand, to obtain a preface by Hitler and on the other to the R. Consulate General in Munich to find out whether the publisher would have any objections based on the contract to an abridged version of the book.

The Berlin Embassy answered as of 17th of this month that the Chancellor would gladly write a preface to the Italian edition of "Mein Kampf" and that it would be sent over as soon as it was received.

The R. Consulate in Munich has not yet answered and we shall send in a reminder.

---

303. The signature is probably not that of Valentino Bompiani.

In any case in the future I think it will be best if you do not address your letters to me personally but simply to the Press Office of the Head of the Government—Ministry of Foreign Affairs so that even during my momentary absence the file may follow its course.

Kindly receive my best regards
Signed:
Sapuppo

A42

Telexpress n. 5468/336

Press Office   Addressed to
Of the Head of the Government   R. CONSULATE GENERAL
Foreign Section   OF ITALY

Munich, Bavaria
Rome, October 23, 1933 Year XI

(Re) "Mein Kampf"

(Text) We kindly request that Y.E. press for a response to telexpress n. 5095/302 dated September 25 regarding the Italian edition of "Mein Kampf".

Signed:
Sapuppo

A43[304]

Consulate General of Italy
Munich, Bavaria

Telexpress n. 9728/923
R. Ministry of Foreign Affairs
Rome
Munich (Bavaria) October 28, 1933 XII

Position: Press
Re: Book by Hitler "Mein Kampf"
Ref: Ministerial telexpress n. 5095/302 of last September 25

Regarding the telexpress mentioned above, I can reply that due to the continued absence from Munich of the publisher Aman [*sic*] we have only just been able to obtain from Franz Eher Nachfolger publishing company the authorization for the Bompiani publishing company in Milan to abridge the work "Mein Kampf" by cutting those parts that are of least interest to the Italian reader.

I therefore transmit the enclosed written confirmation from Mr. Aman.[305]

At the same time I inform you of the request from Franz Eher Nachfolger publishing company to receive as soon as possible two galleys of the translated work per Article 6 in the contract.[306]
Enc. 1

Pittalis

---

304. Annotation by Ciano on the paper: "Thierry to discuss with me. Urgently." Carlo de Thierry was one of the secretaries in Ciano's Press Office.
305. See Doc. A44.
306. See ahead Doc. A63.

A44

Frz. Eher Nachf. G.m.b.h. München
ZENTRALVERLAG DER N.S.D.A.P.

Buchverlag WB/Ki.

München 2, NO, Den 27 Oktober 1933.
Thierschstrasse 11
An das
kgl. italienische Generakonsulat
München, Königstr. 20.

Wunschgemäss, bestäntigen wir Ihnen hiermit auch schriftlich, dass wir nichts degegen ein-zuwendedn haben, wenn Sie in der italienischen Ausgabe von "Mein Kampf" von Adolf Hitler jene Stellen kürzen, die für den italienischen Leser belanglos sind.

Mit vorzüglicher Hochactung!
Frz. Eher Nachf. G.m.b.h
Verlagsbuchandlung
Amann[307]

A45

VALENTINO BOMPIANI
PUBLISHING COMPANY S.A.

Milan, November 2, 1933-XII

Honorable PRESS OFFICE of
THE HEAD OF THE GOVERNMENT
ROME

His Excellency Minister Sapuppo has informed me that President Hitler is willing to write a preface for the Italian edition of his book but

---

307. "Following the request made, we confirm in writing that we have no objection that the Italian edition of *Mein Kampf* by Adolf Hitler be abridged in those segments that of little interest to the Italian reader. With best regards. F. Eher Publishing, [signed] Amann"

that the answer has not yet reached the R. Consulate in Munich regarding the authorization to publish an abridged edition of the book.

Regarding this matter I would like to point out that the American edition of the same book which has just been published was abridged to only three hundred pages which is much more than we were planning. We would be very pleased to receive both the preface and the authorization we discussed as soon as possible in order to avoid delaying the publication of the book.

With our deepest respects,

Valentino Bompiani
Publishing Company Inc.
The Managing Director
V. Bompiani

A46

Rome, November 8, 1933-XII

Palazzo Chigi
5663/1345
Dear Mr. Bompiani,

I am pleased to inform you that Eher Publishing Company in Munich has given authorization (copy enclosed) for the cutting or reducing in the Italian edition of "Mein Kampf" by Chancellor Hitler, of those passages that are of less interest to Italian readers.

With best regards.

Ciano

Dr. Valentino Bompiani
via S. Paolo, 10
Milan

A47

VALENTINO BOMPIANI
PUBLISHING COMPANY S.A.

Milan, November 14, 1933-XII

Illustrious Count Ciano,

I send you my deepest thanks for your kind message about the edition of the work "Mein Kampf" by Chancellor Hitler.

With best regards I remain Yours,

Val. Bompiani

Illustrious Count Ciano
Press Office of the Head of the Government
ROME

A48

R. Embassy of Italy
Telegram-Mail N. 6391/2946

Paris, Nov. 18, 1933-XII

Addressed to: R. Ministry of Foreign Affairs
Press Office
ROME
(Re) French translation of the book "Mein Kampf" by Chancellor
Hitler

(Text) The R. Embassy has been informed that in the next few days—it appears to be a Catholic publisher—the French translation of the book by Chancellor Hitler "Mein Kampf" will be published in Paris.

It seems that the German Embassy and the Quai d'Orsay know nothing about it.

Pignatti

A49

VALENTINO BOMPIANI
PUBLISHING COMPANY S.A.

Milan, December 12, 1933-XII

Honorable PRESS OFFICE of
THE HEAD OF THE GOVERNMENT
ROME

Having completed the translation of the book by Adolf Hitler "My Struggle" and having started the typesetting, we respectfully request whom we should ask about the preface by the Author that had been promised to us.

Respectfully yours,
Valentino Bompiani
Publishing Company Inc.
The Managing Director
V. Bompiani

A50

INCOMING TELEGRAM
N. 11747 P.R.
From: R. Embassy   London, 12-16-33-XII 20:00 hours
London   Rome, 17 "   "   02:00 hours
Assigned to: Press
Re: Book "Mein Kampf" by Adolf Hitler

985-Perhaps Y.E. will be interested to know that I asked yesterday which book was selling the most these days in London at the most prestigious book store in Piccadilly Circus they replied "Mein Kampf" by Adolf Hitler."

Grandi

A51

PRESS OFFICE   Telegram n. 13160 R/462
Of   Outgoing
THE HEAD OF THE GOVERNMENT
FOREIGN DEPARTMENT
Addressed to ITALDIPL
BERLIN
(Re:) "Mein Kampf"
In code

Rome, December 16, 1933 24:00 hours

(Text) I refer to your telexpress n. 1902 of October 17 stop Since Bompiani publishing has completed the Italian translation and started to set type of "Mein Kampf" could Y.E. kindly send a reminder about the preface that had been promised by the Chancellor for the Italian edition.

Ciano

A52

Incoming Telegram
N. 11764 P.R.
From: R. Embassy   Berlin, 12/17/33 XII 15:45 hours
Berlin   Rome, "   "   "   "   18:00 hours
Destination: Press
Re: Request "Mein Kampf"
    762-Telegram from Y.E. n. 462.

I have already solicited the preface that the Chancellor had promised on my own initiative three times. The last time it happened on the occasion of H.E. Suvich's visit to Berlin. I shall continue to insist.

Cerruti

A53

PRESS OFFICE   Telegram n. 452 PR/9
Of   Outgoing
THE HEAD OF THE GOVERNMENT
FOREIGN DEPARTMENT
Addressed to ITALDIPL
BERLIN
(Re) "Mein Kampf"
Rome, 1/16/1934 24:00 hours

(Text) Reference is made to my telegram 462 of December 16 to kindly request that Y.E. solicit the sending of the promised preface by the Chancellor for the Italian edition of "Mein Kampf" as the publication by Bompiani publishing is ready.

Ciano

A54

Incoming Telegram
n. 419 P.R.
From: R. Embassy   Berlin, 1/17/1934 XII 14:30 hours
Berlin   Rome, "   "   "   "   17:00 hours
Destination: Foreign Press-Rome
Re: "Mein Kampf"
    17- Telegram from Y. E. n. 9

I once again insisted with the Secretariat of State at the Reich Chancellery[308] who promised to request the promised preface from the Chancellor.

Cerruti

---

308. Hans Heinrich Lammers, head of the Reich Chancellery.

A55

VALENTINO BOMPIANI
PUBLISHING COMPANY S.A.

Milan, January 13, 1934-XII

Honorable PRESS OFFICE of
THE HEAD OF THE GOVERNMENT
ROME

As we are very close to publishing the Italian edition of the book by Adolf Hitler "La mia battaglia," we respectfully ask your Office to please request the promised preface from Chancellor Hitler for the Italian edition.

With sincere regards
Val. Bompiani

A56

Press Office
Of
The Head of the Government
FOREIGN DEPARTMENT
Protocol n. 294/58

Rome, 22 Jan. 1934 Year XII

In reply to the letter dated January 13 B/P, we are honored to inform the publishing company that following the intervention of this Press Office, the R. Embassy in Berlin has again insistently requested from the Secretary of State at the Reich Chancellery, that promised to remind the Chancellor about the desired preface for the Italian edition of "Mein Kampf."

As soon as we received any information this Office shall immediately inform Y. E.

Respectfully yours

Signed: Mascia[309]

To Valentino Bompiani Publishing Company
via S. Paolo, 10
Milan

A57

Incoming Telegram
Clear by Courier
N. 759 P.R.

From: R. Embassy   Berlin, 1-24-34-XII
Berlin   Rome, 27 id.
Destination: Press
Re: "Mein Kampf"
027-For the Head of the Press Office

My telegram n. 17—I once again approached the Secretary of State at the Chancellery to insist with Chancellor regarding the preface in question. I was told that Hitler, who had been informed about my requests, had actually replied that it would be best to wait with the translation for the publication of the third volume the compilation of which he was working on. In the third volume the Chancellor intends to erase the fear and suspicion that exists in many foreign countries because of the concepts and political theories that are expressed in the first two volumes.

I was not told specifically that the preface would not be written and I therefore feel it is better to wait a few more days before finding out what Hitler actually intends to do.

Cerruti

---

309. Luciano Mascia, a first secretary of legation, second class, was secretary of the Press Office.

A58

VALENTINO BOMPIANI
PUBLISHING COMPANY S.A.

Milan, February 12, 1934-XII

Hon. PRESS OFFICE of
THE HEAD OF THE GOVERNMENT
Foreign Department
ROME

We don't wish to step out of line but, as we already informed your honorable office as of January 13th, the book by His Excellency the Reich Chancellor "La mia battaglia" is ready.

In spite of the kind messages from your honorable office as of January 22nd and despite our direct contacts with the publisher of the original German edition we still have not received the preface to the Italian edition that had been promised.

We take the liberty of asking whether we should continue to wait, or if some communication has reached the Royal Embassy in Berlin or we should proceed with the publication of the book without the preface, which would no doubt be detrimental to the sales of the work.

With best regards,

Valentino Bompiani
Publishing Company Inc.
The Managing Director
Valentino Bompiani

A59

PRESS OFFICE of the
HEAD OF THE GOVERNMENT   Telegram n. 1513 PR/41
Foreign Department   Outgoing
Addressed to ITALDIPLI
BERLIN
In code
Rome, February 16, 1934 24:00 hours
(Text) Y.E. telegram n. 27. Bompiani publishing insists on the immediate publication of the book delaying the publication of the third volume for a later date.

Kindly telegraph if you think you can secure the quick delivery of the promised preface which would otherwise be dispensed with.

Ciano
(Sapuppo)

A60

732/157   Rome, February 17, 1934-XII
Dear Mr. Bompiani,
    I am answering your letter of the 12th.
    I had not answered your previous requests since Berlin had led us to believe that delivery of the preface was imminent and they had told us they were under the impression that Hitler preferred to delay publication of the Italian edition of "Mein Kampf" until after the publication of the 3rd volume which he is in the process of compiling right now in Germany so that all three volumes could be published at the same time in Italy. We have cabled Berlin as of today to say whether the 3rd volume could be published later on and asking if we could still expect to receive Hitler's preface in this case adding that in the final analysis we could also do without it.
    I shall send you the response we receive from Berlin.
    With very best regards,

Sapuppo

Mr. Valentino Bompiani
via S. Paolo, 10
Milan

A61

Incoming Telegram
N. 1496 P.R.
From: R. Embassy   Berlin, 2/17/34 XII. 13:20 hours
    Berlin   Rome, same 14:30 hours
Destination: Press
Re: Bompiani Publishing
55- Y.E. Telegram n. 41

I conferred with the Secretary of State at the Reich Chancellery. Hitler is in Bavaria and shall return only in the next four days. We agreed that I would then be finally told whether or not we will get the preface.

Cerruti

A62

VALENTINO BOMPIANI
PUBLISHING COMPANY S.A.

Milan, February 19, 1934-XII

Excellency,

I thank you for your kind letter. At the same time I received from the Secretariat of the National Socialist Party in Berlin the enclosed letter[310] where as you shall see there is the mention of a contract of which I was unaware requesting that proofs be sent for correction.

In my previous letters to the Press Office of the Head of the Government I had mentioned that the book was already in print; it is now entirely printed.

According to the authorization sent to me by the Head of the Press Office in his letter 5663/1345 on November 8, the book is in an abridged edition and we have included the entire second part containing the movement's program while we abridged the first autobiographical section.

---

310. See A63 where Bompiani provides an editorial translation.

A letter from Your Excellency n. 5473/1304 dated October 21, 1933 informed me that "The Embassy in Berlin answered as of the 17th of this month that the Chancellor has stated that he would gladly write the preface for the Italian edition of "Mein Kampf" and reserves the right to send it as soon as he obtains it." It is possible that the Secretariat of the National Socialist Party was not informed of the promise made which explains what was said in the enclosed letter.

Awaiting a further communication from Your Excellency I remain with highest regards

Valentino Bompiani

To His Excellency G. Sapuppo
Press Office of the Head of the Government
Rome

A63

VALENTINO BOMPIANI
PUBLISHING COMPANY S.A.
<u>Franz Eher, Munich, February 14, 1934</u>

"Regarding Your letter and the telegram[311] about the Chancellor's preface for the Italian edition of his book LA MIA BATTAGLIA, we inform You of the following:

The Chancellor has until now refused to write introductions or prefaces for the foreign editions of his book. It is therefore not possible to satisfy Your request to provide a preface by the Chancellor.

At the same time we wish to point out that in the course of the agreements we entered into with the Consulate General of Italy there was no mention of a preface.

We have noted with satisfaction that the Italian edition of the book is very close to publication. According to paragraph 6 of the contract dated May 30, 1933, we have the right to check the Italian edition for its accuracy with respect to the German edition. Kindly send us the proofs of the book. It is especially important to us that the Italian edition correspond exactly with the German edition."

---

311. Bompiani had already written directly to Eher Publishing (see Doc. A58).

A64

Rome, February 22, 1934-XII
809/168

Dear Mr. Bompiani,

I immediately answer your letter of February 19th.

There actually is a contract that was negotiated on a pro forma basis only with the German publisher "Mein Kampf"[312] however article 6 reads as follows:

"The translation expenses from German to Italian shall be borne by the Italian Publishing Company. The translator must be an Italian citizen.

To ensure that the Italian text corresponds in its meaning to the original German Fr. Eher Suc., declares that it is willing to place a German speaker at the disposal of the Italian publisher to examine the Italian manuscript to ascertain that the meaning of the translation coincides with the original. The related expenses shall be incurred by the Italian publisher.

In any case the Publisher.................................... may use the services of this person offered by Fr. Eher Publishing Company only if it is deemed necessary and convenient and it shall be free to accept or reject the corrections that are proposed."

Given that now through our assignment and transfer your company is the Italian publisher, the interpretation of article 6 offered by Mr. Frz. Eher is not correct because the article itself does not mention the right to control but only <u>their</u> right to use "only if they should find it necessary or convenient the work of the trustworthy man placed at your disposal by Frz. Eher Publishing Company."

I think I should inform you at this time that the only demands that Frz. Eher Publishing can make where you are concerned are those in articles 3, 4, 7 and 8 which I am sending you in the enclosed paper.

I don't think that You will have any problem fulfilling those requirements. On the other hand by the letter of November 8 we sent

---

312. This is an obvious slip.

you a copy of the authorization given by Frz. Eher Publishing to abridge the German edition.

Finally I inform you that on the 17th of this month the R. Ambassador to Berlin cabled that Chancellor Hitler was in Bavaria and would return after 4 or 5 days and only then would we be able to know whether or not the preface would be available.

Kindly accept, dear Mr. Bompiani, the expression of my best regards.

Sapuppo

Mr. Valentino Bompiani
via S. Paolo, 10
Milan

A65

VALENTINO BOMPIANI
PUBLISHING COMPANY S.A.

Milan, February 26, 1934 XII
Reply to the Registered Letter 22/2 809/168

Excellency,
Many, many thanks for your clarifying letter. I shall stick to what was established in the clause of the contract that you sent me as we still wait for the answer on the preface from Chancellor Hitler.

Respectfully yours.

Valentino Bompiani

To His Excellency SAPUPPI [*sic*]
Press Office of the Head of the Government
Foreign Section
Rome

A66

Incoming Telegram
n. 1981 P.R.
From: R. Embassy   Berlin, 3-3-34 – XII 20:12 hours
Berlin   Rome same   24:00 hours
Destination: Press
Re: Bompiani publisher
81-My telegram n. 55
The Reich Chancellor has sent me the text of the preface for the Italian edition of his book "Mein Kampf."

    I will send it in the next pouch.   Cerruti

A67

TELEGRAM FROM BOMPIANI
MINISTER SAPUPPO MINISTRY OF FOREIGN AFFAIRS ROME
Milan, March 5, 1934 1840 hours

    Grateful for a reply regarding the preface by Hitler kindly excuse this request.
    Regards Bompiani

A68

995/217

          Rome, March 5, 1934-XII

<u>URGENT</u>
    Dear Mr. Bompiani,
    Further to the letter of February 22 I am pleased to inform You that our Embassy in Berlin has cabled that it has received the text of the preface from the Reich Chancellor for the Italian edition of his book. The text will arrive with the first pouch from Berlin. As soon as we receive it I shall be sure to send it over to You.
    With best regards.

          Signed: Sapuppo

Mr. Valentino Bompiani
via S. Paolo, 10
Milan

A69

Press Office
Of the
Head of the Government
Foreign Section

Telegram n. 208 PR
outgoing

Addressed to Bompiani Publishing
via San Paolo 10
Milan
Re: Preface by Hitler
Clear transmission
Rome, 3-6-1934 23:00 hours

(Text) Preface by Hitler will reach Rome next Thursday. Sapuppo

A70[313]

R. Embassy of Italy
Berlin

Telexpress N. 0985/390
Addressed to
Press Office of the Head of the
Government—Foreign Section
Rome

(Position) St. 6

Berlin, March 6, 1934—Year XII

(Re) "Mein Kampf" Preface by Chancellor Hitler
(Ref) My telegram n. 81 of the 2nd of this month

Following my telegram as mentioned above I have the honor to send the enclosed the preface written by the Reich Chancellor for the Italian edition of his work "Mein Kampf".[314]

I should point out the mistake that is in the copy of the text itself because instead of "Nationalsozialismus" one reads "Nationalismus."

I also thought it best to provide a "literal" translation of the preface[315] that may be useful to the publisher in drafting a better and

---

313. The page has the mark that Mussolini viewed the document and also underlined the "Ref."
314. See photo.

more fluid text which before publication must be quickly returned to my attention to be sent to Chancellor Hitler as he requested.

I shall certainly be sure to inform Rome of the go ahead for this translation as received in order to avoid any further delay in the publication of the Italian translation of "Mein Kampf".

V. Cerruti

A71[316]

LITERAL TRANSLATION

Peoples that are struggling for sublime national ideals possess life strength and the promise of the future. They hold their own destiny in their hands. Their forces often build alliances and gain international value that are more beneficial for the coexistence of peoples than the "immortal ideas" of liberalism which confuse and poison the relationships between Nations. Fascism and National Socialism, which are intimately akin to each other in their basic ideals are called upon to show new paths for fruitful international cooperation. To understand their deepest meaning and their essence means to serve World Peace and therefore the well being of Peoples.

Berlin, March 2, 1934
Adolf Hitler

---

315. See the following document.
316. A copy of this translation is also in ASDMAE, MAE, Gabinetto 1919–43, b. Gab. 354, f. Pubblicazioni di Adolf Hitler. Con annotazioni di Suvich [Publications by Adolf Hitler. With annotations by Suvich.]

A72

1100/236

Rome, March 10, 1934-XII

Dear Mr. Bompiani,

I send you the preface by Chancellor Hitler for the Italian edition of his book "Mein Kampf" as soon as we received it from the R. Embassy in Berlin in its original German text to which the R. Embassy has added a literal translation.[317]

I would be grateful if you could have the same person that handled the translation of the book draft a better more readable translation and return it to my attention very urgently since Chancellor Hitler informed us that he wishes to see the Italian text of his preface before authorizing publication.

With best regards

Sapuppo

Mr. Valentino Bompiani
via S. Paolo, 10
Milan

A73

VALENTINO BOMPIANI
PUBLISHING COMPANY S.A.

Milan, March 12, 1934 XII

Excellency,

I confirm receipt of the preface by Chancellor Hitler for the Italian edition of his book "Mein Kampf" and send you a copy of the translation that will be included in the Italian edition. I would be very grateful to have the authorization sent by telegram.

With warmest regards.

Valentino Bompiani

To His Excellency Minister Sapuppo
Rome

---

317. See Doc. A71.

A74[318]

VALENTINO BOMPIANI
PUBLISHING COMPANY S.A.

<u>Preface to the Italian Edition</u>

Those peoples who are fighting for sublime national ideals possess life forces and a rich future. They hold their own destiny in their own hands. Often their forces create a community having international values with better results for the coexistence of peoples than the "immortal principles" of liberalism that muddy and poison the relationships among Nations.

Fascism and National Socialism, intimately connected in their basic attitude and worldview, have as their mission to open new paths toward fruitful international collaboration. Understanding them in their deepest meaning and their essence means to contribute to world peace and therefore to the welfare of peoples.

Adolf Hitler

Berlin, March 2, 1934.

A75

Press Office	Telexpress n. 1147/37
Of the Head of the Government	Addressed to:
Foreign Section	R. Embassy of Italy
	Berlin

Rome, Mar. 13, 1934 Year XII

(Re) Italian edition of "Mein Kampf"

(Text) Enclosed is the translation of the preface that was dictated by the Chancellor for the Italian edition of his book in the text drafted by the translator of the Bompiani edition and we will be grateful if you can possibly send your approval by telegram.

Signed: Sapuppo

---

318. Final text as published.

A76

Incoming Telegram
n. 2761 P.R.
From: R. Embassy   Berlin, 3-23-1934- XII 14:18 hours
Berlin   Rome   "   17:00 hours
Destination: Press Foreign-Rome
Re: Preface Italian Text
104 –Telexpress from Y.E. n. 1147/37.

Hitler has approved the Italian text of the preface.

                                          Cerruti

A77

Press Office   Telegram n. 2712 P.R.
Of the   outgoing
Head of the Government
Foreign Section
Addressed to Mr. Valentino Bompiani
via San Paolo 10
Milan
Clear transmission
Rome, 23 MAR 1934 Year XII- 24:00 hours

(Text) Italian translation of preface approved.

                                        Sapuppo

A78

La mia battaglia [*Mein Kampf*]

Il Popolo d'Italia, April 3, 1934, p. 2

The publication by the Bompiani publishing company of—*Hitler: La mia battaglia*—is certainly of great current interest.

After hearing all kinds of things about National Socialism and its Führer, Hitler's book provides a clarification that will be very effective in allowing us to understand the man in his dimensions, his ideas, his struggles and fortunes and the movement which we still cannot determine whether it is tied to the movements of yesterday or more decisively to a new Germany in its historical, environmental, political and doctrinal genesis and in its future strength.

The historical part of the book is alive, captivating and fascinating. The other part is original yes, but rather boring such as the philosophical systems, and German ones particularly, even though they may be interesting and contemporary such as Hitler's.

The political and ideological views of this successful agitator are extremely simple and began to form during the war then crystallized in his mind and spirit immediately after the war ended.

He patiently and meticulously worked on it like a chemist and once he was ready he joined the German Workers Party that had a total of seven members in 1919. And he marched ahead.

The project and the system that follow the preliminary views held that:

1. Nationalist racism and dynastic patriotism are different.

2. The victorious march of the best race is the condition for the progress of the whole human race and this belongs to the Aryan race responsible for all of civilization's achievements.

3. It's not enough to engage in a positive struggle for one's objectives, in order to conquer the soul of the people one must destroy those who oppose one's goals. Success is the only measure in this world of what is right and wrong with such an enterprise.

4. The Nation or better, the race, consists not of language but only of blood.

5. The State is not an end but a means. It is not the promise of the creation of a superior human civilization but its cause, which is the proper race for civilization.

6. As a State the German Reich must include all Germans and has the duty to select and preserve among the people the most precious of the original elements of race and slowly but surely take them to a predominant position. It will be a greater honor to be a street cleaner in that kind of Reich than to be king in a foreign country.

Then he turned to the targets of the struggle and set them as the bourgeoisie and Jewish Marxism. The seven men, in seven years, became the entire German people.

Since then the goals and the terms of internal, economic, religious, international and world policy were clear: the supreme triumph of the German race in the world.

Reading these pages, that are more methodical than passionate and filled with a transcendental mysticism and courageous realism including a cynical kind of brutality, places us in front of the spirit and the anxious meditations of the entire German setting: Arminius, Luther, Frederick, Kant, Marx, the Wilhelms, Bismarck, Liebtenecht [*sic*] Einstein, Hindenburg, Hitler: the contingent, the worse and the excellent.

In his preface Hitler states that Fascism and National Socialism are intimately connected by their attitude toward a vision of the world whose mission it is to open new paths.

The entire book however underscores differences rather than similarities. Berlin is doggedly attached to the idealistic prejudices of a preset system closed within the German idea, seeking absolute, universal domination by one race over all the others.

Rome, free and elastic in its human realism and the strength of its universal ideas, seeks to teach.

This is what is suggested in this book. Let us wait for the verdict of history.

Farinata

Appendix B[319]

Excerpts of "Mein Kampf" read by Mussolini

From the book "Mein Kampf" by Adolf Hitler pp. 741–744[320]

The "populist" political movement must not be the advocate of foreign peoples but the vanguard of its own people. It becomes useless any other way and has above all no right to sulk about the past, because otherwise it acts exactly like it. Just as old German policy was very much influenced by dynastic considerations, that of the future, in order to avoid repeating the same mistake, must not be allowed to be overtaken by internationalist sentimentality. In particular we must not be policemen protecting those well-known "poor" and "small peoples" but only be the soldiers of our own people.

---

319. Italics are used in the original as in the titles. At first there was another "chapter" planned but it does not appear to have been compiled: "Ideas on Russia and Germany's Eastern policy." We have checked this "translation" against the cit. Houghton Mifflin edition of *Mein Kampf,* while respecting the Italian interpretation, which is sometimes very different.

320. On the front page are the following notes initialed by Suvich: "Make one more excerpt of the whole section that is in the news at this time in M.K." Also: "What happened with the publisher, etc. Ciano has to give me 250.000 lire. Suvich." In different handwriting and almost certainly that of Mussolini himself: "Received from Torella 16 December XII," meaning 1933. Raimondo Torella was the Secretary of the Cabinet at the Ministry of Foreign Affairs. It is based precisely on the indications above that we can attribute to Mussolini—who was the minister—the pencil underlining that we indicated. The pages had reached him obviously in "clean" condition and he proceeded to underline them without initialing them; they thus were not underlined a second time by the staff because they were intended to remain as reference texts. On the other hand any additional notes by the staff (more often the Under Secretary) were initialed.

We National Socialists must proceed yet further: the right to have land can become a duty when a people appears destined to face ruin without additional territory. Even more so when this doesn't concern some small Negro people but that of the great Germanic mother that has given the fruit of its culture to today's world. Germany will either become a world power or it will not exist at all. But to become a world power it requires the kind of magnitude that will insure its importance at this time and provide for the livelihood of its citizens.

(Return to the subject of Eastern policy)

In this way we National Socialists consciously put an end to the foreign policy initiatives of our pre-war era. We begin where it ended, six centuries ago.

We stop the centuries-old movement of the Germanic people toward southern and western Europe and turn our eyes toward the lands to our East. We finally end the colonial and commercial policy of the pre-war period and initiate the future policy of territorial expansion. But if we speak today of new territories in Europe, we can only think first of all about Russia and the border states under her control.

Destiny itself appears to want to show us a sign.

By handing over of Russia to Bolshevism it deprived the Russian people of its intellectual class, which had until then determined and guaranteed its existence as a State.

Because the creation of a Russian state organism was not the result of the constructive political qualities of Slavism in Russia but rather simply the marvelous example of the creative activity of Germanic elements within an inferior race. Many powerful kingdoms on this earth were created this way. Inferior peoples having Germanic organizers and leaders at the helm increased many times over until they became huge states that lasted as long as they kept the nucleus that had created the State. Over the centuries Russia used up this nucleus of top ruling classes. Today it must be considered destroyed and extinct. The Jew has taken its place. Just as it is impossible for the Russians to rid themselves of the Jewish yoke on their own it is also impossible for the Jews to preserve the powerful state. The Jew is not an element that organizes but a ferment of decomposition. The gigantic Eastern Empire is ripe for collapse. And the end of the Judaic domination in Russia will mark the end of Russia as a State. We have been chosen by destiny to become the witness of a catastrophe that shall be the most powerful confirmation of racial theory supported by the populist movement.

Our task, the mission of the National Socialist political movement, is instead to bring our people to political awareness by revealing its goal for the future, not in the exhilarating vision of the new expedition of Alexander the Great but rather in the patient work of the German plough to which the sword will only provide the soil.

(*Bismarck's policy through Russia*)

It is natural that the Jews should be resolutely opposed to such a policy. They better than anyone else understand how important this kind of action is to their future. This very fact should be enough to persuade all really national minded men of the correctness of this new orientation. Unfortunately it is the opposite that takes place. Not just within German-nationalist circles but even among the populists there is strong opposition to the idea of such an Eastern policy, and as always in such circumstances, they invoke the authority of a great man. They cite the spirit of Bismarck to defend what is in fact an unreasonable policy that is impossible and highly damaging to the German people. Bismarck is said to have always thought that good relations with Russia were very important. In a certain sense this is correct. <u>But they forget to mention that Bismarck also thought it was just as important to have good relations with Italy, for example; that the same Mr. Bismarck once allied himself with Italy in order to better finish off Austria. Why is this policy not continued today? They will answer that today's Italy is not the same as it was then. But dear gentlemen, you must then accept the fact that today's Russia is not what it used to be. Bismarck never had in mind to lay down a general political directive,</u> in his political game that was meant to last forever. He was much to effective as the "master of the moment" to be tied to such a commitment. But then shouldn't the question be: "What did Bismarck do at that time?" but rather "What would he do today?"—and it is much easier to answer the latter question. In his political wisdom he would never ally himself to a state that is destined to ruin.

Furthermore Bismarck had already engaged in German colonial and commercial policy with a very different vision because he was above all interested in securing the best internal consolidation of the state system he had created. This was the only reason he welcomed the Russian alliance at that time which covered his back giving him a free hand in the west. The difference being however that what was profitable for Germany at that time would be damaging today.

I[321]

IDEAS ON AUSTRIA

as expressed by Hitler in "Mein Kampf"

During the time he spent in Vienna especially Hitler thinks like a German irredentist "a rebel not against the Nation or the State but against a system that threatened to be the cause of the demise of the Germans." The dynastic interests of the Habsburgs had not simply paralyzed the Germanic mission of the Eastern Mark, but also threatened to destroy its German identity. This idea reinforced [missing word] antipathy toward the Habsburg state that had become the scourge of Germanism. His heart was separated from Austria and had a single burning dream: "the annexation (Anschluss) of his birthplace which he loved so much to the common homeland, the German Reich."

Vienna was corroded by the infiltration of many Slavic elements, especially the Czechs and was polluted by a mass of Jews. This metropolis—he writes verbatim—made him think of a huge incest. Every form of politics originating in Vienna, be it internal or foreign, was mistaken and illogical. He was uncomfortable with parliamentarism, not from a personal standpoint or because he already favored dictatorship, but because he saw the Austrian variety as unworthy of the great English model and because the Germans had been reduced to a minority.

---

321. The text bears the "seen" mark and underlinings by Mussolini.

Even religion is considered only from the national point of view. The decision made by the Habsburgs to convert Austria into a Slavic State to preserve territorial unity had brought many Czech priests to German parishes. As a reaction to this attack the cry "Away from Rome" (Los von Rom) was being increasingly repeated, which according to pan-German deputy Schönerer, who was an uncompromising man, could actually mend the fateful division of the Church in Germany if it took hold. However, both the assumptions and the conclusions of this religious struggle were wrong.

A wise and positive middle ground to save Austria without ruining the Germans and the Catholic religion had been followed by the Christian-Social party under the leadership of Burgmeister Lueger "the most important German Burgmeister of Vienna of all time" who failed to reach his objective for two reasons: religious anti-Semitism[322] and his lack of clarity as to the means to be used to achieve his ends. The end result being that both the house of Habsburg and the Catholic church failed to get the boost they hoped for. The Habsburgs lost their throne and the Vatican lost the support of a great State.

Hitler was most sympathetic towards the pan-German Party not only because one of its members had the courage to cry out in the Austrian parliament "Long Live the Hohenzollern," but also because he took every opportunity to declare that the Germans in Austria were simply part of the German Reich. The deputy Schönerer had understood very clearly the fateful end awaiting Austria.

Hitler laughed at those harboring illusions of being able to preserve for a long time the disjointed mosaic of the Habsburg State. Since "his heart had never throbbed for that State but only dreamt of a German Empire, he happily waited for the hour of its demise because that would mean the redemption of the German nation." He therefore decided to leave Austria and go to Munich in Bavaria. When he heard the news that the Archduke Ferdinand of Austria had been assassinated at Sarajevo at first he feared that the shots had been fired by German nationalist students. As soon as it became clear that those who did the shooting were Serbs he trembled that an inscrutable destiny had exacted its strange vengeance: the greatest among Slavophiles had been

---

322. "Meaning: confessional and nonracist." Translator's footnote.

murdered by Slav fanatics. At the same time he intuitively understood two things: first of all that war was inevitable, and second that the Habsburg State would be forced to keep its alliance with Germany which Hitler always doubted especially if Germany was the one to initiate hostilities. Austrian political trends would have certainly shown no interest in Germany's fate.

Hitler therefore exonerates Viennese government circles from the accusation of having pushed the State into a war that could have been avoided. The Serbs were relentless provocateurs. Furthermore Austrian and German foreign policies had made the mistake of delaying this inevitable war until the most unfavorable moment. The war would decide the fate of the German nation. From that point of view Austria's disappearance was a fundamentally positive outcome.

Regarding the Triple Alliance and Italy, Hitler writes on page 142:

"Had the history and psychology of peoples been better studied in Germany it would have been unthinkable for the Quirinal and Vienna's Hofburg to be side by side in case of war. Italy would have exploded like a volcano sooner had a government dared to send even a single soldier to the battlefield alongside Austria that was hated with such fanaticism. I was able to witness at various times in Vienna the passionate contempt and unlimited hatred with which the Italians showed their "attachment" to the Austrian State. The House of Habsburg had accumulated too many sins against Italian freedom and independence during the centuries for these to be forgotten even with every good intention. Goodwill incidentally didn't exist either in the people or in the government. Italy was therefore placed in front of two alternatives with respect to Austria: either alliance or war."
December 19, 1933-XII

II.[323]

HITLER'S IDEAS ON ITALY AND ALTO ADIGE

extracted from "Mein Kampf"

Italy does not appear as a main topic; therefore a complete picture is not available; ideas are offered off and on.

The most important angle from which Hitler approaches Italy concerns its feelings towards Germany and therefore the possibility of an alliance. The Alto Adige issue is also viewed from the point of view of international relations.

On page 162 in discussing the Triple Alliance he writes: "Germany lost its best opportunities for alliances because of Austria; actually it experienced growing tension with Russia and Italy. In spite of all this the mood in Rome was pro-German since all Italians were often raucously and violently anti-Austrian."

On page 699–700 in discussing the alliances that Germany could enter into for its daily struggle for existence he indicates only England and Italy. "Italy cannot want French hegemony in Europe to increase. Italy's future shall always necessarily be tied to the fate of the Mediterranean. Italy was pushed into war not by the desire to aggrandize France but rather by the possibility of inflicting a mortal blow to its hated Adriatic rival. Any further strengthening of France on the continent is an obstacle to Italy in the future. One should not be deluded by the idea that the close affinity of peoples might eliminate their rivalries."

On page 755, in reexamining the issue of Germany's future alliances he states: "If Germany approached England and Italy this would certainly not create a danger of war. France, the only power who would react against this new bloc, would be unable to go to war. The alliance would allow Germany to quietly make those preparations that

---

323. In the margin there is a notation by Suvich: "When was this written?" A note from the Cabinet answered this question on January 10: the first volume up to p. 405 was published in 1925; the second, pages 406–782 in 1927.

will become necessary given this coalition for a reckoning with France. The most important characteristic of this alliance would be that upon its conclusion Germany would no longer be faced with the threat of enemy invasion and would have split the alliance of the Entente that was the cause of so many disasters for Germany and consequently France, Germany's mortal enemy, would be isolated. Assuming even that at first it would only be a moral success, its effect would suffice to give extraordinary freedom of movement to Germany."

Hitler's ideas and statements about Alto Adige are clear and explicit.

Page 520: "I have had to use all my energies many times to make sure that the ship of our movement is not rocked by artificial waves. The last such occasion was when our infernal press succeeded in puffing up the issue of Alto Adige in a way that could become fatal to the German people. Out of cowardice towards public opinion that is being fanned by the Jews, many so-called "nationalists" have joined the chorus that was protesting against a regime that we Germans precisely because of the situation we are in, should consider a ray of sunshine amid this decaying world. While the international Jew is clutching at our throat, our so-called patriots scream against the man and the regime who dared at least in one point of the globe to free themselves from the Judeo-Masonic pincers!"

Page 707: "I must refer to another favorite subject of the Jews: Alto Adige. I wish to point out that I for one belong to the group of people who having to take a position on the fate of Alto Adige—from the beginning of August 1914 to November 1918—were on the side that was actually doing something to defend that territory by serving in the army. I didn't fight so that the Alto Adige would be lost but to keep it in the homeland just as any other German region. Since the preservation of Alto Adige was not protected by the shameful harangues the brilliant parliamentarians on Vienna's "Rathausplatz" (Municipal Square) or in front of the "Feldherrnhalle" (national war monument) in Munich but only by the battalions fighting at the front.

Those who broke that front have betrayed Alto Adige as much as every other German territory. However those who think they can resolve the problem of Alto Adige today by protests, statements, processions and the like is either a wretched man or a pacifist to the bitter end.[324] We must be convinced that the taking back of lost regions cannot happen with solemn appeals to Almighty God or by cultivating pious hopes in a League of Nations, but only by force of arms."

Page 709: "There is something truly delightful, which is to see how the Viennese legitimists now raise their head to reconquer Alto Adige. Seven years ago their august dynasty took a false oath making it possible for the world coalition could also acquire the Alto Adige. These circles then supported the policy of treason of their dynasty and did not care a fig about Alto Adige. It is naturally much easier to begin once more today the fight for these lands since we are using "spiritual" weapons. Instead the reason why certain circles have turned the issue of the Alto Adige into the focal point of Italo-German relations is obvious. The Jews and the Habsburg legitimists have the greatest interest to want to thwart a German policy of alliances that could one day bring about the rebirth of the free German homeland. All the noise made today doesn't originate out of love of the Alto Adige—which is far from helpful and actually damaging—but out of the fear of a possible Italo-German understanding. These lying and infamous circles claim that we "betrayed" Alto Adige. No! Alto Adige was "betrayed" by:

a. all those who did not give their all for the homeland in 1914–1918;

b. all those who didn't commit themselves completely to more resistance;

c. all those who tolerated or helped the revolution of November 1918;

d. all those political parties and politicians who signed the shameful treaties of Versailles and Saint Germain.[325]

Today I begin with this realistic point of view: lost territories can't be reconquered with wordy sentences but only through a bloody struggle. I do not hesitate to say that, since the die is cast, not only do I feel that it is impossible to recapture the Alto Adige through war but

---

324. Hitler's original text reads "speissbürger" and the Houghton Mifflin edition translates it correctly as "petit bourgeois." The Italian version given here was completely "Italianaized" using the term "panciafichisti" a slang term that originated during World War I.

325. Point d. was omitted in the Houghton Mifflin edition.

also that I would personally be opposed to it convinced that in this case it would be impossible to muster the enthusiasm of the entire German people required for victory. On the contrary, I think that if one day we must sacrifice our blood it would be a crime to do so for two hundred thousand Germans while some seven million other Germans are suffering under a foreign yoke and while the region that is a vital artery for the German people has been turned into a square where hordes of African Negroes are bivouacked.

If the German nation wishes to put an end to the current state of affairs that could lead to its extermination it must not repeat the prewar mistake and make enemies of God and the rest of the world; it will have to discover the most dangerous enemy and attack it with all its strength. If this victory can be achieved elsewhere through sacrifices then future generations will not condemn us. They will know how to appreciate the serious needs, the profound worries, and therefore also the bitter decisions, the success coming from that sacrifice will be glorious."

Fascism and its leader are mentioned only twice but always with sympathy.

On page 774, in discussing the struggle of the German people against Marxism he says: "At this time—I must sincerely confess—I have felt the deepest admiration for the great Man south of the Alps who, because of his fervent love for his people did not make any deals with Italy's internal enemies but attempted to destroy them by every necessary means. What will give Mussolini a place among the great men of this world is his determination in not allowing Italy to fall apart because of Marxism and having saved the homeland by bringing ruin to internationalism."

On pages 720–721, speaking of fascism's war on Freemasonry he says: "Only in a <u>single</u> State can state authority be considered strong enough and serving the country's interests so well that one can no longer talk about its political requirements being thwarted by internationalist Judaism. The struggle by Fascist Italy against the three main weapons of Judaism, even though it [Fascist Italy] is not fully aware of it (of which I am not convinced) is the best indication that, perhaps indirectly, even the poison teeth of this supra-state power can be torn out. The suppression of secret Masonic societies, the persecution of the supranational press, the final ruin of international Marxism and, conversely, the constant consolidation of the idea of the fascist state will allow the Italian government in the next few years to serve the interests of its people disregarding the hiss of Judiac hydra." December 22, 1933-Year XII-

III.[326]

HITLER'S THOUGHTS ON FRANCE,
THE TREATY OF VERSAILLES, AND THE RUHR

extracted from "Mein Kampf"

France is considered mainly from the geographic, historical, political and military vantage points.

The geographic position (page 625): "France is protected by nature in its southern borders with Spain and with Italy. It is safe on the German side due to the impotence of our homeland. Its coast extends over a long front is located in front of the vital centers of the British Empire. The English vital centers are good targets for French long-range cannon and planes. A submarine war against England coming from the Atlantic coast of France and its possessions in Africa and the Mediterranean would have disastrous effects on England."

The mongrelization of the race (page 730): "Should France continue to develop as it is doing now for another three centuries, the last remnants of Frankish blood would disappear in a new state of part-European and part-African mulattos. It would become a compact and enormous territory from the Rhine to the Congo, filled with a lower race produced by continuous mongrelization."

The historical enmity (page 699): "France is and will always be the mortal, inexorable enemy of the German people. It does not matter much to know who was reigning over it, whether it is the Bourbons,

---

326. On the first sheet there is Mussolini's mark "seen." Further down one underlining.

the Jacobins, the Napoleonic people, the bourgeois democrats, the clerical republicans or the red Bolsheviks. The final goal of its policies will always be to take possession of the border of the Rhine and control that river, breaking up and scattering Germany."

Political goals (page 696): France will always want to prevent the formation of a unified power in Germany and to perpetuate therefore a system of small German states, in a balance of power amongst themselves, without a common guide, while France occupies the left bank of the Rhine as a requirement of its hegemony in Europe.

Page 765: "I am firmly convinced that France's intentions toward us will never change because of the simple fact that they are part and parcel of the spirit of self preservation of the French nation. If I were French and loved the greatness of France as much as I love and hold sacred that of Germany I also would not and could not act any differently than Clemenceau."

Page 766: "As long as the centuries old duel between Germany and France shall be fought only as a German defense against a French attack it will never come to a decision and Germany will lose its positions from one century to the next. All one needs to do is follow the movements of the German linguistic borders, from the 12th century until today to become painfully convinced that we Germans have already been seriously injured."

Page 705: "What France, spurred by its obsession with revenge and led by the Jews, is doing in Europe is a political crime against the existence of the white race and will bring upon that people all the thunderous vengeance of a generation that will discover that the capital sin of humanity is in the mongrelization of the race. The French threat makes it a duty for Germany to set aside all sentimentalism and extend its hand to he who threatened as he is like us, will neither suffer nor tolerate the domineering tendencies of France. Germany can have only two allies in Europe in the near future: England and Italy."

Regarding the *Treaty of Versailles* Hitler's ideas and judgments are strangely very short and not very clear.

On pages 518 and 523 the only mention is of National Socialist Party propaganda against the treaty.

Only one strong but isolated sentence is at page 714: "When in 1919 the peace treaty was imposed on Germany one would have thought that this instrument of oppression would have favored German aspirations for freedom. Peace treaties whose clauses strike at peoples likes a whip are often the signal of a future revolt."

There are instead many more judgments by Hitler on the *Rhur.*

Page 767: "By occupying the Rhur, France was hoping not only to break Germany's moral pride forever but also to lock her into an economic web to force her willingly or not to accept the heaviest obligations... Instead through this occupation, fate has once again extended to the German people the hand that would help it rise again."

Page 619: "The occupation of the Rhur that took place during the first months of 1923 was of great importance to the development of National Socialist squad fighters. It is not possible or advisable for reasons of national interest to speak or write about it too openly. I can only say that this subject has already been discussed in public proceedings and therefore the public is well enough informed."

Page 768: "The occupation of the Rhur has changed Italy's feelings toward France: the post war resentment having turned into hatred. This was the great historical moment where yesterday's allies could become the enemies of tomorrow. If things went differently and the allies didn't fight among themselves from one minute to the next, as it happened in the second Balkan war, the reason is that Germany didn't have an Enver Pacha but Chancellor Cuno instead..."

Page 769: "France by occupying the Rhur had accomplished a conspicuous breach of the Treaty of Versailles and clashed with various guarantor powers and especially England and Italy..."

IV.

HITLER'S THOUGHTS ON ENGLAND

extracted from "Mein Kampf"

Hitler's ideas on England can be summarized in a few basic concepts:

Prewar Germany had a mistaken opinion of British psychology. England sought to maintain a balance on the European continent allowing it to move freely in the rest of the world by preventing a single European state to rise and dominate the others. When Germany intended to overtake England the latter used the first opportunity to strangle its rising rival. It even went to war but without reaching a result that was commensurate with its goal. Since Germany is no longer a world power, England has changed its opinion but is still drawn in by the Judaic influence.

Here are Hitler's exact words:

Pages 158–159: "In Germany through education, the press and satirical magazines create a false view of the English mentality, which everyone considered as basically nothing but <u>a smart and cunning but fundamentally cowardly businessman</u>. This misconception would later take its bitter revenge. I still remember the amazement on the faces of my comrades when we faced the "Tommies" in Flanders. No one could believe that those Scotsmen were not identical to those they knew from the satirical magazines and the articles written by our journalists."

Page 746: "I remember the childish hopes of our "populist" circles in 1920-21 when they thought England was about to give up because of India. Some smart Asian, perhaps a true supporter of Indian independence, succeeded in spreading this idea, (it contradicted the other that held that India was of capital value to England) and penetrated the mind of those people ready to accept preset ideas…"

On page 747: "The hopes placed in the legendary revolt in Egypt are also just as meaningless. The "holy war" may give our soft types the thrill of seeing others ready to bleed each other for our benefit: but it is also certain that such a war would quickly end under the fire of machine guns and a rain of British bombs."

Pages 691–699: "For three centuries the history of our continent was determined by England's efforts to further its worldwide plans using indirect agreements among European states. The traditional direction of British diplomacy, which Germany opposed only with the Prussian army, had been set since the times of Queen Elizabeth at preventing any great European power from rising above the rest and using any means to do so, even war if necessary."

"England viewed Germany as a nation that had increased its world economic reach to the point of becoming equal to that of England."

"The British world empire struggled four and a half years to break the perceived supremacy of a continental power. A sudden collapse seemed to wipe that power off the map. Then there was such a lack of that innate spirit of conservation when the equilibrium of Europe seemed shaken by one event that lasted just 48 hours: Germany was annihilated and France had become the top continental European power..."

"England had no interest in having Germany disappear from the face of the earth; on the contrary, the awful collapse of December 1918 placed British diplomacy in front of a new and unexpected situation: England had not reached its war goal; it had actually helped another European power impose itself, more so even than Germany, thus disturbing the balance of the continent... The final objective of French diplomacy would always be opposed to British statecraft..."

"England doesn't want Germany to be a world power; France on the other hand doesn't even want there to be a Germany. This is a big difference. Today we are not fighting to be a world power but only to conserve the existence of our homeland, the unity of our nation, the daily bread of our children. If starting from that point we look for allies in Europe only two states remain: England and Italy..."

Page 721: In England a country of the "deepest democracy" the Jews (contrary to the case of Italy) are indirectly dominant and almost unchecked through public opinion. Yet there is also a relentless struggle among those who represent British interests and those wishing to institute a universal Jewish dictatorship...

Page 702: "Jewish finance, contrary to British interests, would like to bring about not just the economic destruction of Germany but also its complete political enslavement."

V.

HITLER'S IDEAS ON "RACE" AND "JUDAISM"

extracted from "Mein Kampf"[327]

In the scattered forest of Hitler's ideas, the most revolutionary in "Mein Kampf" (a book that is guided by an autobiographical line), the most original and the most interesting is race, since its corollary anti-Semitism explains several measures taken by Hitler once he became Head of the Government.

But it is best to let Hitler speak for himself:

Page 428: "The character of a people, or better its race, is not to be found in language but in the blood..."

Page 316: "Everything we admire on this earth today—science, art, technology, and discoveries—is the inventive product of a few peoples and perhaps at the origin of a single race...All great civilizations of the past perished only because that initial creative race became extinct following a poisoning of the blood (mixture)..."

Page 312: "Any mix of two human beings who are not perfectly equal produces an average result that is half that of his parents. This means that the Son will be higher than the lower half (by race) of his parents but will never reach the height of the half that is superior. Consequently in a struggle against this superior half he will necessarily be defeated. But this coupling is contrary to nature's will since it tends to perfect life. Such a result is not attained by the union of superior elements with those that are inferior but from the unconditional victory of the first. The strongest is the one that must dominate and not couple with the weaker one, thus sacrificing his own greatness..."

Page 313: "History offers us numerous examples in support of this fact—it teaches us with impressive clarity how all minglings of Aryans with inferior peoples have as a final result the disappearance of the civilizing element. In North America the majority of the population is made up of Germanic elements who do not mix with inferior *colored*

---

327. On the first sheet, "V. [seen] Head of the Government. Acts." Several underlinings follow.

elements, and offers a human type and a civilization that are different from Central or South America where the majority of latin immigrants mixed with the aborigines…"

Page 436: "Our Germanic nationality, unfortunately, is no longer based on a single racial background. The process of fusion of various component parts has not progressed to the point where one can speak of a new race. On the contrary: the poisoning of the blood that has penetrated the body of our people especially following the Thirty Years' War has produced a decay not only in our blood but also in our soul. The open borders of our homeland, the contact with foreign non-Germanic elements along those borders especially the infiltration of foreign blood toward the center of the Reich because of its constant renewal, will not allow an absolute fusion. A new race is not created because foreign elements continue to coexist next to one another with the result that especially at critical moments when the flock gathers together, the German people scatter in every direction instead. Nordic men live in the proximity of Eastern peoples; the Dinarics are also near them and the Westerners are close by: in between there are also many mixes. This is a great disadvantage because the German people lacks that secure animal instinct that comes with the unity of the blood and saves nations from ruin during the most dangerous moments. The conservation of our basic elements of race that have remained intact is the reason for what we call "superindividualism." It can be sometimes useful during periods of peace; but all things considered, we must say that it is responsible for the fact that we do not dominate the world. Had the German people had in its historical evolution the kind of animal unity that helped other peoples, the German Reich would today be master of the globe."

Page 428: "I myself still remember how in my youth everyone was filled with a false idea of the word "Germanize." Even within pan-German circles one could hear that the Germans of Austria had they been helped by the government could have "Germanized" the Slavs within the Monarchy; but no one could see that an efficient "Germanization" could only be applied to the soil and never to the people. What was being attempted then was simply to externally impose the use of the German language. But how can anyone believe that a Negro or a Chinese could become German just because they learned the language and could use it in the future or perhaps join a German political party? No one understood that a "Germanization" of this kind was actually a "de-Germanization.""'

Page 443: "Any race mixing sooner or later inevitably brings about the ruin of the mix it created as long as the superior part of the mix continues to exist elsewhere as a pure race. The danger for the product of the mix disappears only once the last pure element of a race is also mongrelized."

Page 446: "A state that is concerned with the welfare of its people must make race the centerpiece of life in general. It must strive to keep the race pure. It must proclaim that the child is the most precious among things. It must be careful that it is healthy and can procreate other children; it must spread the idea that the greatest shame is to give birth to children when one is sick or unhealthy and that instead it is an honor to avoid it. On the other hand those who deprive the nation of healthy children must be punished.

.... The State must provide the most modern medical tools to serve this truth. It must declare unfit to procreate anyone who appears to be sick or afflicted by a hereditary disease and apply this rule.... (page 448) It must work this way without regard for understanding or misunderstanding, approval or disapproval."

Page 629: "We witness the carnage of our people because of the mongrelization with the Jews on a daily basis and we should consider that the poisoning of the blood can be cured only after many centuries or perhaps even never. We think that this racial decay has lowered the last Aryan values of the German people and often destroyed them resulting in the constant lowering of our strength as a civilizing nation and we are vulnerable to the danger at least in our large cities to end up like southern Italy today."

Page 360: "All the strongest symptoms of prewar decadence derive essentially from issues of race."

Page 310: "The final and deepest cause for the ruin of the old German Reich was to not have understood the race problem and its importance for the historical development of peoples. Since all events in life of nations are not the result of chance but of natural causes tied to the instinct for preservation and reproduction of the species and the race even though men are not aware of deeper motivations of their actions."

Page 481: "It shall therefore be the State's task to provide a continued renewal of the intellectual classes through national education by bringing in fresh blood from the bottom to the top..."

Page 468: "It shall finally be the task of a State interested in the future and the welfare of its people to make sure that a universal history be written that elevates the racial issue to a top position."

Before we add up Hitler's attacks against the Jews it is necessary to know what he thinks of the Aryan peoples to whom he dedicates a short special 12-page chapter (317–328.)

It would be completely useless to seek out which race was the first to create human civilization that can be considered as molding what we call "humanity." It would be much simpler to ask this question with regard to the present time when the answer is simple and clear. Everything we see today with our own eyes that is civilization, art, science and technology are the almost exclusive product of the Aryan creative spirit..."

... "The progress of humanity resembles the long ascent of an endless staircase: you cannot get to the highest steps without having gone up the middle ones. So the Aryans must take the path that reality has assigned to them and not the one drawn by the dreams of a modern pacifist....

Therefore it comes as no coincidence that the first civilizations appeared when the Aryans came into contact with inferior peoples, subjugated them and subjected them to their will. They then became the first tools to serve the new civilization... Once the defeated nations came closer to the victors even in their language the separation between the master and the servant was broken ...the purity of Aryan blood was then corrupted and the Aryans lost the paradise they had created... Anything in this world that is not of a good race is as worthless as the chaff..."

"Should anyone inquire as to the real reason the Aryans managed to reach such superior importance we would have to answer that it will not be found in a superior instinct for self preservation but rather in a special way of showing it...

...The reason for the spread of the civilization of the Aryans is not only due to their intellectual attributes...The first condition of any true civilization is in the readiness to place one's ego second to the conservation of the collectivity...In the dedication of one's life for the collectivity to live on is the crowning of every sense of self sacrifice...The German language has a specific word that describes this action perfectly: fulfillment of one's duty...The purest idealism equals the deepest knowledge...

Human civilization cannot be separated from the existence of the Aryans. Their disappearance would plunge the world in the darkness of a period deprived of civilization."

On page 329 continuing the short chapter on the Aryans, Hitler attacks the Jews in these terms: "The Jew stands in the most strident contrast with the Aryan. No people in the world have developed the instinct of self-preservation as well as the so-called chosen people. What other people has undergone fewer changes in his internal psyche in the last two millennia than the Jews? What other people has emerged unscathed from so many catastrophic events? What a tenacity of life: ... The intellectual capabilities of the Jews have sharpened during the last millennia. The Jew is reputed to be "intelligent" today, but in a certain sense he has been that way at all times. His intelligence however is not the product of his own evolution but of education by third parties... Since for obvious reasons the Jew never possessed his own civilization, the foundations of his spiritual work were always provided by others... Despite his apparent intellectual capabilities, the Jew does not possess a true civilization: and in any case that civilization would not be his own. The apparent culture of the Jew today is something that comes from other peoples that he has damaged... There has never been a Jewish art. In architecture and music, the two queens of all the arts, the Jews have never produced anything original... The best proof that the Jew absorbs other civilizations is his successes in the dramatic arts where he can develop without any true greatness his histrionics and aping aptitudes... No, the Jew has no civilizing strength because he lacks the idealism barring which there can be no true elevation of man... Since the Jew never possessed a state having territorial limits and therefore a civilization of his own, many have the mistaken idea that he should belong to the nomadic peoples... No, the Jew is not a nomad; but has always been a parasite within the body of other peoples... Another trait coming from this parasitic behavior led Schopenhauer to say: "The Jew is the grandmaster of lies."

Before we continue researching of Hitler's ideas on the Jews it is best to point out the subjective reasons for this antipathy as shown on pages 54 and 64.

"It would be difficult, if not impossible, for me today to recall the moment when for the first time the word "Jew" got me thinking. At home, as long as my father was alive, I don't remember having ever heard the word... Even at school I had no opportunity to hear about it... It was only at age 14 that I often heard the word "Jew," but it was mostly in political speeches. I sensed a slight hostility... There were only a few Europeanized Jews living in Linz whom I thought of as "Germans"... I went to Vienna... Even though there were two hundred thousand Jews out of two million people I didn't pay attention at first... I also didn't like the religious intolerance of the anti-Semitic press because it smacked of the Middle Ages... As for the Jewish press, if I was impressed by the quiet and dignified tone it used to answer the anti-Semitic attacks, I didn't like the slavish way it glossed over every minimal event that took place at the Habsburg Court... Another point that got on my nerves a lot was the odious cult those newspapers displayed for France ... One day in the street I bumped into a man dressed in a long caftan with curly hair. Was he a Jew or a German? ... Little by little I found out that the hand of the Jew was in every pornographic publication and event... I paid attention to the vices one finds in the streets and I noticed how prostitution was encouraged, propagated, and exploited by the Jews... I became indignant... My sympathies for democratic liberalism were offended... Later on I discovered that the social democratic press was mostly directed by the Jews... Then I thought of ways of saving the great masses at the cost of much sacrifice and patience... I was still very young and naïve to think that I could explain to the Jews the insanity of their theories and convert them... I wasted my breath because no Jew would change his thinking... I began hating them... Under the pressures of daily life I studied the origins of Marxism and discovered...the Jew. It was then that the great transformation took place inside me; from an

international petty bourgeois I went to being a fanatical anti-Semite..."
(page 69).

Page 337: "To get to know the Jew it is best to follow the path he
followed along the centuries in the midst of other peoples... The first
Jews entered Germany in the wake of the Romans, acting as merchants
as usual. The vortex of the migrations of peoples made them
apparently disappear so that a second period of a new and lasting
Jewish infiltration in Central and Northern Europe must have started
when the first Germanic states were formed. The Jew appears suddenly
as a modest merchant almost without a mask. Then he develops an
economic activity not as a producer but only as an intermediary. He
acquires stability and dedicates himself to trade and money related
businesses where he creates a monopoly... He then begins to display
his true character: he begs favors and safe conducts from the Princes,
gets close to heads of State and catches them in his web. However,
until Frederick the Great he remains a "foreigner." In the meantime,
having learned the German language to perfection in the course of one
thousand years and once the power of the princes began to crumble
and the civil rights appeared on the horizon, the Jew proclaims himself
"German"; this is the real reason for his emancipation from the
Ghetto. —He suddenly becomes a benefactor, a liberal, the precursor
of a new era. Little by little he takes possession of all the ways he can
dominate public opinion and the State: the press, the stock exchange,
finance, Freemasonry, and created his universal language: Esperanto.

Page 211: "The First World War broke out: there were very few
Jews at the front. Instead, the headquarters at the various command
posts were all filled with Jews: every clerk was Jewish and nearly every
Jew was a clerk. What about supplies? The Jewish Hydra sucked the
people's blood from all its pores...by 1916 all production was under
the control of Jewish finance..."

Page 359: "The race problem and the Jewish peril were one of the
deepest reasons for Germany's collapse in 1918..."

Page 585: "However, the real organizer of the revolution, the
international Jew, understood the new situation very well, that the
German people was not ripe for Bolshevism..."

Page 227: "Just like he knew before the war how to deflect public
attention from his intrigues to provoke the war, he excited the so-called

national elements in Germany against one another, conservative Bavaria against Prussia. This Jewish ability to deflect public opinion from itself is still a topic of investigation today."

International Judaism has created plans for world domination: Freemasonry (page 345) Socialism (page 64), Bolshevism (page 751) the dictatorship of the proletariat (page 357), Marxism (pages 350–352).

There is an identity between Jewish and French interests (page 704): "There is a huge danger to Germany in this similarity of interests... The French people, destined as it is to be even more mongrelized with African Negroes, is tied to the Jews for the purpose of world domination and is an ever lurking danger for the white race in Europe..."

Page 628: "In 1918 there was no organized anti-Semitism. I remember how many problems we encountered every time we began talking about the Jews. Our first attempts to show the public who his real enemy was had no effect and only very slowly did we begin to have some success."

Page 629: "In spite of everything the Jews have reached their purpose: Catholics and Protestants are happily fighting each other while the mortal enemy of Aryan and Christian humanity is secretly laughing."

Index*

---

* The names of Hitler and Mussolini have not been indexed. Page numbers in italics refer to footnotes.